A PALETTE, NOT A PORTRAIT

Stories from the life of Nathan Garrett

Nathan Garrett

iUniverse, Inc.
New York   Bloomington

A Palette, Not a Portrait
Stories from the life of Nathan Garrett

Copyright © 2010 Nathan Garrett

iUniverse books may be ordered through booksellers or by contacting:

iUniverse
1663 Liberty Drive
Bloomington, IN 47403
www.iuniverse.com
1-800-Authors (1-800-288-4677)

ISBN: 978-1-4502-4875-4 (pbk)
ISBN: 978-1-4502-4876-1 (cloth)
ISBN: 978-1-4502-4877-8 (ebk)

Printed in the United States of America

iUniverse rev. date: 8/25/2010

To my wife, Wanda; my children Devron, Shahida, Nathan, Jr.;
and my sister, Gloria.

Contents

CHAPTER ONE

My Foundations

I was the only hot weather baby mother had. August 8th, 1931 in the front bedroom at 514 East St. James Street, Tarboro, North Carolina. No air conditioning. No anesthesia. No doctor. Just Mother, Nurse McMillan and me. Daddy was at his drugstore.

Tarboro is a town of now 10,000 people that was started in 1760 on the west bank of the Tar River in eastern North Carolina. It is an important marketing center for tobacco, peanuts, cotton and other products grown nearby. On the east bank of the Tar is Princeville, now a town of 1,000, founded by former slaves in 1865.

The house where I was born was a quarter of a mile from the Tar River. The river starts in the north-central part of the state near the Virginia line and meanders eastward through nine counties on its way to the Pamlico Sound, whose eastern border is North Carolina's Outer Banks.

My parents were York David Garrett, Jr. and Julia Bonds Williams Garrett. I was their youngest, preceded by York III, Gloria, and Oliver.

The house was one of the nicer homes on East St. James Street. I am told that there was a stable in the rear at one time. An uncle who died long before I was born had kept a horse called Frolic there. According to my father, Frolic had been owned by a wealthy Philadelphian and when the horse could no longer race, he gave it to Andrew Taylor, my Dad's cousin. Cousin Taylor did odd jobs for the wealthy man, including occasional care of his animals. Cousin Taylor had the horse shipped to Tarboro as a present for Judson, Dad's older brother. Judson, I was told, was already a dashing figure and became more so as he trotted around Tarboro on tawny-colored Frolic.

HISTORY REPEATS ITSELF

A thousand times around the dinner table, during evenings when we just sat and talked, and on those long car trips to New York, Houston, Atlantic City, Chicago and Detroit, I listened with half an ear to my father, York David Garrett, Jr., telling as much as he knew about our family origins on both the Garrett and Williams side. My mother, Julia Williams Garrett, for reasons of her own, opted not to contribute to these discussions. Mother died in 1977 and five years later, on April 11, 1982 following dinner at my house, my wife, Wanda, decided to turn on our tape recorder. With modest success, we interviewed my father, his sister, Sarah Beatrice Parker Burnette, and my first cousin on my mother's side, Mariah Burke Creed (Popsie). Dad was then 88, Aunt Bea 90 and Popsie 61. The trouble with the interview was that the three of them were, perhaps, the most talkative of all my relatives and weren't the least bit constrained by the questions I asked them to address. Dad controlled the conversation, as always. He intimidated Aunt Bea and overwhelmed Popsie. When I listened to the tape a few days later, I concluded it was almost worthless. Dates were not agreed on, recollections on events were usually challenged, and three voices at once made the tape undecipherable in many spots.

Fifteen years later, and after Aunt Bea and Popsie had died; I sat at my computer with my father at my side and typed his responses to my inquiries. He digressed a lot, but he agreed to get back on the subject when I gently urged him to. I knew I had to do it gently because I was present when a young doctoral candidate who was interviewing him got frustrated and asked him (not gently) to get back on the subject. Dad told him he would hear his story the way he wanted to tell it, or not at all.

It seemed that history had changed on several points, but by listening to the 1982 tape several times, poring over the typed responses and checking with: Wanda; my sister, Gloria Pratt; my first cousins Judson Parker, Julian Williams, Sylvester Price, Francis Price, Hobart Price; and my second cousins Leon and George Creed on the stories they had heard, I found a good deal of consistency in the following early history of my family.

Most of my ancestors were employers rather than employees. They were successful professional and/or business people. My careers as a certified public accountant, a lawyer and a leader of small businesses were definitely influenced by my knowledge of what my forebears did. The greatest influence was my father from whom I learned much of the basics of small business operation. From my talks with him, it is clear to me that he, in turn, had been influenced by his father who died before I was born. My mother's father died when I was 13, but although he stopped operating his barbering business ten years earlier, I was generally aware that he did not work for others; people worked for him.

I don't believe in destiny. We are created with mental and physical characteristics drawn from the genes of our parents. How we use those characteristics in our careers as earners, our roles in our families, and our participation in our communities are determined by one thing only: how we react to the people and events we encounter.

GARRETT SIDE

Great-Grandfather and Great-Grandmother

Great-Grandfather York Garrett came from somewhere in Europe, perhaps Scotland, to Washington County in eastern North Carolina about 50 miles northeast of the point where the Tar River enters the Pamlico Sound. According to an analysis of my Y chromosome, he shared ancestry with the Ewe people of what today is Ghana. He might have been born in either Scotland or Ghana and might have been an indentured servant in Scotland. Some Scots found it profitable to lease indentured servants to Americans for periods of time.

Washington County is bordered on the north by the Albemarle Sound. The sound is separated from the Atlantic Ocean by the outer banks of North Carolina. Exactly when, how and why he came is unknown, but he brought the Garrett name with him. He became a slave and married my Great-Grandmother who lived on the same farm. Her last name had been Spruill, probably the name of her owner, but Dad and Aunt Bea never knew her first name. She had a brother named David.

York and his wife were bought by the Powells who ran a farm in Edgecombe County near Tarboro, 80 miles west of Washington County.

Three children were born to my great-grandparents: Eliza around 1846; Sarah Emma around 1857 and York David Garrett on July 5, 1859.

It is likely that Great-Grandfather York and his family could not read or write. North Carolina's 1854 Revised Code, Chapter 34, Section 82 stated: "A fine of up to $200 is to be levied against any white person who attempts to teach any slave to read or write (figures excepted) or who gives a slave a book or pamphlet." If one of the very few Free Negroes sought to teach a slave, the law provided "A fine, imprisonment or between 20 and 39 lashes for attempting to teach any slave to read or write ..."

I can't begin to imagine the pain and disfigurement that would result *from 20 to 39 lashes, but to put the $200 fine in perspective, a family of six people would have spent a total of under $700 a year for their needs in 1854. Clearly the punishment for helping a slave to read or write was severe.*

Whether or not he could read and write, Great-Grandfather York was a "finished" harness, saddle and boot maker. In addition to his work on the Powell farm, he was hired out by Powell to persons who needed such work as far away as southern Virginia, around 60 miles north. The custom was that Great-Grandfather York would travel alone to the customer and return once the job was completed.

Although this "hiring out" might well have occurred, it would have been against Chapter 105, Section 28 of the North Carolina Revised Code, which stated: "A master is prohibited from hiring out the time of a slave to another person. Violation results in a fine of $40 against the master and the slave can be indicted for the offense and publicly hired out by the sheriff for one year ..." Also, allowing a slave to hire himself out or to go at large subjected the owner to a $100 fine under Chapter 106, Section 29.

However, as I was told, at the end of one of his engagements in 1863, Great-Grandfather was late returning and was to have been beaten for it. To avoid the beating and slave life, York ran away. No one knows where he went, though it was rumored he went west. Perhaps he was aided in some way by the confusion resulting from the Civil War that had begun two years earlier and by the Quakers, many of whom lived in central North Carolina.

Help for a runaway slave would have been hard to find. Anyone who harbored or helped a runaway slave would have been required to pay $100 to the owner and would have been liable for other damages according to Chapter 34, Section 81 of the North Carolina Code.

We have met black Garretts from Memphis Tennessee, Baton Rouge Louisiana and Texas near the Arkansas line, but have never been able to establish a connection to York.

York's escape was accomplished when his children were seventeen, six and four years of age.When my father and his older sister, Aunt Bea, told the story of Great-Grandfather York running away, it was told with pride in his defiant attitude. However, as I think of the fact that Great-Grandfather was a valuable property to the Powells, I conclude that it was unlikely that the punishment would have been so severe as to cripple or kill him. How could the Powells continue to use and sell his services if he was crippled? By running away, Great-Grandfather avoided the beating, but he also abandoned a wife and three young children. I have wondered about what he and Great-Grandmother (and perhaps the children) talked about before the decision was made to run away. A return to the farm was not a possibility nor was there a means of communicating with his family. Did Great-Grandmother encourage him to leave? What impact did his leaving have on her and the children? Was she beaten in his stead? How did the children suffer as a result of his departure?

After slavery ended, Great-Grandmother remained on the Powell farm as housekeeper for several years and reared the children. The children were able to go to school through the 5th grade.

Around 1867, when York David, Sarah Emma and Eliza were 8 and 10 and 21 respectively, Great-Grandmother married again, this time to a man named Bowens whom she had known when they were slaves in Washington County. Six years after the marriage, she and Bowens moved back to Washington County to the town of Plymouth but left the children, now 14, 16 and 27 to continue to work on the Powell farm. She and Bowens had several more children, one of whom was named George. She died in 1897. There was a dentist in Durham, Curtis Bowens, and I suspect that we were cousins. His family is from Martin County, which is adjacent to Washington County.

Eliza moved to James City near New Bern where she had a child, possibly out of wedlock, who was named Edna Bell Garrett. Edna Bell married Edward Brooks and from that union came Nathaniel Franklin Brooks. Nathaniel married Martha Hamlin and that couple had four children: Theodore Hamlin, Mildred, Carl and Vernon. Theodore married Blondena Nichols and gave birth to two boys: Theodore, Jr. and William Nathaniel. Theodore, Jr. is a dentist now living in Durham and we claim each other as cousins. It was interesting to find that Mildred Brooks married a Bennie Garrett and their son, Benjamin, took as his third wife a woman named Gloria Garrett. Gloria is my sister's name.

I have also speculated that Great-Grandfather York, before he and his wife were sold to the Powells, might have fathered children in Washington County who were given his last name.

As is the case with many black families, tracking relatives is both frustrating and fun. Frustrating because of the lack of records. Fun, because relative-suspects pop up everywhere. Those of us who meet people - either black or white - whose ancestors lived as slaves or were a part of the slave owner's family on the same farm often conclude that we are cousins. When I run into people named Powell, Bowens, Brooks, Spruill, Robinson, Harrison or Garrett, I try to find out if they have an eastern North Carolina connection. Recently I ran into a man, Fred Hines, whose mother grew up with the name Florence Garrett and was, according to Fred, born in Washington County on Garrett's Island. His mother told him that her last name was derived from the Garrett Island Plantation.

Grandfather York David and Grandmother Sally

York David and Sarah Emma stayed and worked on the Powell farm after their mother left. At age 17, Sarah Emma had a child by a West Indian named Taylor, who was the principal or a teacher at the graded school she attended. The child was named Andrew Garrett. York David, Sarah Emma and Andrew left the Powell farm in 1880 when York David was 21 and took up residence in Princeville.

York David met Sally A. Robinson sometime before he and Sarah Emma left the Powell farm. Sally, who was born March 15, 1860, came to the Powell farm from Nashville, some 25 miles west, to visit an uncle named Pappy K who also worked for Powell.

Sally was the daughter of Frank Harrison from Nash County. Nash is just west of Edgecombe County. Frank had lived as a slave on the Harrison farm near Nashville, a small town in Nash a few miles west of Rocky Mount, the county's largest town. When Union troops occupied the Nashville area, Frank was freed and was sent to New Bern where he enlisted to fight alongside the Union troops until the end of the war. Great-Grandfather Frank hated his former master and, after slavery, he changed his name to Robinson after the John Robinson Circus. Frank became a farmer and businessman in Nash County. He ran a farm with eight horses and sold ice for many years in Rocky Mount. He carried the ice to and from his wagon on his shoulders and the long years of exposure to the cold caused him to become partially deaf.

Frank married a Native American Indian and had five children; the oldest was Grandmother Sally.

The oldest boy was Frank, who ultimately moved to Norfolk. There was a sister named Mariah who died in 1903. Next were Luther and Carlton. We don't know anything about Carlton, but Luther grew up to be a brakeman for the Atlantic Coastline Railroad. At the time Luther worked for the railroad, the family lived within sight of the rail line and the engineer would blow when the train passed the Robinson house. Luther was killed when he fell between the coupling mechanism for two freight cars and was pounded to death.

That sort of accident occurs even today. Because of a Supreme Court decision written by Clarence Thomas, it is now more difficult to get damages in such cases. In Norfolk & Western Company V. Hiles, a 1996 case, Hiles had been injured by a misaligned coupling. According to an article in the August 2001 issue of The American Lawyer, Hiles argued that the railroad was strictly liable under an 1893 act that required automatic couplers so that railroad workers would not need to get between moving cars. According to the article, Thomas ruled that the law did not apply, saying that a misaligned coupler was not necessarily a defective one. Thomas likened the device to an unplugged appliance for which the manufacturer should not be held liable. "Coupling accidents accounted for 11 of the 76 deaths among railroad workers during a recent six-year period" the magazine stated.

Carlton never knew his mother because when he was barely two she left the family and ran off with another Native American Indian. In those days the children of a broken marriage had a better chance of being fed and clothed if they stayed with the father, especially if the father had a farm as did Frank. It also helped that Grandmother Sally was, by the time her mother left, old enough to assume the care of her younger siblings.

Grandmother Sally's name was changed to Sarah with the middle name of Frances, though there is no record of when or why this was done.

Business and Civic Leadership in Princeville and Tarboro

Sarah (Sally) and York David married in 1882 and the couple, Emma and baby Andrew lived in Princeville.

Princeville is located in a flood plain on the east bank of the Tar River across from Tarboro. A bridge connects the two communities. At the end of the war, Union troops occupied the Tarboro area and bivouacked on the land that is now Princeville. Many slaves in Edgecombe and surrounding counties left farms and plantations and migrated to the vicinity seeking freedom and federal protection. The land had been owned by two white planters: John Lloyd and Lafayette Dancy. Originally the former slaves called it Freedom Hill, but it was chartered in 1885 and named Princeville for Turner Prince, an early resident and town leader. It was one of two all- black towns established in North Carolina. *(The North Carolina Historical Review Volume LXIII, Number 3, July 1986)* The first was James City, the town Eliza moved to. James City was established in 1863 across the Trent River from New Bern at a time when Union Troops held that eastern North Carolina city.

Although the federal government advised former slaves to return to plantations to work for their old masters, many of those who settled Princeville chose not to and, instead, supplied the labor for the homes and businesses across the river in Tarboro. This suited the needs of Tarboro because the blacks were conveniently nearby, but in a separate community.

Emma died while still a young woman and Andrew was reared by Granddaddy York and Grandmother Sarah in Princeville.

Barely over 23, and with a family, York David found work at a grocery and dry goods store owned by a white man named William Judson Gantt. The store was on the east side of Main Street between St. James and Church, the present location of the Tarboro City Hall. Gantt died and the store was sold to a Mr. Fuller, who kept York David on the payroll as a clerk in the store. Fuller contracted tuberculosis, sold the store to York David and financed the purchase. York David renamed the store: "The Y. D. Garrett Plain and Fancy Grocery Store," The store had a bar in back, but although the grocery portion of the business catered to customers of all races, the bar portion was open only to whites. York David, himself, never drank. The bar was ended by Prohibition. At the turn of the century the family moved to Tarboro.

York David's progress was remarkable given the tenor of the times. At the end of slavery the nation began the painful period of reconstruction. In 1866 North Carolina passed Chapter 40 of its Public Laws entitled "An Act Concerning Negroes and Persons of Color or Mixed Blood." The chapter repealed most, but not all, of the laws in the 1854 code that discriminated against slaves and free Negroes. In general the new chapter guaranteed Negroes that they would be entitled to the privileges and subject to the same disabilities as "free persons of color" prior to emancipation. Among the disabilities imposed on free Negroes with which York David had to contend were:

In order to "hawk" or peddle, a Negro had to give evidence of good character to seven justices. The license was good for one year.

In order to own a weapon, a Negro had to apply for a permit a year before getting the weapon.

Negroes could not be witnesses against white persons.

A North Carolina Supreme Court opinion in an 1850 case stated: "...A free negro has no master to correct him, ... and unless a white man, to whom insolence is given, has a right to put a stop to it, in an extra judicial way, there is no remedy for it. This would be insufferable. Hence we infer from the principles of the common law, that this extra judicial remedy is excusable, provided the words or acts of a free negro be in law insolent."

According to Theodore B. Wilson in his The Black Codes of the South, at page 13: "When the Negro slave came to be regarded as some sort of subhuman, the concept applied with equal force to the Negroes who were free. ... (T)he theory of Negro inferiority ... was fraught with grave and long-lasting consequences. In conjunction with the institution of slavery, it gave impetus to the gradual development of a mass of prescribed behaviour which came eventually to regulate virtually all the relations of the white and black races in America. That highly structured and patterned relationship in reality constituted a new, though unrecognized institution ... which included all the Negroes ... and all those white persons who had face-to-face contact with Negroes." Wilson designated that new institution as the "Gray

Institution." On page 24 of his book, Wilson wrote: "The gray institution provided (for) 'proper' ways to manage all the intercourse between the races; 'proper' attitudes to be maintained by Negroes in the presence of white persons; 'proper' practices, also, to be observed by all white persons in their relations with Negroes."

However, on the positive side, this was also a period during which, through the help of church groups and northern philanthropists, several schools were established for Negroes which exist today. Shaw University and St. Augustine's College were established in Raleigh. The first state normal school for Negroes was established in Fayetteville and was the root for the present Fayetteville State University. A normal school was also established at Elizabeth City in northeastern North Carolina and led to Elizabeth City State University. The North Carolina Agricultural and Mechanical College was originally established by the state as an annex to Shaw. It was moved to Greensboro (central North Carolina) in 1893 and ultimately became North Carolina Agricultural and Technical State University. Slater Normal was created in 1895 and later became Winston-Salem State University in the foothills of the Appalachians.

Between 1876 and 1894, we had the right to vote and elected 52 Negroes to the legislature. George White, a Negro from eastern North Carolina was elected to the U. S. Congress.

It was almost one hundred years between White's election and the election of North Carolina's present two black Congressional representatives.

But in 1900, North Carolina set up property and literacy qualifications for voting through which few blacks could squeeze. To vote, a person had to satisfy the registrar that he could understand the Constitution unless his grandfather had been a registered voter in 1867. Registrars were subjective in determining whether or not the candidate had sufficient understanding of the Constitution, and, of course, most blacks had been slaves until 1865.

York David was civic minded. He was treasurer of the State Grand United Order of the Oddfellows for 25 years or more. He also served as a member of the Grand Lodge of the Free and Accepted Order of Ancient Masons for 25 years. He was a Justice of the Peace, a deacon and treasurer of Union Baptist Church and, according to the *Southerner (December 10, 1928),* was *"...one of Tarboro's most worthy and respected Colored citizens."* In 1898 he ran as a Republican and won election to the North Carolina General Assembly. However, when he went to the Capitol in Raleigh he was not seated because the "Red Shirts" convinced the Legislature that the election allowed the "wrong" people to vote and therefore was invalid. The purpose of the Red Shirts was to disfranchise blacks. Once when the whites, in order to intimidate black voters, formed a cordon of armed men through which voters had to pass, York David loudly announced he would defy the cordon and vote. He never failed to vote in an election from age 21 until his death.

My Garrett Aunts and Uncles

Sarah gave birth to ten children and also reared Andrew, the child of her husband's deceased sister, Emma. But when Andrew became an adult, he left the York David household, moved to Philadelphia, dropped the Garrett name, and took the name of his father, Taylor.

The first child was born to York and Sarah on December 4, 1882 and was named Mary Emma. She went to Estes Seminary at Shaw University in Raleigh. Shaw is a historically black college formed in 1865. During its heyday, in addition to its undergraduate offerings, Shaw had a four-year school of medicine, a school of dentistry, a school of pharmacy, and a school of nursing. It no longer has the health science professional schools but it now has a school of religion and several graduate programs. Mary Emma died of tuberculosis in her early twenties after teaching a few years in Princeville. She had no issue.

The second was James Patrick. He was born June 4, 1884 but died at six months.

Third was William Judson (named for York David's first employer in Tarboro), born November 23, 1885. He finished Shaw College in 1908 but died within four months of tuberculosis at age 22 without issue. His ambition had been to get a degree in medicine at Shaw.

The fourth and fifth were the twins Hattie and Mattie respectively, born May 4, 1888. Hattie went to school at St. Paul's College in Virginia and to Cheyney State College in Pennsylvania. Both colleges were founded to educate blacks. After college she returned to Tarboro where she taught school and practiced as a seamstress. She had learned dressmaking at St. Paul's. In 1920 she moved to Chicago to work as a seamstress at the urging of her first cousin, Andrew Taylor, who had moved there from Philadelphia. She lived with Andrew and his wife on Prairie Avenue. There, Hattie met and married George Sylvester Price from Texas, near the Arkansas line. Though the family was domiciled in Chicago, Hattie went home to Tarboro to give birth to their first son, George Sylvester, Jr. They later moved to Ann Arbor Michigan to provide financial and family support to George Sylvester's younger brother, Hobart Garrett Price, who was a student at the University of Michigan. In 1924, while living in Ann Arbor, a second son, Francis Garrett, was born. When

York Sr.'s health began to fail in 1927, the Price family was asked to return to Tarboro so that George Sylvester Price could run the store. While living in Tarboro, a third son, Hobart Carlton, was born. The family left Tarboro in 1931 and moved to Jamaica, New York. Despite the Great Depression, the couple was able to buy a home in South Ozone Park, New York. Hattie and George Sylvester always told their sons that the best way to achieve success was to get a college education. All three boys became professionals in the City of New York. George Sylvester, Jr. became an orthopedic surgeon, Francis Garrett pursued a career as an educator and high school administrator, and Hobart Carlton became a physician who practiced cardiology and internal medicine. Hattie died in Queens New York at age 97.

Mattie did summer school work at Hampton, Shaw, A&T and Johnson C. Smith, all historically black institutions, and became a teacher. She gave up teaching to work with her younger brother, York, Jr. in his drug store. She married a man named Mattocks, a minister who had gone to Howard University. They separated after six months but never divorced. They had no issue. Mattie died at age 93.

The sixth was Annie Lillian Gertrude. She was born November 30, 1890 and died at age eighteen of tuberculosis. No issue.

On January 24, 1893, Sarah Beatrice was born. She graduated from Elizabeth City Normal with honors in 1910. She taught in the schools of Tarboro and was a strong leader and secretary for the NAACP statewide for 35 years. She married Isham Lemuel Parker and they had one son, Judson Garrett. She divorced Isham and later married Earl Burnette from a small community between Tarboro and Rocky Mount. No issue from that union. Judson graduated from North Carolina College at Durham and earned a degree in pharmacy from Philadelphia College of Pharmacy. He later earned a Master of Social Work at Columbia. Judson married Arona McDougald and to that couple was born Gwendolyn (a lawyer, author and TV producer), Judson, Jr. (a self-employed businessman) and Anthony (a pilot and executive with Federal Express). Arona and Judson were divorced after many years and Judson married Faith, a divorcee with a child, Nicole. Judson and Faith had a child, Sarah Grace (a junior executive with a marketing firm). Bea died at 103 years.

Mable Blanche was the ninth child, and was born June 26, 1897. A male child whose name is not given in the family bible was born December 22, 1898. These two died of Chicken Pox at very young ages. York, Jr. and Bea caught the disease at the same time as their younger siblings. The custom at that time was to withhold water from a child with Chicken Pox. However, Bea and York Jr. were old enough to get water on their own and therefore survived.

My Father, York David Garrett, Jr.

The eighth was my father, York David, Jr., born December 10, 1894. He completed eight grades in Princeville Graded School taught principally by two black men: R. L. Jones who had graduated from Wilberforce, another historically black college, and William Augustine Perry who had graduated from Yale. York then went to Elizabeth City Normal and finished the two-year program in one year, graduating as salutatorian in 1912. Following Elizabeth City he went to Shaw but became ill after ten days. Sarah, his mother, went to Shaw on the train and brought him back home in fear of losing yet another child who had matriculated at Shaw. (Mary Emma and Judson had both died shortly after attending Shaw.) Following his recuperation, he taught for two months in Hattie's slot in the Edgecombe County School. Hattie had left to get a better teaching job in the Princeville School.

Dad entered Howard Academy in the fall of 1913 and finished the three-year program in two years, graduating in 1915. Courses included algebra, plane and solid geometry, trigonometry, chemistry, physics, history, English composition, French, and Latin. He excelled in the math and sciences, and was good at everything else, except Latin. He was captain of the Academy baseball team and played second base even though he was left-handed. Left-handed players were relegated to outfield or first base but, at five feet two inches tall, he was too short for first base. He also played offensive and defensive end for the Academy football team.

He entered the School of Pharmacy in 1916 and remained until drafted into the Army on August 1, 1918. The drafting had been delayed as long as possible by the head of the Tarboro Draft Board, George Howard (son of Judge Howard, one of the richest men in Tarboro), so as not to interrupt the education of York Sr's son. In the Army, Dad served as clerk of Company B 825th Reserve Labor Battalion at Camp Green, Charlotte. He entered the army as a corporal.

At the time he was inducted, there were no black officers in the South by order of U. S. President Woodrow Wilson. One of the officers who befriended him was Captain Swinson from Bemidji in Northern Minnesota. Bemidji is a small town named for the Ogibwa Tribe. A major attraction in Bemidji is a huge statue of Paul Bunyan and his blue ox.

Dad was released in March 1919 and while waiting for return to Howard in the fall went to a ten day, all expenses paid, course on race relations in Atlanta, sponsored by the U. S. Government. There were separate courses in other towns for whites. The purpose was to smooth race relationships between civilians and returning service men. The white person chosen from Tarboro was pastor of the Episcopal Church in Tarboro, but he was never willing to meet with York, Jr. after they returned.

Dad went back to Howard in the Fall of 1919 and received his Doctor of Pharmacy degree in 1920. At the end of his freshman year in the School of Pharmacy he joined Chi Delta Mu, a fraternity of medical, dentistry and pharmacy students that started at Howard. It was the worst initiation anyone could imagine. The motto was "whip his ass some more." The initiations were held in their own fraternity house at 3rd and T at Ledroit Circle in D. C. The whipping started on the third floor and you were a member if you made it to the bottom. At the bottom floor a member hit your bare ass with a red-hot poker. My father still had the brand when he died at age 104.

Some classmates in the Howard Academy, pharmacy and other professional schools were E. Spurgeon Neal from Winston Salem, Brooks from NY (father was pastor of an AME church on Fifth Avenue), the Hardwick brothers from Northern Virginia, Pannell and B. A. Coles from Charlottesville Virginia, Benton Rupert Lattimer from Warrenton, Ga. (Lattimer became a Captain and led the Army's Rainbow Division in France during WWI), Barbara Jordan (who became a dentist and married a pharmacist named Waters in New Jersey), and Oscar and Sydney Brown of Chicago. York Jr., Brooks, Neal, Brown and Coles were the "Stumps." Lattimer, Pannell, and the Hardwicks were satellites of the Stumps because they were too tall.

In 1920 Dad took the NC Board of Pharmacy Exam, but they refused to pass him because the policy was not to pass a black applicant on the first try. When York reviewed his exam paper with Zuellen, the president of the board who lived in Tarboro, he was told that he had passed all subjects. Zuellen promised Dad that if he would take the exam again, he could be assured of getting his license. During the six months wait to take the exam again, Dad planned for the store, found a location on Main Street near the Princeville bridge and a block from his father's store, ordered furniture to be constructed, and ordered his inventory. He was able to use his father's credit and good reputation to finance the venture.

Garrett Grandparents Die; Leave Some Wealth

York David died December 8, 1928 at age 69. He suffered from asthma all of his life. When he died, he owned four houses. His will left the first home he built to York Jr.; the second house to Sarah Beatrice; the third house was nearby at 401 or 403 St. James Street and was left to Mattie; and the last house was on St. David Street behind the house on St. James and was left to Hattie. The will instructed the children to care for their mother. Sarah Frances died four years later in 1932.

13

WILLIAMS SIDE

Grandpa and Grandmother

Both my maternal grandparents were born as slaves in the City of Tarboro North Carolina or in Edgecombe County in which Tarboro sits.

Grandpa Nathan Williams was eleven years old when slavery ended. He was a handsome man with dark, slightly curly hair. He was around five feet four inches tall. His mother was black and his father was his mother's master. The master's name might have been either Williams or Davidson. It was the custom in that part of North Carolina to give children born in slavery the last name of the slave owner.

Grandpa's mother must have been of light complexion, because Grandpa looked totally like a white man. He had a half sister, Laura, whose father was black. Laura was dark complexioned. Laura married a Wilkins and had a daughter, Gertrude. Both Grandpa and Laura were life long residents of Tarboro.

We know virtually nothing of Grandpa Nathan's father. I surmise that he must have been a man of means; he had several children and hired private tutors to instruct them. Grandpa was tutored along with his half brothers and sisters in his father's home.

Grandpa's job, as a young slave boy, was to help make the rest of the family comfortable at the dinner meal. The dining room was equipped with a large wicker fan suspended from the ceiling. The fan could be pulled back and forth by a chord attached to it near the bottom. At dinnertime Grandpa was dressed up and his job was to pull that fan back and forth to help with air circulation and to keep flies away.

Grandpa's father owned a barbershop that catered to the well-to-do white men of Tarboro. Since only black people worked as barbers, the shop was an investment rather than a place of employment for Grandpa's father. Grandpa learned the art of cutting hair in that shop, probably after slavery ended. There were three kinds of barbers in Tarboro (all were black). One kind worked in shops that catered to the well-to-do white men of the city: the professional and businessmen. The second worked in shops that catered to the lower class white men: the mechanics, laborers and farmers. The third group of barbers worked in shops that served black men, only. The custom was that the class line was never crossed in the barbershops: the lower class white men were not welcome in the well-to-do shops and the well-to-do never ventured into the shops for the lower class. And of course, the black barbershops were exclusively for black men. Grandpa was known as a "white-trade" barber. He never learned the art of cutting black people's hair, that, generally, is thicker and flatter than the hair of white people. Eventually Grandpa's father turned the shop over to him and he continued to cater to the well to do.

Grandpa's first wife was one of the five Anderson sisters who were born in Tarboro of a light complexioned mother and a slave-master father. The first wife and her child died in childbirth. Later, Grandpa married Mariah Anderson, one of his first wife's sisters. Mariah was my Grandmother.

The Anderson girls, like Grandpa, looked white. They lived on St. Patrick Street across from St. Stephan's Church. Following slavery, three of the sisters left Tarboro. One, named Johnnie, ran a restaurant for blacks in Atlantic City. We do not know of a marriage or children. Another, whose first name we do not know, married a man named Bryant in Boston and she had at least one daughter and two granddaughters (Barbara and Beverly). The third was named Julia, who moved to Connecticut and had a son named Jarvis. There are some white half siblings whose Mother was named Sudie, but we don't know the father's last name. One of the half siblings was a woman who was married to a German named Mallett who acknowledged that she and the Anderson girls were half sisters. Mr. Mallett ran a bakery in Tarboro.

Economic Prosperity and Civic Involvement

Grandmother Mariah and Grandpa Nathan prospered in Tarboro, he as barber and she as a beautician for white women. Grandpa served as a member of the School Board for many years. The Board governed the public schools in Tarboro and Princeville. All the black children attended the Princeville schools. He was placed there to represent the Princeville schools.

During the years of bearing and rearing children, my grandparents lived in a large, attractive brick home on a hill overlooking the Tar River at the eastern edge of Tarboro. After the children were grown or in their mid teens, they built a home on Church Street across from the white Episcopal Church. The location was the last block of black residences before the street became totally white, about six blocks south of Main Street. It was the most attractive residence in that part of town. It had latticework across the roofline and around the supporting posts for the roof of the porch. There was a parlor, three bedrooms, a sunroom, a large dining room and a generous kitchen. There was a gazebo in the left side yard, and near the rear of the yard there was a barn suitable for two horses. A major feature for me was the peach tree with its trunk painted white and surrounded by large white pebbles. A three-foot high white picket fence ran the entire length of the property line with gates for entering the front porch and the side yard. The structure is now occupied by a white family and is on the historic registry.

Aunts and Uncles - Williams Side

Nathan and Mariah had ten children, six that lived to adulthood. Of those who survived, the oldest child was Nathan Jr., the second was Julian, the third was Charlie (Charles), the fourth was Geneva, the fifth was Sarah and the sixth was my mother, Julia. The girls were all pretty and the boys were all handsome.

Williams family, circa 1901. My mother is the baby standing at the bottom.

Nathan, Jr.

Nathan Williams, Jr. was trained as a barber in his father's shop. He did not go to an academy or college. As a young adult he moved to New York where he married a German woman and lived as a white man. He was the chief barber on the Fall River Line, a ship company that carried passengers on overnight trips from New York to Boston. He prospered at this and at running his own shop somewhere in New York. We know of no issue from that union. Nathan, Jr. was very fond of his parents and sisters. He would send dresses home to his Mother and his sisters, Geneva, Sarah and Julia. He also sent his Mother some petite parlor chairs imported from France. In 1963 my Mother made a gift of those same chairs to my wife, Wanda. They grace our foyer, today. Although he visited Tarboro occasionally, Nathan, Jr. never brought his wife with him. He found his visits home were not pleasant because many of the white people he had served while working in his father's shop refused to shake his hand or talk to him as an equal. After Grandpa and Grandmother died, his visits stopped altogether.

Julian

Julian was also trained in his father's shop and continued to work there after Nathan, Jr. left. Julian married Maude Dillard, a member of a prominent black Goldsboro North Carolina family, with whom he had two children, Julian, Jr. and Ethelind. According to Julian, Jr., his father, Mother, sister and he left Tarboro because of the following incident to which he was an eyewitness.

In 1927, when Julian, Jr. was ten years old, the Klan began to agitate for the Williams barber shop to be replaced by a white barber. One of Grandpa's customers tipped him off that the Klan might be planning to harm him in some way. Grandpa donned a Klan robe and attended one of the Klan meetings. He, of course, looked as white as they did. At the meeting he learned that the Klan planned to burn down his home.

He then contacted his son, Nathan Jr., and asked for help. Nathan Jr. responded by getting a machine gun and a pistol and driving to Tarboro immediately. Nathan Jr. was able to get the weapons because he knew the gangster who ran the numbers racket in the area that included his shop. Barbershops were good places for numbers writers and their customers to get together. Customers or others in the neighborhood could give in their number selections, pay for their bets and collect their winnings all at the barbershop. The barbershop owner, though not necessarily directly involved, would wink at the numbers writer's activity. After all, the numbers writer attracted customers.

Nathan Jr. brought his brother, Charlie, with him to Tarboro. Charlie was living in New York at the time.

When the Klan showed up in front of the Williams home on Church Street, Grandpa and his boys were ready. They stood on their front porch and defied one of the Klansmen to light the torch he was carrying. The Klansman lit it any way and Julian shot him with the pistol he held.

The man he shot turned out to be a deputy sheriff. Julian was arrested later that day and was to be tried or arraigned on Monday. But because the prosecuting attorney and the judge were customers of Grandpa's and knew him well, Julian was freed. However, he was warned to leave

Tarboro. Julian left, moved his family to Detroit, and never returned to Tarboro.

Neither Charlie, Mother, Aunt Sarah nor Aunt Geneva ever mentioned this story; but my father and Aunt Bea confirmed that, unlike Nathan Jr., Julian never returned to Tarboro, even for his parents' funerals.

In Detroit, Julian continued as a barber, but not white-trade. Julian, Jr. married Beatrice Goolsby and had two children: Gail Delores and Judith Eileen. Gail, a retired magistrate in Las Vegas, married Robert Lee Smith and had two children: Sheila and Sharon. Sheila and Sharon produced a total of eight children: Nelson, Whitney, Shallante, Alexis, DeAngelo, Robert, Desmond and Dale. Judith, now an attorney in Detroit, married Ozzie Wiggins, Jr. and also had two children: Lynda and Karen. Lynda has a daughter, Kayla Eileen. Ethelind, Julian's sister, married Zaro Simmons and that couple had two children: Gloria and Zaro, Jr. Gloria gave birth to Michelle, Silvia and Cassandra. Julian's second wife was named Lenore. They had no children.

Charlie

Charlie graduated from Livingstone College in theology. Livingstone is a private black college in central southwestern North Carolina that is supported by the African Methodist Episcopal Zion Church. Charlie had a career as a minister and served as the Presiding Elder of Mother Zion Church in Harlem, New York. Charlie was an excellent preacher. He married a woman whose name has been lost and had one child, Lydia Williams Mussenden.

Geneva

Geneva was educated at Barber Scotia, a black teacher training school in Southwestern North Carolina. She taught for a few years and attended Hampton University in Virginia several summers. She married Joe Burke whom I remember as a large man who drove expensive looking cars (one was a Cord according to my sister) and dressed well. He owned a nightclub and restaurant in Norfolk. Their only child was Mariah who was nicknamed "Popsie." Geneva and her husband were not together for long. She remained in Tarboro where, after she retired from teaching, she ran a beauty parlor and served as the librarian for the black community. Her last home in Tarboro was on Water Street, uncomfortably close to the Tar River, which flooded often. Once on a visit with her I recall the water being within twenty yards of her front door.

Popsie earned her baccalaureate and master's degrees at the all black North Carolina College (now North Carolina Central University) in Durham. She worked in several administrative posts at the college, and retired as Registrar.

Popsie married and, subsequently, divorced Leon Vincent Creed of New Jersey. Leon was a Tuskegee Airman; not a pilot, but a combination navigator and bombardier. He retired as a Lieutenant Colonel after service in Korea and Viet Nam. He died in 2002 and was interred at Arlington. Popsie and Leon had two children: Leon Jr., a businessman who lives in California near San Francisco, and George Creed, a veterinarian who lives near Gastonia, North Carolina, southwest of Charlotte. Leon married Susan (a woman of Italian descent) and had two children: Lucia and Leon, III. George married Natalie (Marshall) and had three children: George Bryan, Kevin and Karen. George Bryan has a daughter, Austen. Both Kevin and Karen are physicians. Popsie was more like a sister than a cousin to my siblings and me. She lived with us while she attended college and made her home in Durham after she and Leon were divorced. Popsie died in 1997.

Sarah
Sarah was the spirited one, full of mischief and humor. She went to St. Augustine's College in Raleigh, North Carolina, a school that offered academic, teaching and nurse training for blacks at that time. It is now a four-year liberal arts college. She worked for a time as an agent for North Carolina Mutual Life Insurance Company, a black company founded in 1898. According to Popsie, when Sarah told Grandpa Nathan she was applying for the job, he advised her to send in her sister Julia's picture instead of her own because Julia looked more intelligent.

Sarah married Lovelace Capehart of Raleigh. Lovelace was first a pharmacist and then became a physician. They moved to Harlem in New York where they had an apartment that also contained his medical office on the corner of Seventh Avenue and 120th Street. At various times they had homes in suburban areas near New York City, but his practice remained in Harlem. Both Lovelace and Sarah were white in appearance. This enabled them to buy those suburban homes and allowed Sarah to work at several jobs in New York that were not available to black people.

Lovelace and Sarah had two sons: William and Lovelace (called Brother). William had a son, Billy (called "Bumps"), by his first wife, Dolly. Dolly was Puerto Rican. They divorced and William married a white woman whom I've never met. He worked his whole life in New York as a white man and after Sarah died, he broke off contacts with the family. Brother never had children. He served in the army for about a year as a white man before being discharged due to severe asthma.

My Mother, Julia

Julia Bonds Williams was the baby. She was pretty, five feet one inch tall and, like the rest of the children looked white. But she was an outspoken fighter for racial justice.

Like her sister Sarah, Mother graduated from St. Augustine's College. Mother was one of the speakers, perhaps the valedictory speaker, at commencement the day before her 19th birthday. What follows comes from *The News and Observer* (Raleigh, North Carolina) Thursday morning, May 20, 1919 edition. The headline for the article read: "Joyner Advises Negro Graduates." One of the sub captions read: "Former Superintendent of Public Schools of State Delivers Annual Address Following Reading of Papers by Graduates Demanding Extension of Rights."

"Twenty-one graduates of the school yesterday received their diplomas including seven academic, six normal and eight graduates of St. Agnes Nurse Training School.

"The exercise took place in the chapel of the school, which was crowded long before the hour for the exercises, which opened with processional hymn and prayer by Bishop DeLaney, closing with the creed…

"Failure to Demand is Cowardice

"Julia Barnes [sic] Williams charged failure to demand rights of economic and political equality as cowardice. She defined the social equality asked for as being that guaranteed by the constitution and not racial intermarriage.

"In this period of reconstruction, she declared the time has come for the recognition of the race which was hailed as Americans and members of which participated in the nation's war. Protests from pulpit and platform and from individuals she declared as indication of effectual demands on the part of the negro.

" 'Fifty years ago,' she continued, 'our destiny found us an ignorant and unlettered people, even non-progressive, but since that time we have gradually become educated and thrifty. We are now in the middle of a period of reconstruction; and as subjects of America we no longer need strive after rights that are already ours, but merely expect to be included in the program of social justice with other races of the earth. In such a reconstruction, the old question of keeping the negro out of American politics and perpetuate his position as an inferior being will be wiped way.

" 'The sentiment which lies at the root of democracy is nothing new, for it is simply a desire of the people to have a hand, if need be, a controlling hand, in the management of affairs of its own country.

" 'For fifty years the black man has been knocking at a door that has been bolted and barred against him, and as yet it has not opened. The time is now that the negro has got to show to the world, that he is not an inferior being, that he deserves all that he is demanding.' "

Mother's essay was followed by that of another graduate: Sara Madeline Hudson. Her essay was entitled "Fate of Autocracy" and was reported as follows:

"From the bloodthirsty mob of the South, Sara Madeline Hudson [from Washington County, North Carolina] … wanted protection, and she questioned why the negro should not have a voice in the peace conference where the rights of men are being adjudicated. If the lawmakers refuse to grant the negro the rights the race is demanding, she feared to picture the upheaval which will follow.

" 'The sign,' she said, 'is written across the sky so that those who run may read and any who are too foolish to run must read.' "

After hearing the fiery remarks of these two young graduates of St. Augustine's academic course, the principal speaker felt obligated to rebut with what was the conventional wisdom of moderate white people in North Carolina at that time.

"Dr. Joyner Speaks

"With the utmost frankness Dr. J. Y. Joyner, former Superintendent of Public Instruction in the State, talked to the negroes in a way that apparently struck deep. They gave him close and respectful attention when he discussed the problem of the races. He told them that in the beginning that he was going to say a few words about the racial aspects of the problem and was then going to dismiss this entirely.

"Separation Necessary

" 'There are certain race differences and instinctive race prejudices,' Dr. Joyner said, 'which make necessary racial and therefore social separation. The wise of both races understand this, and unless it is accepted as fundamental in the solution of the race problem in the South, in my opinion, there is no

21

hope for the negro race to receive the just treatment it ought to have and to have the human chance it is entitled to for development along all lines in the South.

" 'Having said this much, I propose to leave the racial phase behind me and discuss it as a great human and economic problem.'

"Dr. Joyner then cited a number of laws which govern humanity.

" 'Their can be no elevation for an individual or a race except through education, the development of the mind, the body and the soul' was his first principle. His second was a natural consequence:

"Must be No Prizing

" 'The doors of opportunity and privilege never swing open to individuals or races without adequate preparation for entrance into these doors, and any suggestion of prizing these doors open before adequate preparation, by revolution, force, blood or legislation, is in violation of God's eternal laws as fixed as the stars.

" 'If any individual or race enters without preparation, …it is a tragedy to him and those whose destinies are linked with him.'

"Deepest Tragedy

" 'I need but to cite you to a tragedy, which I regard as the deepest tragedy of the South – the tragedy of Negro suffrage immediately after the Civil war, a tragedy for them and for us, because the door of suffrage was prized open for a race just out of the barbarism and the bonds of slavery and in the natural process of evolution unprepared for the discharge of the duties and privileges conferred upon it.' "

With Dr. Joyner's words still ringing in her ears, Julia taught in Princeville for two or three years after graduation.

In 1922 Julia moved to Manhattan to be near her sister, Sara, and found work as a seamstress. My father, York David Garrett, Jr., courted her intensely before she left Tarboro and pursued her even after she moved to New York.

Years later in the 1960s and 1970s when I was deeply involved in the struggles for civil rights, justice and greater economic progress for blacks, my Mother's words and the rebuttal of Dr. Joyner provided fuel to keep me going during exceedingly difficult times.

Grandpa and Grandmother Williams Die

Grandmother Mariah died when Mother was thirteen years old. Grandpa Nathan then married Georgia, the daughter of Grandmother Mariah's best friend and a cousin to Mrs. Cottie Moore, wife of the Dr. Aaron Moore who became a co-founder of North Carolina Mutual Life Insurance Company in Durham.

Grandpa Nathan died in 1944 at the age of 90.

CHAPTER TWO

My Early Years

What Durham Had to Offer

The family moved from Tarboro to Durham in 1933 when I was two. Because of the Great Depression, few blacks in and around Tarboro had money for anything beyond the basics. Business at the store was too slow to support a family of six.

Durham had not been Dad's first choice. Winston-Salem, near the North Carolina mountains, was where he wanted to move. The tobacco industry had not suffered from the depression as much as others, and blacks in Winston-Salem worked in the R. J Reynolds cigarette factories.

Dad knew that there were already two other black pharmacies in Durham, but Clyde Donnell, a black physician who had done his undergraduate work at Howard University in Washington and his medicine at Harvard, convinced him to come. Dr. Donnell had a store he needed to sell. He had leased it to another pharmacist who hadn't made a go of it. Donnell promised Dad that he and a few other doctors would channel their prescription work to him. Donnell was the medical director at North Carolina Mutual Life Insurance Company, a black firm established in 1898. In addition to helping the company determine whether or not an applicant for insurance was a good risk, Donnell maintained an office in the company's building and treated its employees and a limited number of other patients.

The deciding factor, however, was that, unlike any other town in North Carolina and almost any other town in the nation, Durham's black population had income streams from businesses and institutions they, themselves, owned and/or operated. The enterprises included the life insurance company, a bank, a savings and loan, a fire insurance company, a brick manufacturing firm, a four-year college, a two-year business school, a hospital, a school of nursing, a library, a first rate kindergarten, a beauty college, a barber college, physicians, dentists, attorneys, a furniture store, a movie theater, a three-story hotel, a printing company and dozens of service and retail establishments that provided automobile gas and repair, groceries, building construction and repair, food service, dry cleaning, burial service and transportation service. Prior to 1933, blacks had either owned or operated two hosiery mills that made socks. At one time, a black man had owned a tobacco manufacturing plant. The black population of Durham was far less dependent on whites for products and services than was the case anywhere. Dad decided we could make it in Durham.

Where We Lived

Our first home was rented from Mr. Fitzgerald, the man who owned the brick-making company and had owned the tobacco-manufacturing firm. After a year we moved to a suite of rooms in the Biltmore Hotel, the building that also housed the drugstore and was owned by Clyde Donnell. After another six months we moved to 1502 Fayetteville Street, one mile from the store, near the four-year college and in Durham's most affluent black neighborhood. That house was owned and occupied by the Garrett Family for 64 years. Mother preferred traditional furnishings with lots of colorful accent pieces. In addition to the regular couches, chairs, tables and lamps, there was a baby grand piano Dad had bought for Mother before we left Tarboro. At one time or another it was home to perhaps 40 of my family members who were either elderly, ill, out of work, pursuing degrees in education, or adults and children in need of shelter due to domestic upheavals. At family gatherings, the house is simply referred to as "1502."

Kindergarten to High School

I was the first or second best student from the beginning at Scarborough Nursery School through Whitted Elementary and Hillside High.

Scarborough Nursery was really a kindergarten. By the time we graduated we could add, spell and read pretty well. The school was run by Mrs. Clydie Scarborough, the wife of Durham's most successful black mortician, J. C. Scarborough. When I attended, the school was housed in a two-story wooden structure on the corner of Proctor Street and Cozart Alley that had served as Lincoln Hospital, the hospital for Durham's black population.

Lincoln Hospital was not connected with local or state government. It was started by blacks with the help of white philanthropists (George Watts and members of the Duke family) and the non-medical staff was all black. George Watts had donated money to create Watts Hospital with separate wings for white men and white women. Some proposed that a third wing for "colored" be added to Watts Hospital but Aaron Moore, a black doctor, and others, convinced Watts and the Duke family that a separate hospital was needed where black physicians could care for their patients. The successful development and management of the facility resulted from the initiative and skill of the black business and professional people. John Merrick, the barber and real estate investor who, with Dr. Moore, had started the North Carolina Mutual Life Insurance Company became chairman of the hospital's board. Dr. Moore became the chief medical officer and William Gaston Pearson, a businessman and educator, became the Secretary. White physicians provided training for the black doctors and there were a few whites on the hospital's board of directors.

Scarborough Nursery, formerly Lincoln Hospital, circa 1920. Courtesy of the North Carolina Collection, Durham County Library.

In the public schools I attended, all the students, teachers and administrators were black. The School Board and the administrators above the level of principal were all white. I rarely saw a textbook, desk or chair that was new. The rule was that the new books went to the white schools first. After a year or two they were passed down to us. As for furnishings, ours were replaced when they were no longer useable. But the replacements were never new. They came to us from the white schools. The white schools then got the new stuff.

Our books and furnishings were not the best, but I was told by many people that the black teachers, on average, were better than their white counterparts. They had better training and were more dedicated to uplifting their students. If you were black, lived in the South and had a college education, there were very few opportunities for employment. You either taught, or were a doctor, lawyer, nurse, pharmacist or minister. Teachers and teaching, like the other professionals and the services they offered, were held in high regard in every black town.

The pay for white teachers was low relative to other employment opportunities for them, but, by law, it was even lower for blacks. In 1901 the pay scales were such that white teachers were paid 25% to 39% more than black teachers. The pay was finally equalized in 1943. However, because we had fewer opportunities, the low pay, when combined with the motivation to improve the lot of our people, was enough to keep our teachers on the job. White teachers, on the other hand, tended to move off into other fields when the opportunities presented themselves.

All teachers were required to continue their education to remain employed. This meant that, if they stayed long enough, most earned masters' and some even became PhDs. Because of the exodus of many of the whites and the persistency of most of the blacks, the average black teacher had more education and more experience.

All the teachers I had were keenly interested in the development of everyone in the classroom. They were tough on us when they needed to be, but were always ready to praise good work. If a student was doing badly, teachers often made home visits. The teachers of whom I have the fondest memories are: Mrs. Clay in first grade, Mrs. Wilson in third, Mrs. Morris in fifth, Mrs. Massey in sixth, and Mrs. Willis, Spaulding, McLester and Turner in high school

Throughout my years before high school, my best friend, George Jones, and I vied with each other for top honors, but that competition ended after I finished the eighth grade. My father insisted that I go to summer school so that I could skip the ninth and go to the tenth. His plan was for me to go to Yale, the school from which William Augustine Perry, his much revered grade school teacher, had graduated. But to go to Yale, Dad reasoned, I would need a year in one of the prestigious New England prep schools such as Andover. He planned for me to graduate from Hillside and then take an additional year at Andover to help assure admission to Yale. By skipping a grade, the year at Andover would put me in at age 18 as a college freshman. I did as he asked.

I hated splitting up with the group I had been with for eight to ten years but especially hated splitting up with George.

Other than ping-pong, my only sport was tennis, but George and I were the only kids who played tennis. I tried basketball in the tenth grade, but at five feet five and 185 pounds (I had lost a little weight), I was no good. I got in one game, took one shot and that shot went over the backboard. I tried football in my junior and senior years. I figured I was heavy enough and low enough to the ground to make it as a guard. I made the team as second-string guard, but the coach just couldn't bring himself to put me in a game. When the first stringer got hurt, he would look at me, hang his head, and send in a second string tackle or even the third string guard. I often wondered, was it my lack of ability or was he protecting Dr. York Garrett's baby boy?

But in ways other than sports, high school was great. I had the leading male role in several school plays. I was valedictorian. I was also both the editor of the high school newspaper and president of my class for my junior and senior years. These experiences were invaluable. With the paper, I not only learned to write better but also how to arrange stories and advertising. The paper was published monthly and with each new issue I spent hours at Service Printing Company watching the paper being put together on the Linotype machines and reading the galley proofs. As to the class presidency, I was introduced to Robert's Rules of Order and gained skills for running meetings that lasted a lifetime.

There were a lot of girls who were my friends, all of them pretty and smart. The ones I liked best were Jackie Townsend, Dorothy McDougald, Elizabeth Ray, Peggy Payne, Hilda Wilson, Lynette Payton, Fredilean Pendarvis, Florida Fisher, Ethel McLaurin, Magalene Markham, Corrine Mabry and Mamie Smith. There were a few from this list that I would have liked to have been my girl friend, but I was too shy to ask for a date. I felt that because I was fat, short and lacked athleticism, they would not be interested in me.

The guys I remember best were Ralph Malone (who introduced me to smoking), Gordon and Wayne Perry, Albert Smith and Elwood Goins (both of whom played good ping-pong), Fletcher Graves, Jake Rainey, and of course, my best friend, George Jones. We all lived within three quarters of a mile from one another.

George Jones and I did our share of hanging out. By age 16 we were driving, drinking beer and smoking cigarettes. I recall one cold and rainy Friday night in winter when he and I took a couple of girls out on the town. Durham had an array of nightclubs where a young man could buy a drink if he didn't look too young or wasn't clearly already drunk. There were no legal bars for selling liquor at that time. But those clubs did a brisk business. There were jukeboxes and, sometimes, live music on weekends. There was limited-menu food service. The clubs had interesting names: The Silver Dollar, The Tree in the House, The Square Club, Miss Minnie Hester's, The Quarter House (shots for 25 cents) and La Petite Birdland where you were greeted by a sign: "Come clean or at least smelling like soap." Dad let me use the car and let me wear his new dark-blue woolen overcoat. We got the girls home by 11:30 and decided to hit a few more nightclubs. I wound up drunk and, on the way out of the last club I stopped to pee in a muddy ditch. I slipped, lost my balance, and my father's new dark blue woolen overcoat and I toppled over into the ditch. To make matters worse, I didn't stop peeing. The coat was a complete mess. George helped me out of the ditch and luckily he and I got home OK, but there was nothing I could do about the coat. Dad knew I had gotten in around 2:30 A.M. By 7:00 A.M. he had discovered the coat and woke me saying he needed me to work at the drug store all day from opening at 9:00 A.M. to closing at 11:00 P.M.. He never said anything about my evening out or the coat, but I didn't get the car again until I was in college. And to this day I have never gotten drunk again.

I asked a girl who was not on the above list of friend girls to be my date for the senior prom. But I got thwarted on my big plans. It was OK that Dad wouldn't let me use the car because I had taxicab money as well as money for the room we were going to use. But Dad insisted on having first cousin Judson ("Yip") and his wife, Arona, to pick my date and me up after the dance for rides to our respective homes. I learned years later from Arona that I had been seen taking a package of Trojans from the condom drawer at the store and the rat, whoever he or she was, told Dad. I should have used some of my intellect and figured that I needed to get the Trojans at some other store.

At the urging of my teachers, I sent my applications to Howard and Yale during the fall of my senior year. I was accepted at Howard right away but was told by Yale that they required me to take the College Entrance Examination. Dad remained convinced that acceptance at Yale would require a year at Andover, however, and he was ready to send me. I took the College Entrance Examination at the all-white Governor Broughton School in Raleigh, some 25 miles from Durham. I was the only black person in the entire room of perhaps 200 people and I got a lot of stares. I don't remember how well I scored, but I did my best because I always did my best on any kind of test. Apparently I did well enough because my score, my class standing at Hillside, and my extracurricular activities were enough to get an acceptance letter from Yale. I wanted to cry. Howard was where I really wanted to go, but I knew dad would insist on Yale. I was to be the fulfillment of the dream he had when he, in the eighth grade back in Princeville, had been taught by William Augustine Perry, the black Yale graduate. Dad decided then that he wanted one of his children to go to Yale. I was it.

The Drugstore and the Neighborhood Around It

Our lives revolved around the drugstore. Located on Pettigrew Street in the Biltmore Hotel, it was thirty feet wide but at least 120 feet deep. The store was handsomely furnished with mahogany display cases and a fountain for dipping ice cream and making ice cream sodas, milkshakes and carbonated soft drinks. Behind a partition was the pharmacy section, storage for inventory and a table for Dad's Wednesday night bridge games.

On the other side of the hotel to the west was the Regal Theater, and, next to it, was an office building for lawyers, doctors and dentists. The ground floor of the office building contained the Donut Shop that offered home made donuts and an extensive menu for breakfast, lunch and dinner. Beyond the Donut Shop was a light industrial building in which hogsheads for the storage of tobacco were made. That operation was one of only two businesses on the street that were not run by blacks. On the east side of the drugstore was a commercial building that housed a seven-chair barbershop and a beer and wine distributorship. An ESSO gasoline station, two restaurants, another large barbershop and a recreation center completed the block.

The next three blocks contained nearly forty other businesses including: The Carolina Times, a black weekly newspaper published and edited by Louis Alston; Service Printing Company, owned by three Hampton University graduates; Katz grocery store, owned by a Jewish family; Baldwin's Furniture Store; Scarborough Funeral Home; Isler's Hotel (the one I didn't get to use); Speight's Pure Oil Service Station and several restaurants and specialty shops.

Garrett's Biltmore Drugstore ground floor left. Photo courtesy of North Carolina Collection, Durham County Library.

Across the street from the drugstore was a dirt parking strip that bordered the railroad tracks that were elevated six feet higher than the street. Two blocks past the railroad was Main Street and downtown Durham. For several blocks to the rear there was housing occupied by low to moderate-income families. It was an excellent commercial location.

Work at the Store

Garrett's Biltmore Drugstore was a family affair. There were non-family employees, but every member of the family played a role. Dad, of course, was in charge of everything. Mother did the ordering of cosmetics and products for Christmas, Easter, Mother's Day and Father's Day and worked as a clerk when we were extra busy or an employee was absent. The male customers loved it when she dipped ice cream in her low cut blouses. She also did the banking each morning at 11:00 AM at the black owned Mechanics and Farmers Bank down town on Parrish Street.

When not in school, Yorkie, Gloria, Oliver and I had shifts doing whatever dad needed us to do. Mostly we clerked, but I also delivered packages on the bicycle. I recall one rainy night in November when I was nine, I had to deliver a five-cent fountain Coca Cola in a paper cup with a napkin over the top. We didn't have plastic in those days. Of course the napkin got rain-soaked from above and from below by the sloshing of the Coke as I pedaled, so that it had disintegrated by the time I reached the customer. The cup was overflowing with rainwater. Nobody was happy with the outcome - not me, not the customer and not dad because the customer refused to pay. I guess I learned from that incident that although you will not always please your customers, they need to know that you tried your best. It was an important principle for me when I developed my own business.

I enjoyed helping Dad fill prescriptions. By age twelve I had learned to read the prescriptions and could assemble the medications. This was important work, and I was as careful as Dad was. I would place the pills or elixir on top of the doctor's prescription for Dad's inspection before he completed the work. Sometimes, after he was satisfied that the medicine was correct, he would let me count the pills, pour the liquids and affix the labels he had prepared. If it was a re-fill I would search for the right number among the neatly stacked high rows of prescription boxes. Each box contained a two-pronged spindle that could file around two hundred prescriptions. The boxes were labeled with the range of numbers of the prescriptions inside. Today, of course, the pharmacist's assistants must be well trained and all the prescription files are on computer.

When I was fifteen, Dad trained me to manage the non-medicine side of the business. I would take inventory regularly and recommend to Dad what we ought to order. When the goods came in I would compare what we received with the invoice and watch for price increases. If the price increased, I had to compute the standard markup and recommend to Dad what the new retail price should be.

Interaction with the vendors gave me my only regular exposure to white people while growing up. The only other exposure that I recall was when a big white man denied me a seat on a city bus. It was the only seat left on the bus, but I couldn't have it because of my race. The law, of course, was "colored to the rear." The bus drivers had to enforce the law or they, themselves, would be charged with breaking the law. I had boarded the bus with a group of kids my age who had just attended an NAACP meeting at the church adjacent to the bus stop.

All of our customers at the store were black. Occasionally, a white person would come to the store to try to get prescription drugs without a prescription, but Dad always handled those visits and dispatched them quickly with a firm *no*. The salesmen who called on the store were all white. They would solicit an order and usually fill the order from whatever vehicles they were driving. I never had a problem with any who served us. They were generally courteous and friendly. Why not? They wanted our business.

I learned to watch both customers and employees carefully to cut down on theft. At the end of the day I checked the register to see if the money agreed with the total sales as shown by the register. The final job was to do a rough calculation to determine if we were making or losing money on the fountain, tobacco and reading material sales. The register provided a breakdown of the sales in each of these categories. I knew what the cost of goods sold should be based on the markup applied to the merchandise we bought for re-sale. The difference between the sales and the cost of sales is called the gross profit or gross margin and it had to be a large enough number to cover the costs of the work force, utilities and supplies for that day. I reported my calculations to Dad at least once a week.

None of my work at the store was drudgery. I enjoyed greeting and serving customers. If a customer had to wait for service, Dad insisted that we speak to the waiting person and assure him that he or she would be served shortly. I wish more clerks would do that today and I must admit that, sometimes when I am shopping, I will offer that advice to clerks who do not do it. More often than not, however, the advice is greeted with a cold stare. I also enjoyed helping Dad with prescriptions and I found the managerial duties especially rewarding.

The store was open from nine in the morning until eleven at night every day except that it closed from eleven to one on Sunday for church. For at least sixty years it was never closed for a complete day. Not for holidays, weddings, births, deaths, sickness or graduations. Dad explained to me that in the retail business it was essential that the customers never doubt that you would be open. They needed to be able to rely on the store being there to serve them and, in exchange, they gave their loyalty.

Dinnertime

Dinner was always at 3:30 seven days a week. Dad would take a break from the store, the children got out of school, and we all arrived by 3:15. Dinner was waiting. Mother did all of the cooking but was assisted during the week by a domestic (there was a series of them - at least eight) who helped serve the meal and cleaned the kitchen afterward. The domestic ate with the family, if she wished.

All seats were designated and no changes were permitted, except when there was company. Dad was at the head of the table with his back to the living room. To his left was Mother and to her left was Yorkie. Gloria sat to Dad's right and Oliver was to her right. I sat at the end opposite Dad and to my right, in the seat closest to the kitchen door, sat Mother's helper.

The glass-topped table and eight chairs were made of mahogany. The buffet table and china cabinet matched the table and chairs. A small chandelier was centered above the table. There were three additional cabinets in the room for storage. The table could be extended to accommodate two additional people when there was company, as was often the case.

The floor was of wood but the area beneath the table and chairs was covered with a woolen rug.

Mother was a very, very good cook and was careful to give us well-balanced meals that were flavorful. We had tossed salads regularly. Macaroni and cheese, potatoes in various styles, rice, greens, peas and beans were rotated throughout the week. Every day we had beef, fowl, pork or seafood. The only thing that didn't vary was sweetened iced tea. That was always a part of dinner. Occasionally, Mother would stew a rabbit or have chitterlings, tripe, haslet or lights (lungs). Brains and eggs or fish roe and eggs were an occasional delicacy on Sunday morning before church. I recall asking Dad what was fish roe and, as he began to explain about the sex life of fish, Mother frowned and interrupted him saying: "York, don't talk about nature!"

Each child had a dessert preference and Mother catered to our wishes. Mine was devil's-food cake. Gloria liked chocolate pie; Yorkie wanted apple pie; Oliver's favorite was caramel cake. We all liked jelly cake with white icing.

Mother's choice was lemon chess pie. Dad liked them all, except one, and I found out about that one during dinner in 1970.

It was Thursday and mother had gotten behind for some reason. She had the fish, salad, potatoes, and iced tea as usual but she didn't have time to make dessert. She said: "York, I'm sorry, but I just couldn't get the lemon chess pie made." To which dad replied: "That's OK Julia. I never liked lemon chess pie anyway." This, after about 45 years of lemon chess pies. She stopped making them after that, and, instead, started buying them at the Woolworth lunch counter.

The menu varied from day to day except for Thursdays. Every Thursday we had fried fish. Mother picked Thursdays because the fish market got its supplies from the North Carolina coast on Thursday morning.

Mother did all of the grocery shopping. She controlled the family car and made the rounds to the fish market, the poultry market, and the A&P. She didn't have to drive to our favorite store, however. That was J. L. Page and Sons. J. L. Page and Sons was on Fayetteville Street just north of the house. It was a house with a front porch that had been converted into a food store. The family lived in the house next to the store. Mrs. Page was in the store most of the time, but suffered from crippling arthritis. They maintained the kitchen in the store and Mrs. Page would cook there and serve her husband and sons. If you came in during meal time one of them would get up and wait on you. You were also offered a sampling of whatever they were having for that meal.

Mother bought fresh produce, dairy products, many of our staples and almost all of the specialty meats, such as lights and chitterlings, from the Pages. In the morning she would call in her order. Anything they didn't have she would buy from the A&P. We had a weekly charge account at Page and Sons and they delivered the groceries at whatever time mother specified. We were good customers for them and they were good customers for us.

Mother and Dad agreed on a daily budget for the house. Every night when Dad got home from the store he and she and any of the children who were awake at 11:15 would have a snack in the kitchen. During or after the snack Dad would give her the money for the next day's expenses.

I never heard them have a dispute about money.

Dinnertime at 1502 in 1962. From left: Yvonne, Yorkie, Doris, Tommy, Oliver (standing), Mother, Leon Creed (standing), Gloria, Popsie Creed (standing), me, George Creed (standing), Marc, Wanda (expecting Nathan, Jr.), Dad. Photo by Alex Rivera

About Mother

Mother did the shopping for all the clothing, Dad's included. From 1933, when we came to Durham, until 1977, when Mother died, Dad never entered a white owned clothing store in Durham. Mother would select the items, including shoes, and bring them home for Dad to try. If they didn't fit they went back. However, he never had her return anything because of style, color or cost. He wore what she brought, and to me he always looked very well dressed. He especially wore good shoes. He was a size 5 ½ and that happened to be the samples size the stores would display. When the stores were ready to discontinue a model they would call Mother to see if she was interested in getting them for Dad at 50% off or more.

Sales clerks in two or three of the stores on Main Street knew Mother's taste and sizes. They would call her when new items came in and Mother would stop in after one of her daily trips to the bank. In the 1930s through the mid 1960s most of the stores would not allow a black person to try on a garment before buying. Blacks had to size it by holding it against their bodies. If you tried it on and it didn't fit, too bad. The sale was final. This didn't apply to Mother, however, unless she was shopping with my sister Gloria whose complexion was two shades darker than Mother's. No one in the store except the clerk knew that Mother wasn't a Caucasian, so the rule didn't apply to her. She didn't ask for this special treatment, but accepted it for herself. She was always one of the best-dressed women in town. As for Dad's clothing, since he wasn't trying it on in the store and since the only person the store saw was Mother, they readily agreed that they would accept the return of things that didn't fit Dad.

In addition to her banking and buying duties at the store, Mother did the public relations. She was a member of several clubs. One of the clubs was The Gourmets, an organization of the wives of the doctors, dentists, lawyers, educators, college executives and business executives in Durham. There were eight of them. They met monthly for a very fancy meal at the home of one of the members. Mother joked to us that after one of the members served chicken, the others whispered derisively: "Chicken. Twenty-three cents a pound." A week before Mother's turn she would try out the meal she planned on us. Based on our reactions she would adjust the seasoning or other particulars of the presentation so as to have it just right. My brother Yorkie would say we were the Guinea Pigs. The club's rules prohibited having any part of the meal prepared by anyone other than the hostess. Of course, these sumptuous meals called for using the gold inlaid plates, the Gorham silver, crystal glasses, the silver champagne bucket and starched linen tablecloths and napkins.

Mother was a member of The Queen High Bridge Club, an especially interesting group of women. Most of them had careers of their own in professions, education or business. Vi Turner was the Corporate Treasurer and Bess Whitted was the Corporate Secretary at North Carolina Mutual Life Insurance Company. Mollie Lee was the chief librarian for the black library in Raleigh, the capital city 25 miles away. Several, such as the historian Helen Edmonds, were PhDs at the college. One was a graduate Registered Nurse. Odessa Turner, whose husband was dean of the law school at the college, was also a pharmacist and worked part time with Dad at the drugstore. This was a power group of women and I am convinced the name was chosen with that in mind.

The all-black Old North State Medical, Dental and Pharmaceutical Society had a Women's Auxiliary and Mother served as president of it for several years. She always joined Dad for these professional meetings throughout the state. The National Medical Association was the national organization for all of the black medical care professionals for many years. Dad served as national secretary for a dozen years. When the pharmacists split off and formed the

National Pharmaceutical Association, Dad joined it and became president. Mother served as president of that auxiliary as well.

Mother did a lot of hosting at home. For the staff at the drugstore there were dinners and parties for Easter, Thanksgiving and New Years. When Dad was host for his bridge club, The Jiggs, Mother made sure everything was perfect for them, including keeping the children upstairs and out of the way.

We all had help from Mother in our schoolwork. I know I benefited greatly from the hours she spent with me. When I was in the seventh grade I entered the Elks Oratorical Contest. The Elks is a national organization that sponsored these contests in every town in which there was a chapter. First there was local competition, then statewide and then the national. The competitors were mostly high school juniors and seniors. The grand prize was a four-year scholarship for college. Even though I was only 12 at the time, I entered because the local president knew my family well and because my teacher encouraged me. My topic was "The Negro and the Constitution." It focused on the 13th, 14th and 15th amendments. I did the research under the direction of my teacher. I first outlined and then wrote several drafts of the speech. Mother critiqued each draft and encouraged me to polish it. She rehearsed me for hours. She corrected my enunciation, worked on my posture and gestures, helped me on pace, and taught me about varying my pitch. By the time she finished with me I was good. *Very* good. I went all the way to the national finals in Ft. Lauderdale Florida before losing to a girl who was a high school senior from Florida. I was first runner-up.

We were encouraged to have lots of friends and our friends were always welcome at our home. Mother taught us to be courteous to all, to display good manners, to be truthful and to speak acceptable English. She emphasized the importance of associating with people from "good" families whose standards were similar to ours. A touch of snobbery was displayed when, on some occasions in a relaxed moment, she would describe a person as being the "wrong kind" or of having "coarse" features. I never asked what she meant but assumed she was talking about people whose standards for personal behavior were lower than hers or whose physical appearance featured broad noses, big lips and thick Negro hair. She didn't mean color because Dad was dark brown in complexion, though he did not have a broad nose, big lips or thick hair.

I think she approved of all of my friends. Most of them were kids who were doing well in school. If they were making good progress in school, it didn't matter to Mother what their family backgrounds might have been. She did not approve of many of Gloria and Oliver's friends, however.

Books, music, movies, New York City and the legitimate theater were important to Mother. She especially liked love stories and historical fiction.

We had a record player at home with an automatic changer that handled the old 78 disks. When feeling really good she would play the piano, though I don't think she knew more than a few songs. I remember one song she played called for her to cross her hands over each other several times. She did this with exaggerated movement, and I thought she was elegant. Plays on Broadway were a must during Mother and Dad's annual trips to New York. Up until the mid 1940s they would stay at the black-owned Theresa Hotel on 125th Street and 7th Avenue in Harlem and drive their car to and from the theater district. In the later 1940s through the 1950s they started staying at the Taft on 7th Avenue downtown just a few blocks from the theaters. The room assigned to them at the Taft was always on either the 2nd or 3rd floor. That was the floor for traveling salesmen. The hotel's policy was not to give rooms to Negroes on the upper floors where the vacationing guests might complain. The restaurant Mother enjoyed most was Pier 52, around the corner from the entrance to the Taft.

My parents always seemed to get along very well. If they didn't, it was hidden from me. I can only remember one argument and that was about the store. Mother complained that Dad did not think her work at the store was as valuable as she thought it was. I don't know whether the argument was over money, lack of appreciation or her practice of dipping ice cream in low-cut blouses.

But I know there was one thing about Dad that Mother disliked intensely.

When we would take trips by car before the 1964 Civil Rights Act and the Supreme Court's decisions that Congress had the right to pass laws relating to public accommodations, we could not stop at restaurants for meals. In the major North Carolina cities and in Atlanta, Richmond and Washington, D.C. we knew of black-owned eating establishments. But if you are on a major highway and trying to "make time," as Dad always was, you needed to find a place where you could pull off, get something to eat and be on your way quickly. A few places near the larger cities in the South had windows for "colored " customers where we could buy the food and take it with us so as to avoid contact with the white patrons inside. But if you happened to get hungry and could not find a place with a window for "colored," you were out of luck. But not Dad! He would park the car in an isolated area maybe 50 yards away from the restaurant, order us to stay in the car and out of sight and have Mother go into the restaurant to get food. She hated doing it, and she hated him for asking her to do it. But the children needed food and drink, so she acquiesced.

About Dad

During the school year we came down to breakfast and were gone before Dad reached the kitchen. School opened at 8:30 and the store at 9:00. During the summer and on weekends we were either off early to play with friends or trying to sleep late. Usually we were asleep at the 11:15 pm snack time. So, we saw Dad briefly at the 3:30 mealtime and at the store when we had a shift to pull. After dinner Dad took a nap and returned to the store at 6:00 where he stayed until closing at 11:00.

Bridge, baseball and the movie on Thursday night were his primary local distractions.

The Saturday night Bridge games on the thick white glass-top table in the back of the prescription department at the store often lasted until the wee hours of Sunday morning. They also often got very noisy and frightened a few customers from time to time. The regulars at Bridge were: Professor F. D. Marshall, principal of one of the elementary schools; Dr. J. W. V. Cordice, a surgeon who lived across the street from us; Dr. William Cleland, our first board certified pediatrician; Dr. R. P. Randolph, a family medicine practitioner; and Dr. Alphonso E. Elder, the President of North Carolina College.

Dad's favorite team was the Brooklyn Dodgers. Very late in life he adopted the Atlanta Braves as well. He never liked any of the American League teams. He attended at least one game of any World Series that was played in New York City. He also never had a ticket for a game when he left home. Buying a ticket from someone who could not attend the game or purchasing a box office a ticket for standing room only and then finding a seat by tipping an usher added to the enjoyment of the excursion.

Dad played baseball and football at Howard but he enjoyed all sports and encouraged all of us and other young people to participate in sports as a means of building character.

The Howard Academy baseball team, circa 1915. Top row: Neal,
Parker, Jones, Mattocks. Middle row: B. Q. Coles, O. Brown, Lofton,
Holmes, Dabney. Bottom row: Cameron, P. Hardwick, Grakins,
York D. Garrett (Dad), S. Brown, B. M. Coles, H. Hardwick.

He and Mother had a standing date to go to the nine o'clock show at the
Center Theater every Thursday night. Mother would pick him up at the store
at 8:40. The Center was downtown and segregated. They bought their tickets
at a side window and then trudged up four or five flights of stairs that led
from a side street up to the "colored" balcony. The theater was well appointed;
even the "colored" section. It was Durham's premier theater complete with
a huge Wurlitzer Organ. I think they preferred the Center to the Carolina
Movie Theater because there were fewer steps and because of the organ. The
programs at the Center included a musical interlude by the organist, an RKO
Pathe news reel, a "short subject" such as a ten minute comedy film with actors
like Andy Clyde and Arthur Kennedy, a "sing along" session with old tunes
and the "bouncing ball," coming attractions for the next week and then the
feature film. When the movie was over they would go back to the store so Dad
could check the day's receipts and put the money in the safe.

During his many years of practice Dad was directly responsible for developing at least five black pharmacists who otherwise might not have had an opportunity. There are hundreds of people who, as youths, worked as clerks and delivery boys who are now solid, contributing citizens in their communities.

At one time Dad had three drugstores. When we left Tarboro and opened the Biltmore, he placed his sister, Mattie, in charge of the Tarboro store and arranged for a part-time pharmacist to handle the professional end. After assisting his sister Bea's son, Judson Garrett ("Yip") Parker, to get a degree in pharmacy and to pass the N. C. Board, he opened a second Durham store called Garrett-Parker on Fayetteville Street, one-half mile from the Biltmore and about the same distance from our house.

With the Biltmore store open 14 hours a day for six days and 12 hours a day on Sunday, Dad had no time for civic activity. He kept up with local politics through his customers, some of whom were the most influential blacks in town. They would sometimes have meetings in the rear booths in the store.

He expressed neither support nor objection to the push for public accommodations in which my wife, Wanda, and our children were involved in the late sixties and early seventies. Almost all of the protest marches to downtown passed by the Biltmore. He felt strongly that job discrimination needed to end but was ambivalent about desegregation of the theaters, hotels, eating establishments and schools. He recognized that his business and that of the other retailers around him would always serve black customers exclusively. Whites were not coming to our section to buy. Only to sell. I think he realized that one day the protesters would march downtown and never return to do business with him. I clearly recall the day the white merchants finally agreed to open their lunch counters and other establishments to blacks. Wanda and I went to 1502 and, in the kitchen, were joyfully telling Mother and Dad the details of the great changes that had come about that day. They listened intently, but their mood was reserved.

Dad was a strongly independent person. He worked as hard as anyone could to make a way for his family. He did whatever he had to do in the store to make it work. He knew how to do almost every job he hired someone to do, but he couldn't do plumbing, electrical work or carpentry. He often said to me that he had never found a left-handed hammer, screw driver or pliers. He was left-handed. But, whether janitorial, clerking or bookkeeping, if it needed to be done in the store, he would do it. Only in this way could he know what the work was worth. He knew how much a person could accomplish at the task per hour. He knew how much strength and how much brains the job demanded. He set the standards and decided how much to pay for the work.

Any small businessperson would do well to follow this example. I know I did in my business and advised my clients to do the same.

Dad was so independent that he refused to accept Social Security payments until he was 79. He thought it was welfare and would have nothing to do with it. I had to convince him that he had been paying into the system through the self-employment taxes he paid as an unincorporated business and that the money he would be getting was really his. I went back through his tax returns for twenty years and extrapolated for another twenty years to show him that if he began to accept payments right away, he would not collect all he had put into the system until he was nearly 100 years old. He finally consented so that he and mother began to draw checks. She was 72 when she got her first payment.

Although he had no time for civic involvement, he always voted. His father had been a Republican, but Dad, because of the single party system that developed in the South, was a Democrat. The Republican Party had become so weak that they fielded very few candidates and those candidates never won. The Democratic primary elections were the only elections that mattered because the primary winner always won against the Republican. Therefore, if you wanted your vote to count for something, you had to be a Democrat and vote in the Democrat primary. Though he was a registered Democrat he voted for whomever he considered the better candidate for the U. S. President. But he told me that none of the presidential candidates for whom he voted ever won. When Clinton ran against Bob Dole in 1996, at the age of 100 and for the first time in his adult life, he didn't vote. He explained that he couldn't bring himself to vote for Dole and that since his vote was obviously a jinx; he decided not to vote for the candidate he preferred, Bill Clinton.

Ultimately, Urban Renewal took both locations in Durham as well as all the other businesses along Pettigrew and Fayetteville Streets. The first to go was the Garrett-Parker store. "Yip," the nephew with whom dad had owned the Garrett-Parker store, had given up pharmacy as a career and had moved to New York. After Yip's departure, dad sold the store to William Wimberly, a young black pharmacist whose father (also a pharmacist) had gone to school with Dad at Howard. The Tarboro store had been taken several years earlier by Urban Renewal in Tarboro. A few years before he was forced to vacate the Biltmore, he opened a store with my brother, Oliver, who had returned from Los Angeles. With legal help, Oliver had gotten his North Carolina pharmacy license. He passed the pharmacy exams in both South Carolina and California, but failed the North Carolina test three times. Oliver argued that he should be given reciprocity in that a person who passed other boards could get licensed in North Carolina without taking the North Carolina test. The Board of Pharmacy argued that because Oliver took and failed the North

Carolina test, he could not be granted reciprocity. The only way for him to get a license was to pass the North Carolina test. Dad took the matter to our good friend, Lawyer M. Hugh Thompson. Lawyer Thompson wrote to the North Carolina Board that their position denied Oliver equal protection of the laws as required by the 14th Amendment to the United States Constitution. The Board capitulated and Oliver was licensed shortly thereafter.

When Urban Renewal finally took the Biltmore, Dad was eighty-six, but he did not retire. Oliver had not been able to make a go of the store Dad had opened with him and had taken a job in pharmacy at Duke Hospital. Dad moved his pharmacy into the store Oliver had run. He did not offer anything other than prescription services; no fountain, no patent medicines, no cosmetics or magazines; just prescriptions. As was his custom, he stressed customer service and even when he was over 100 years old he would personally deliver medicine to his most loyal customers.

My father was very generous with his family if he approved of the way you lived your life. His priority for his children, nieces and nephews was to get a college education. Any who were seriously working toward a baccalaureate and stayed out of serious trouble with the law found him a willing supporter. "Yip" Parker, his sister Bea's son, and Mariah (Popsie) Creed, the daughter of Mother's sister Geneva, lived with us while pursuing college work at the local college. Judson's pharmaceutical degree was at least partially underwritten by Dad. My sister, Gloria, Oliver and I had no debt when we finished college.

His generosity also extended to non-family employees at the store. He aided clerks who wanted to go to college. His arrangement was to reimburse them for tuition and fees at the end of any period during which they passed all courses.

I have sometimes wondered how he was able to do all that he did. His businesses were successful, but not wildly so. He was frugal as to his personal needs. He dressed well, but was not all that interested in clothes. He neither drank nor smoked. He provided the family with luxury cars, but we did not change cars often. Home was beautiful and well appointed but not nearly as fancy as most of the other professional's houses. When others built new homes, we stayed put. 1502 was the family home from 1934 until Dad died in 1998. Traveling was limited to the annual trips to the National Pharmaceutical Association meetings and the mandatory one- week stay in New York City. He budgeted carefully and monitored expenditures for both the business and the house, although once the household budget was agreed upon, Mother alone decided how to spend it.

Dad was proud of his nieces and nephews. His sisters produced four nephews, all of whom did well. "Yip," who initially became a pharmacist, later earned a master's degree in social work. Two others became physicians. One earned a master's degree and was a school principal. The children of these four all went to college and three have earned graduate degrees. Mother's siblings produced six children: all attended college and at least three earned their degrees. All except one had steady employment, got married and enjoyed a good family life. Of the thirteen children reared by these nieces and nephews seven are business or professional people and four are presently in college. I don't know about the final two. Their father married a white woman, passed for white, and cut off all communication with the family.

I think Dad's biggest disappointment was that two of Oliver's three children did not finish college. Both opted for careers in entertainment. Tommy, the oldest, was an internationally famous model and singer who lived in Paris for many years. Yvonne, the middle child, was also a singer but later focused her working life on community development. Yvonne spearheaded the project in Knoxville Tennessee to have an impressive statue of Alex Haley, the author of Roots, erected in one of the city's public parks. Now a citizen of Newark, Yvonne came in third in a 2010 race to unseat Corey Booker as Mayor. Although those two met with success, Dad always felt they should have at least completed college. A college degree, he felt, was the best insurance we could get against a life of dependency. Oliver's third child, Michael David, made Dad very happy by finishing undergraduate school. In 2005, and at the age of 35, Michael earned a Master's in Business Administration while working full time.

Dad stopped driving when he was 101. Before then he drove himself to the store seven days a week and would drive to deliver medicine to the customers who couldn't come to him. He drove to church on Sunday. On occasion he would drive to D. C. to see Gloria or to New York for a medical appointment with his nephew, Hobart Price. After Wanda and I moved from Southeast Durham, about 3/4 of a mile from 1502, to Southwest Durham, some five miles away, he got lost a few times and stopped trying to drive it. We provided the needed shuttle service.

When he went in for his license renewal at age 101 he could not read the road signs to the examiner's satisfaction. He was told he needed glasses. He had never worn glasses for driving. On occasion, at the store, he would use a magnifying glass to read small print or difficult handwriting. He went to another drug store and bought eyeglasses, but could never get the right ones. Since his long time friend, Dr. Dawson, the ophthalmologist, had retired, Dad decided it was time to give up driving. He was not going to go to a doctor he didn't know. The decision not to drive, however, also meant he had to discontinue the drugstore operation.

He surrendered his pharmacy license when he was almost 102. The state pharmacy board published an article about him in their newsletter. The article praised Dad for his years of work and for always completing the required professional education in spite of his age.

When Mother died in 1977, none of us thought Dad would survive even a year without her. But his work at the store, his love of travel, his enthusiasm for sports and the love of a multitude of friends and family members sustained him.

Our son, Nathan, Jr. and his wife, Gail stayed with him during the early part of their marriage starting in 1990. Later, Michael David, stayed with him until a few months before Dad died. He never had assistance at home beyond a part time housekeeper who cooked and cleaned.

Wanda and I made sure he kept himself presentable. We went to church with him. We took him on most of our motor trips to Detroit, New York, Philadelphia, and D. C. We made sure to have him for meals regularly. Wanda or I would drop by to see him three to four times per week. We were in touch by phone at least every other day when we were out of town and almost every day when we were in Durham.

Dad never used a cane. The only medicine he took was a vitamin and a heart pill. Sometimes when he was not feeling well, the best medicine was a chopped barbecue sandwich with "not too much slaw" from Dillard's Barbecue, a black restaurant located two miles down Fayetteville Street from 1502. It was not unusual for him to call Wanda at any time of day or night to pick up a sandwich for him, and she always complied, lovingly. He always insisted that if he ever needed to be hospitalized, I was to take him to the VA Hospital in Durham. In December 1998 when he was 103 he asked me to take him to the VA because he was not feeling well. I complied. The doctors and staff were truly amazed at his mental and physical condition and, in my opinion, subjected him to more tests than were appropriate, given his age. I know that he got uncomfortably cold while waiting in hallways for one test after another. Following that visit, which consumed around six hours, he never regained his usual vigor and demeanor. He died December 30th 1998, twenty days after his birthday, at the age of 104.

CHAPTER THREE

Brothers and Sister

Yorkie - Born White, Died Black, Lived in Full Color.

In 1923 Mother left Tarboro to try life for a while in New York City. Perhaps she had decided that Tarboro with all the racial bias and few employment opportunities was not what she wanted. Maybe she should be in New York. Perhaps Mother's brother, Nathan, and her sister, Sarah, both of whom lived in New York City, convinced her that even in New York, her prospects for employment were much brighter if she did not disclose that she was not Caucasian. Certainly, both of them did so whenever they chose to. If Mother did pass for white it would have been inconsistent with her fiery valedictory speech about racial discrimination and the denial of rights to black people. It would also have been inconsistent with the extreme displeasure she felt much later in life when Dad insisted that she pose as white to get food for the family at whites-only highway eating establishments during our motor trips below the Mason-Dixon Line. In my youth, she taught me the importance of racial pride and had me read books and news articles about black leaders. However, I know that in my own life, there have been occasions when the social and economic pressures of the moment caused me to compromise my values and my normally preferred courses of behavior; sometimes to my regret. A huge example of such a compromise is described in chapter six of this book.

In New York, Mother lived with Sarah and her husband, Lovelace Capehart, and found work. Mother nearly gained employment as a chorus girl in the 1923 version of the Ziegfeld Follies. She had passed the first screening but she declined the invitation for a second screening because she discovered she was pregnant. Yorkie arrived on October 1, 1923. Dad was running his pharmacy in Tarboro. Apparently he did not arrive in time for the birth because the hospital assumed Mother's race to be Caucasian and, accordingly, the birth certificate for York David Garrett III showed him as white.

It was a complicated birth. The doctors had to use forceps and that resulted in slight brain damage to the newborn child. After a brief recovery period in New York, Mother returned to Tarboro with the new baby. The doctor in Tarboro discovered that Yorkie also had an irregular heartbeat. The combination of the heartbeat and the brain damage led doctors to predict only a few years of life for him. Mother's loving care confounded that prediction; Yorkie lived a life filled with love, humor, pain and joy for 54 years. He lived with Mother and Dad his entire life and never married. My son, Marc, as a sub teen, often said that when he grew up, he wanted to be like Uncle Yorkie.

Yorkie had the lightest complexion of the family except, of course, for Mother. He was, what we called, *very* high yellow. He grew to the height of 5' 4" and was rotund, slightly cross-eyed and slightly pigeon-toed. He had a healthy appetite and was outgoing. He was mentally retarded.

Dad accepted, but never related well to Yorkie. As his first-born and his namesake, Yorkie was a deep disappointment. I don't recall a single instance when Dad treated him with kindness or sympathy. Instead, Dad would criticize his behavior, mock his shortcomings and, in the main, avoided involvement with him. Dad wasn't cruel. He just was not as loving to Yorkie.

Yorkie was retained for a year three different times between the first and sixth grades. He probably never passed any of the subjects but, because he was the son of York and Julia Garrett, teachers or the principal would give him social promotions. There was a change of schools for his seventh grade. Yorkie was nearing 16 while his classmates were only 12. The change placed Yorkie among students and teachers that he did not know. He became a disciplinary problem, probably because of the taunting and snickering of the other students, so the administration decided that his parents needed to keep him out of school. When his schooling ended he could spell a few words, write using block letters, and add. He could read surprisingly well. He had a really good memory for dates and events and got decent grades in history.

Yorkie had a difficult time accepting the arrival of our sister, Gloria. On one occasion after bathing Gloria, Mother returned to the bedroom to dress her. She discovered that the clothes she had laid out for the baby were gone. Then she caught the odor of burning cloth coming from the fireplace in the next room. Yorkie had taken the baby's clothes and thrown them in the fire. Mother told us that she guessed Gloria was to have been next.

Six years later, Yorkie made it clear to Gloria that she was not a welcomed companion when they walked home from school in Tarboro. He insisted that she walk behind him and would throw rocks at her to make sure she stayed far to his rear. Fortunately, he couldn't throw straight or hard. His throwing motion was more like a basketball player shooting a free-throw than a pitcher throwing a strike.

We were all disciplined by Mother; often with a switch. Yorkie got his share; maybe more than the rest of us. There was this time when Mother was really mad at me for having torn my pants. They were my Sunday pants and I knew I should not have been wearing them on Friday. Yorkie was in the room watching and listening. We were in the kitchen. Mother's voice kept rising in greater and greater anger as I tried to lie my way out of my predicament. Suddenly Yorkie ran out the back door. I wondered why. Maybe he thought he might be next for something he had done. Just when Mother seemed ready to really explode, Yorkie came up behind her and said: "You want a switch Momma?" He had one in his hand.

Yorkie loved baseball. He probably learned to love it from observing Dad's great passion for the game. Yorkie was at nearly every home game of the Durham Bulls, our minor league team. Mother or Dad would drop him off at the ballpark and he would hitch a ride back to the drugstore with anyone he knew. His main transportation back from the park was Lawyer Hugh Thompson, a good family friend. Yorkie knew the lawyer's car and where he parked it. I remember Lawyer Thompson telling Dad that often when he got to his car, Yorkie was sitting in it. Nobody locked their cars back then.

He listened to the radio and later watched television whenever a Yankees' game was broadcast. He was a true Yankee fan and bragged loudly whenever they won. And they won most of the time. This was the late 1940s when Jackie Robinson had just broken the color line and was playing for the Brooklyn Dodgers. Every black person in Durham, except Yorkie, was a Dodgers fan. When Larry Doby broke the color line with the Cleveland Indians of the American League, our loyalties were with that team; that is, all of us except Yorkie. And, of course, when the Dodgers and Yankees played in a World Series, Yorkie got to be very unpopular around town.

In addition to baseball, he loved church, apple pie, soap operas, *I Got a Secret* and working at the drugstore, pretty much in that order.

Church was a must for him. Every week he was at Sunday school, the eleven o'clock service and the Wednesday night prayer service. He walked the six tenths of a mile between church and home. Reverend Fisher and the church leaders recognized that Yorkie had the mental age of a six year old and gave him little chores that Yorkie could handle and feel good about. For instance, from around age thirty, although he was not a member of the Gospel Chorus, Yorkie's job was to place the hymnals in the seats to be occupied by the chorus and to collect them following service.

He also became an assistant usher and was assigned to pass the offering plate. If a worshiper did not contribute, Yorkie often would either comment about it to the person or pass the plate to him a second time. His comment was loud enough for worshipers nearby to hear. Mother tried for years to get him to stop doing that. Yorkie would promise, then forget, and revert to the practice. Apparently, the pastor, the head of the usher board and the chairman of the board of deacons didn't see any harm in letting him continue.

His was a busy life and if you interrupted his routine he'd give you trouble. I recall when Mother and Dad had been away for ten days to the national pharmaceutical convention with a side trip to New York, he got really upset. The domestic came each morning to fix Yorkie's breakfast and to straighten up the house a bit. I came in to see how he was doing and found him and the domestic in the kitchen. Yorkie was sitting in front of a bowl of grits and stamping his feet. Suddenly, he shot a fierce look at the domestic and shouted: "Grits a-damn-gin. If you think I'm going to eats grits every day for the rest of my life, you crazy." Then he turned to me and said, almost pleadingly: "I ain't had apple pie in a long time, either."

Ma Perkins and *Stella Dallas* were Yorkie's favorite radio series. When we got television in the late '50s, he watched all the soaps; his favorites were *The Guiding Light* and *As the World Turns.* During the Watergate hearings much of the afternoon programming was preempted, meaning the soap operas were off the air. Yorkie was upset, big time. He was sick and in his room when I stopped by to see him one day during the hearings. I heard the television through the door of his bedroom and went in to see how he was feeling. There was Yorkie bent over from the waist with his pajama pants down around his ankles and his bare behind pointed at the television screen. I exclaimed, "Yorkie!" He replied very angrily, "That's what I think about Watergate."

I think working in the drugstore extended his life greatly. People he had met at sports events, school and church came regularly to buy and visit with Yorkie. He was actually good for business.

Two large display windows flanked the entrance to the store. One of them contained a large pendulum clock that advertised a product named "666" used as a laxative and for colds. The rest of the window was devoted to displays for cosmetics and patent medicines. Nothing was sold from that window. The other window contained a fantastic array of comic books, newspapers and magazines such as *Ebony, Jet, True Confessions, Life,* and *Look.* All the merchandise inside the store was either behind very handsome display cases with sliding doors or inside three round mahogany glass top tables that had been fitted with two doors that could be locked. The cigar counter had glass on top and three sides of glass. Behind that counter the various brands of cigarettes were stored in slots. Next to the cigar and cigarette area was the soda fountain. It was equipped with a carbonated water spigot and five porcelain containers with pumps for coke, strawberry, cherry, lime and chocolate syrup. The fountain also had freezer spaces for six five-gallon ice cream containers complete with metal lids that hinged in the middle.

Yorkie's main job was to sell magazines, cigarettes, candy and fountain items. There was a chart to tell him how much sales tax to charge. The registers we used were mechanical, not electronic. You pushed the keys to indicate the amount of the sale and then pushed the keys and the "tax" key to show the sales tax. The machine gave the total. If the customer did not give you the exact amount, you had to figure the amount of change to return to him. Dad had taught Yorkie a system for giving the customers the right change and he seldom got mixed up or frustrated. He could dip ice cream for our customers, although Dad complained that he usually made the scoops too large. He could put the syrup, ice cream and milk needed to make a milkshake into the large metal container, but he didn't have the dexterity to put the metal container on the milkshake machine. The few times he tried were met with disaster. He just couldn't secure the container to the shaker so that it wouldn't fall off as the electrically driven mixing shaft did its work. The machine had a slot at the top into which the top edge of the container was supposed to fit and a small ledge near the bottom to hold the container upright. After a few cleanup jobs, Dad required Yorkie to call someone to do the mixing for him.

Dad's policy was to wrap customer purchases of cosmetics and patent medicines instead of using bags. The wrap was cheaper. But, on those rare occasions when Yorkie made a sale of a patent medicine, he couldn't wrap it. So, Dad decided to bear the additional expense of buying bags especially for his use.

It was Mother who pushed Dad to give Yorkie a job in the drugstore. Many families with retarded children hid them away, partially to protect them and partially for the embarrassment of it. We were fortunate that the store was there as an outlet for him. But I think that even if we hadn't had the store Mother, with her great love for him, would have found a way for Yorkie to have a full and meaningful life.

Yorkie liked the movies. The Regal Theater was two doors from the drugstore. It was a black-owned enterprise and offered great variety in programs: love stories; musicals; "chapter pictures" as we called them, such as the Green Hornet; suspense plots; and lots of action films, especially Westerns. All movies that featured black artists came to the Regal. Full-length movies such as *Green Pastures* and *Carmen Jones* were very popular. Shorter films featuring comedians "Pigmeat" Markham (originally from Durham), Mantan Mooreland and "Stepin' Fetchit" were often seen as was Herb Jeffreys, the black singing cowboy. Musical short features by Nat King Cole and Cab

Calloway were welcomed offerings. Dramatic actors and actresses such as Rex Ingram, Paul Robeson, Hattie McDaniels, Nina Mae McKinney, Louise Beavers and Lena Horne were always a hit in whatever roles they played. If there was no black talent in the film, the audience identified with the swarthy ones - Sabu, Anthony Quinn, and even Dorothy Lamour.

Yorkie would often sit through the programs two or more times. I recall that a regular customer of the drugstore once stopped by after a movie and told Dad that Yorkie was telling anyone sitting near him what was going to happen next in the movie. He could do this, of course, because he had already seen it at least once. Later that evening when the theater closed, Dad confronted Yorkie about the problem and told him that if he didn't stop doing it, the people sitting near him would get mad and have the manager put him out. "Unh unh," Yorkie replied, "No they won't. They get mad all right, but *they* go out."

He had a hearty laugh and laughed often. He also showed wit. I recall one hot day our brother Oliver and I were in his car and we spotted Yorkie walking to the church to attend a mid-day funeral service. We stopped and Yorkie got in the back seat. Oliver, who had recently graduated from pharmacy school, chastised Yorkie for not waiting for someone to drive him to the service. Oliver said "Yorkie this hot weather could cause you to have a heart attack and die." Yorkie replied, meekly, "All right, Oliver," and fell silent for a moment. Then he added: "I didn't know you were a *medical* doctor."

He was generous. I recall on a road trip when Yorkie, Wanda and I were in the front seat with Oliver's two children and our children in the rear. We stopped for gas and I bought Yorkie a soda with ice in a large paper cup with no plastic lid. As we drove along, Yorkie was sipping the soda and Yvonne said from the rear, "Uncle Yorkie, let me have some soda." Yorkie said "all right Yvonne" and, without turning his body, immediately swung his arm straight up and in an arc over his head to pass the cup back to her. We heard Yvonne shout "Uncle Yorkie! No!" Too late. When the cup passed the top of his head Yorkie flexed his wrist slightly to get it closer to her, and Yvonne got drenched.

Yorkie died of rectal cancer. I believe he was in considerable pain for the last year of his life. I learned that he secretly brought home bottles of aspirin from the store and would take them when no one was around. Dad and Mother discovered empty aspirin bottles in his room and chastised him for consuming them. They explained how harmful aspirin is in large doses. Yorkie had complained that he wasn't feeling well, but was unable to describe what was bothering him with specificity. During his final year, Mother was also in very bad health and did not have the strength to see to Yorkie's needs as she always had.

Mother died in June 1977 and Yorkie followed two months later in August. I had gone to the hospital to visit with him and was told that he had just passed. The doctors asked if they could remove his brain so they could study it. "Absolutely not!" I responded.

He was loving and colorful. I'll never stop missing him.

Gloria Williams Garrett, the Queen

She was born June 5, 1925. My view of her from my earliest recollections until she was around 30 was that she was very pretty, very smart, very spoiled and mean. From age 30 until now she is still very pretty and very smart. The other two traits have been replaced by kindness, thoughtfulness and generosity.

In some ways, Mother and Dad both were closer to Gloria than they were to Yorkie, Oliver and me. As a senior citizen myself with a daughter, granddaughter and four great granddaughters of my own, I can understand it. But I surely didn't like it back then.

She was the queen of every contest she entered. Gloria and Mother shared with us the story of Gloria's coronation at around age 13 (I was six at the time) as The May Queen. On the day of her coronation, Gloria had on her costume, complete with a long train held by eight attendants, and was being escorted to her throne that was awaiting her in the center of a grassy field. Suddenly, Mother told us, Gloria veered off course followed by her train and attendants and went back inside the school building. Mother and the other assembled parents wondered what had happened, but ten minutes later the Queen and her attendants emerged from the building and resumed their march to the throne. At home, after the ceremony, Mother asked about the detour. Gloria responded that she had to go to the toilet, to which Mother replied: "Queens just don't do that."

Before reaching the age for entering high school, Gloria was a part of a group of boys and girls whose parents were professional people and business leaders in our town. However, for their high school years, most of them were sent to Palmer Memorial Institute, a private boarding school for blacks 50 miles west of Durham. The school was started and led by Charlotte Hawkins Brown. It was accredited as a high school. The children of many of the upper income families from many Northeastern, Southern and Southwestern states went there. Gloria went to Hillside High, the Durham public high school for blacks at that time. In 1938, the year she was ready for high school, the nation was still mired in the Great Depression and Dad could not afford the cost of private schooling. He always regretted the "Palmer denial" and tried to make up for it in numerous ways later in her life.

She was a very good student at Hillside and finished near the top of her class. Although she was very popular in high school, her social activities were circumscribed because Mother disapproved of some of her would-be close girl friends and boy friends that attended Hillside.

At home, Gloria had the single room; the three boys shared a room. She had the clothes because girls needed more clothes than boys. She got her favorite dessert (chocolate pie) much more often than we boys got our favorites.

Gloria at the cigar counter in the drugstore, circa 1942. Photo courtesy of the North Carolina Collection, Durham County Library.

She was sympathetic with Yorkie, but toward Oliver and me she was a shrew. When Oliver was around eleven she told him he was adopted. She said: "Look at yourself. You're tall, you're skinny, and you've got red hair. The rest of us are short, plump and have dark brown hair." And then the clincher: "Mother and Dad found you in a garbage can." Oliver believed it.

For me, it was my obesity and large tits that she hit with. From the time I was three or four I was fat. When I was in first grade, I participated as the dancer in a skit that was presented to the students at Duke University. The skit was done to the song, *Mr. Five By Five*, a popular tune in 1937 recorded by

Louis Jordan and his "Tympany Five.". The words to the song were: "Mister Five by Five. He's five feet tall and he's five feet wide. He don't shake it no mo' from head to toe than he do from side to side." I recall the horror of seeing my tits sprout. First they appeared near my arm pits and then traveled to my chest. I agonized over whether or not I was a hermaphrodite and would check myself often to be sure there was no vagina. By age thirteen I was 190 pounds and had a full bosom. Once, when she saw me stripped to the waist, Gloria laughed and told me I needed a bra. Then she went into her room and tossed me one of hers. (I have since learned that the condition is called gynecomastia.)

When she went off to Howard University, Oliver and I were glad, but we still didn't get to use the Queen's room. It had to be kept pretty and fresh for the Queen's visits at Christmas, spring break and summer.

She majored in economics at Howard and compiled a very good record. In her senior year Dad made an installment on his obligation for the "Palmer denial" and gave her a white Kaiser automobile. The car had a bison hood ornament. The bison is the Howard symbol.

She married her college sweetheart, Bill Haynes. After finishing Howard undergraduate, Bill went on to finish Howard Law as well. He was from Chicago and the couple moved there after Bill finished law school. But Bill was an alcoholic. He never took the Illinois Bar Examination because, he said, he was too busy handling the estate of his deceased father. He didn't have time to study or get a job.

When the National Pharmaceutical Association convention was held in Chicago, Mother and Dad attended as they did every year and they, of course, spent time with Gloria and Bill. During one of their gatherings, Bill was drunk and was verbally abusive to Gloria. Two months later Dad flew to Chicago, told Gloria to go out and pick out a car. She selected beautiful green and gold Mercury. Dad paid for it and the two of them packed all her belongings and drove back to Durham. The second installment on the "Palmer denial."

Once in Durham, Gloria filed for divorce.

She drove the Mercury back to live in D. C. after about a year and found employment in the U. S. Department of Labor, where she stayed until retirement. She rose through the ranks at Labor and at the pinnacle of her career was the Chief of the Branch of Foreign Economic Policy. That position required her to review prospective U. S. and foreign trade polices to determine the potential effect on labor in this country. She traveled to every continent except Africa to represent the U. S. during her years at Labor. She even lived in Geneva, Switzerland for two years as a part of our delegation to the Kennedy Round of Tariff Negotiations. Gloria also became a member of the Senior Executive Service, a distinction earned through meritorious service and special course work. The SES is as high as you can go as a federal government employee without being a Presidential Appointee.

Before she retired, Gloria married Judge Carlisle Pratt whom she had known for several years. Carlisle's first wife, Peggy, died when their two children, Sharon and Benaree, were quite young. Later, Carlisle married Jean, a friend of Gloria's, but that marriage ended in divorce. During this period, Gloria was married to Don Vernon, an administrator at the Howard University School of Dentistry. Several years after her marriage to Vernon was dissolved, and Carlisle and Jean had divorced, she and Carlisle decided to wed

The two girls have done very well. Benaree, the younger, lives in Boston with her husband Fletcher Wiley and has met with great success in business. Sharon (Kelly) became a lawyer, then Mayor of D. C. and is now in business, also.

Carlisle died after he and Gloria had been married for fifteen years. He was a super brother-in-law and was a great friend and inspiration to me. We had many long talks about the law as it applied to a variety of things I was involved in. He is a big part of the reason that I went to law school before my career as an accountant ended.

Gloria was devoted to Mother and Dad. During her stay in Geneva she had Mother to fly over to spend some time with her touring Europe. It was something Mother had always wanted to do. A year later Gloria returned to the U. S. via a cruise ship and played Bridge with the Bridge great, Goren.

After Mother's death Gloria stayed close to Dad. He always enjoyed driving to D. C. to stay with her a few days. She would cook for him and often she and friends would drive him to Atlantic City for a night or two at the Claridge Hotel and Casino where Dad had a favorite slot machine. What would have made Dad happiest would have been for Gloria to move to Durham and take care of him. She didn't, and it's a good thing that she didn't. For one thing, she really loves living in D. C. Second, in Durham she had very few friends left and virtually no outlets other than family for her interests. And third, it allowed Wanda and me to get to know my father better through taking responsibility for his care.

Gloria is also very good to her nieces, nephews and cousins. They are always welcome to stop with her when in D. C. She remembers them at Christmas and other special occasions. Wanda and I also love to visit her. We have a lot of common interests in politics, sports, racial progress, economics and Bridge.

Somewhere along the way Gloria learned how to be a truly great sister. I cannot imagine having a better one.

Oliver, The Maverick I Didn't Understand But Idolized.

Oliver Thomas Garrett was born November 17, 1927 and was the sibling I idolized.

He was four years older and taught me to play tennis, ping-pong and pool. He was naturally left-handed but, luckily for me, he played ping-pong and served in tennis with his right hand. But since he played pool left handed, to this day I shoot pool the way he did.

Oliver, Yorkie and I shared the "boy's room" at home. "Queen" Gloria had a room all to herself.

Oliver and I slept together on a double bed and Yorkie had a single bed adjacent to ours. The room was actually quite small but the three windows avoided that closed-in feeling. There were two very small closets for hanging our clothes. The rest of our belongings fit into the two chests of drawers.

We did the usual roughhousing in the "boy's room" including pillow fights, jumping on the beds and wrestling. Yorkie's favorite activity was to sit astride the footboard to his bed and pretend to ride it like a cowboy. He would shout: "Boogidy-boogidy up the hill, boogidy-boogidy down the hill, boogidy-boogidy cross, boogidy-boogidy un-cross."

Keeping the room straightened up fell to Oliver and me. Yorkie was not much help. When we made the bed it always seemed that Oliver got his side straight first and always commanded me to "pull it on your side." Even today when I am helping Wanda make our bed I remember Oliver when she says: "pull it on your side."

Oliver was smart, but not as good a student as I was. Unlike me, he was considered a regular guy and was very popular in school.

The girls loved him because he was handsome, slim, around 5 feet 10 inches and a good athlete. His hair was a reddish brown. His complexion was medium brown.

The boys liked him because he was friendly and willing to try almost anything. He wasn't exactly reckless, but definitely venturesome. He'd walk across the railroad trestle when others were afraid. With odds and a point spread he would take a bet on who would win any event. He wasn't afraid of critters of any sort. Snakes, spiders, bats, even rats didn't bother him at all. He played a little trumpet, saxophone, and clarinet; he didn't want to be a serious performer, he just wanted to amuse his friends and himself.

As a teenager Oliver spearheaded the creation of a young men's social club called the Gaylords. To be a member you had to enjoy music, dancing, partying and women. Social status and family background were of no importance. None of the members were involved in anything more illicit than the under aged occasional drinking of beer and peach brandy. You just had to want to have a good time. They pooled their money and talents for picnics, parties and formal dances. Many of the Gaylords went on to become solid citizens of Durham: Attorney William Marsh, Dr. (Ph. D.) Walter Brown and restaurant owner Claiborne Tapp, to name a few.

The existence of the Gaylords prompted the creation of the Gayladies who usually collaborated with the boys on events. To me, those "older women" were the prettiest group in town.

The sports he loved most were football and tennis. He was second-string running back - scat back- they called it in high school. He excelled in tennis, however, and for good reason.

Our house was four doors from the Algonquin Tennis Club. The Algonquin was a membership organization and the Garretts were members. The complex consisted of a two story white frame house with dining and party facilities downstairs and rooms for black tourists up stairs. It was managed by a succession of elderly ladies. Behind the house was a generous and well-kept lawn that sloped down to three red-clay tennis courts that were on two levels. There was a wire fence around three sides of the courts and behind was a thickly wooded area, a stream, then more woods until they gave way to the recreation fields for Hillside High. There were umpire stands for each court. For court two, which was about six feet lower than court one, there were seats for spectators built into the embankment that separated the upper from the lower courts.

The older members of the club took delight in teaching the kids how to play. Their attention was not limited to the children of members, however. The only condition placed on help with learning the game was that the child had to have a tennis racquet and proper tennis attire. You didn't have to come from a wealthy family to learn, but you weren't likely to be able to manage the equipment and attire if your family was truly impoverished.

Ms B. J. Whitted - "Miss Bess" as we called her - was especially active with the youth group. She was an executive at North Carolina Mutual and her active playing days were over, but she would spend time on weekends and in the summer early evenings teaching the game.

The courts, being clay, required a lot of maintenance. The lines were a mixture containing white lime and were painted on by brush. When it rained or after heavy play, the lines had to be swept or completely re-done. The courts had to be compacted periodically by using a water-filled metal drum with a handle attached to bars that ran through the center of the drum. In dry weather the courts had to be sprinkled to keep down the dust. The nets had to be moved indoors when the courts were not in use to protect them from the ravages of weather and to discourage play by nonmembers

The maintenance on the courts was done by Sam Moore whose

woodworking shop was adjacent to the tennis courts. Sam made crates and pallets for a living. He also was a good teacher of woodworking arts. He was personally responsible for two of Durham's black Soap Box Derby champions. He helped design the cars and the kids built them under Sam's supervision.

Sam did the work on the courts for little pay but was given the right to play. This was the entry for the children from families of less means. Sam would allow the kids to come into his shop and make tennis paddles from scrap sheets of wood that were always around. The kids who made decent paddles were welcome to play with Sam and one another as Sam's guests through his "sweat equity" membership. Many of Sam's kids got to be pretty good and it was not unusual for the "racqueted" kids to lose to Sam's kids in some of the club's tournaments.

So, Oliver learned tennis and taught it to me. He served right handed, then switched and played the rest of the point with his left. He was better than almost all of the teenagers with whom he played and many of the adults.

Oliver had friendships from every corner of the city, because he was popular at Hillside High, the only high school for blacks. Durham High was the school for whites. Most, but not all, of his friends met with Mother's approval, but Oliver resented the fact that not all of them were acceptable to Mother. She would ask him what he knew about his friends' families but Oliver would seldom share any information. They were his friends, regardless of their backgrounds.

This was an issue that he and Mother never resolved and his feelings about it broadened into a general view that Mother was snob. He felt that she patronized the employees at the store. He concluded that the women in her two clubs, because of their social and economic status, were also snobs. When Dad tried to explain that he and Mother were concerned with Oliver's safety and development, it didn't help. They were both wrong, he thought.

When Oliver finished Hillside High the diploma only called for completion of the eleventh grade. The next year they added grade twelve. He had not done well enough for admission to Howard, so Dad and Mother sent him off to Cambridge, Massachusetts for a year at Cambridge Latin High. While there, he lived with Mother's cousins, the Cottens.

The experience strengthened him enough to win admission to Howard. But that lasted only one year because he was having too much fun. The next September he enrolled at North Carolina College for Negroes, which was six blocks down Fayetteville Street from 1502.

He married Doris Delaine, a beautiful dark brown skinned woman from Manning South Carolina whom he met in college. Doris was also a tennis player. They seemed to be a natural fit: Oliver was playing number one for the college tennis team and each had a great sense of humor. They were married a year after both had graduated and after Oliver completed basic training in the Air Force. They made a great couple for several years. He was assigned to an Air Force Base near Orlando Florida and while living there, their first child, Oliver Thomas Garrett, Jr. - "Tommy" - was born in 1954.

Southeastern Tennis Tournament circa 1963. Fourth person from top left is Doris Delaine Garrett, fifth is Oliver Garrett. Fourth person from top right is me. First person from bottom left is Yvonne Garrett (Doris and Oliver's daughter). Second and third persons from bottom right are my son Devron Marc and Doris and Oliver's son, Oliver Thomas, Jr.

Following military service, Oliver was admitted to the Philadelphia College of Pharmacy. PCP, as it was called, was considered one of the very best schools of pharmacy in the country. Oliver's decent grades in college, good performance on the entrance exam and the help of Oliver Winters, an influential black dentist in Philadelphia got him accepted. Winters had been a close friend of Dad's at Howard. In fact, Oliver had been named for him.

I was surprised to learn that Oliver had chosen pharmacy as a career. Though he, like all of us, had his duties in the drugstore, he always said that he hated pharmacy and the drugstore business. The hours were too long and the compensation was too weak.

While Oliver attended PCP, Doris got a job teaching Physical Education at Hillside and she and the baby lived at 1502. Mother and Dad were delighted to have them both. There was plenty of room since Gloria, having already graduated from Howard, was living in Chicago and I was living in Detroit. Before he finished PCP, Oliver's second child, Yvonne Delaine, was born.

When Oliver returned to Durham following graduation, he worked for Dad at the store. However, he did not do all he needed to do to get his North Carolina pharmacy license. Two things were required: he had to pass the written examination and he had to complete an apprenticeship. Oliver did not prepare well enough for the examination and refused to complete the workbook that the State Board required as evidence of the apprenticeship. He felt that his degree from one of the finest schools of pharmacy in the nation meant that he had the knowledge needed to pass the written exam and that the apprenticeship workbook was a ridiculous requirement. Rightly or wrongly, he concluded that the Board's denial was based on his race, not his ability. He knew that Dad had faced a similar problem nearly thirty-five years earlier.

To help the young couple along, Dad bought a two-story house three blocks north of 1502. The mortgage was held by Mutual Savings and Loan; black-owned. The house had upper and lower apartments. Oliver, Doris and the two children moved into the lower apartment and Dad arranged for Oliver to assume the mortgage. The rent from the upper apartment went to Oliver and, instead of paying rent to Dad, Oliver was responsible for making the mortgage payments.

Unfortunately, things began to go wrong. Because Oliver did not have a license, his income was not what he needed it to be. Also, Oliver's popularity with his old classmates, both the women and the men, continued and served as a major distraction from his duties as a family man. He and Doris began to have terrible fights and she was able to get a court-ordered separation including a restraining order requiring Oliver to move out of the house and stay away from the family. Oliver moved back to 1502.

Things went along fairly smoothly until one night after a few drinks Oliver decided he wanted to see Doris. He went up to the apartment and banged on the door but Doris would not let him in. Suspecting he was drunk, she called the police. Before the police came, however, Oliver found a baseball bat and broke every ground floor window in the apartment. After he got out of jail and paid a fine, I asked him what made him do such a thing. He knew I wouldn't understand so he tossed it off by telling me: "It seemed like a good idea at the time."

For her safety and that of the children, Doris relinquished the apartment to Oliver and moved back to 1502. Both Mother and Dad welcomed them. Eventually, however, after the divorce was granted, she decided to move to Newark, New Jersey where her very good friend, Ethel McLaurin Tapp had recently gone. Ethel had been a classmate of mine and had gone through a divorce from Claiborne Tapp, Oliver's good friend.

After his family left, Oliver decided to take the South Carolina pharmacy examination. He studied hard and passed it. But his request for reciprocity to North Carolina was denied. The North Carolina Board's position was that reciprocity was not available to anyone who had taken, but not passed, the North Carolina examination.

With no family, no license and little income, Oliver decided that perhaps Durham was a curse for him. He had just managed to buy a navy blue convertible Mercury when he called me to say he had decided to drive out to California to look around to see if he liked it. I responded: "I think that is a good idea. When are you leaving?" Oliver replied: "In about five minutes." I said: "Gee, Oliver, when did you decide to do this?" His reply: "About five minutes ago."

I always envied Oliver's ability to act spontaneously. My whole life, I have been slow to act and when I do, I choose the safest path open to me. I choose to be reliable and steady rather than Mercurial. I thought Oliver was wrong to terrorize his wife and children the way he did, but I so wished to have the guts to just pick up and leave a bad situation. My style is to stay and try to work it out.

Oliver left, and no one knew where he was. I went to his apartment every day to collect his mail. I would open his credit card bills to get clues. When one month's worth of charges proved to be all in Los Angeles, we called James Hubbard, a dentist from Durham who had relocated to Los Angeles to see if Oliver had been in touch. Hubbard had been in touch and gave us an address and phone number.

After three months in Los Angeles without making any payments on his car, Oliver went out one morning to find it gone. He knew it hadn't been stolen. He simply got on the bus and went to work. After another three months with no payments on the mortgage for the house, the S&L announced to Dad that they were foreclosing. Dad asked me if I was interested in bringing the payments up to date and assuming the debt. At first I said no. We didn't want to live in an apartment and we couldn't afford the outlay, even though we had accumulated enough savings to catch up the missed payments. I also did not want the responsibility for managing rental property. I was then told that we wouldn't have to carry the debt for long because the city was planning to widen the street and would demolish the house. Wanda and I agreed to the transaction and after a few more months the house was taken by the city. However, they only needed twenty feet of the land for the project. They tore down the house but left the remaining land in Dad's name. They paid enough to satisfy the mortgage, so Dad came out OK. The land that remained was more valuable than the amount Dad had paid as down payment on the property when he bought it for Oliver. I felt OK about the deal because what Wanda and I paid to catch up Oliver's arrearage was more than the principle payments he had made. Dad refunded the money Wanda and I put out to save the foreclosure by taking out a small loan on the raw land which was then free and clear of debt. Fifteen years later, I was accused of profiting from the deal by Marion Garrett, Oliver's second wife. My conscience is completely clear. I explained what happened only once and decided not to discuss it further when the accusation resurfaced on several occasions.

Oliver passed the California pharmacy examination and found work in one of the chain stores in L. A. After two years he married Marion, a girl he had met before he left Durham. Marion was also pretty, a graduate of North Carolina College for Negroes (by then the name had changed to North Carolina College at Durham), was a tennis player and taught physical education. To that marriage was born a son, Michael David. Mother and Gloria flew to California when the baby was born.

More trouble came Oliver's way. He was caught in a sting operation when he sold narcotics without a prescription. Perhaps he needed the extra money and perhaps he had concluded that the sale was not immoral even though illegal. Once, on a business trip to L. A., I went to a party with Oliver where the people were using cocaine. Before they broke out the drug, I thought that this was a very religious group; everyone wore a cross. When the white powder came out and everyone started to scoop it up with the crosses, I was amazed. I had never seen anything like it. Square me.

Oliver did a little time in prison, lost his license and he, Marion and Michael David moved back to Durham. They stayed at 1502 for a little while but soon found a house. Marion taught and Oliver resumed work with Dad.

But old habits returned and soon Marion and Oliver were estranged. He left Durham in late 1976 to take a job in South Carolina but told no one where to find him. He just happened to come back to 1502 for a visit on June 25th 1977 and learned that Mother had just died. Dad, Gloria, Popsie, Marion and I each thought that one or the other of us had been able to contact Oliver and that was why he had come. We were all seated in Dad and Mother's room when Oliver asked where was Mother. When Dad told him, Oliver shouted: "No one told me Mother was dead," broke down and sobbed heavily. Gloria took the lead in trying to comfort him.

He stayed in Durham after Mother died and worked again with Dad. After he was able to get his North Carolina license he took a job as a pharmacist at Duke Hospital. But he lost his job at Duke for complaining too bitterly about the way the hospital treated the black employees. Oliver always identified more with labor than with management.

Shortly after leaving Duke he developed testicular cancer and was operated. During his recuperation he had a tube in his left side that had to be drained twice a day. For a while, a home duty nurse did the draining, but Oliver could not afford to keep her. By this time, Dad had moved his downgraded pharmacy operation and his income was limited. The answer was for me to do the draining and I did it faithfully until he healed. When I was absent, Wanda drained it.

The cancer was not gone, however, and two years later he died at Veteran's Hospital. Before he died, his ex wife, Doris, came to visit and sat with him hour after hour. When she had to return to Tennessee where she was then living, Wanda and I would sit with him as much as we could. He slipped into a coma and she and I would take turns talking to him. It didn't matter what we said, but we felt that just hearing familiar voices would keep him alive. I recall clearly that on his last evening, Wanda, Cousin Popsie and I were with Oliver and talking. Wanda left the room to walk Popsie to her car. I stayed behind and talked but left the room briefly to take care of my perpetually weak bladder. When I returned three or four minutes later, Oliver had stopped breathing. I recall asking out loud as tears welled up in my eyes: "Is that all?"

Living room at 1502, circa 1947. Left to right: Oliver, Yorkie, Beft, Mother, Gloria, Dad, me.

CHAPTER FOUR

Yale

I entered Yale in September, 1943. I was seventeen.

Mother, but not Dad, accompanied me. Mother came despite the fact that she had suffered a bad burn on the right side of her face that was still painful and bandaged. I tried to dissuade her from making the trip by assuring her that I was man enough to handle the transition. She, however, was not about to let her baby boy go without a last chance at mothering. Dad kept the store open, as usual.

Traditionally, Yale freshmen were housed on Old Campus, a quadrangle of buildings surrounding grass, walkways and benches. Two additional buildings are inside the quad. One of them, Connecticut Hall, has a statue of Nathan Hale (a Yale graduate) in front of it. That building was constructed in1752. Old Campus is adjacent to the New Haven Green on one side, a variety of privately owned businesses on another, and other parts of the university on the other two sides. However, around 150 members of the class of 1952 and I were assigned to the barracks that had been occupied by Navy men who attended Yale during World War II. The barracks were about a mile and a half from Old Campus.

I had a double room and my roommate was Robert Byas Ward from Dallas. He, like I, had gone to a public high school and was 16 days younger than I. He wasn't expecting me and I wasn't expecting him. We only learned whom we were sharing a room with when we met in the room assigned. When I got there, Bob was already settled in. I could see the shock on his face when I struggled through the door with my luggage. He had taken the top bunk and after a very brief, pregnant pause, he hopped down and offered to help me.

I got along quite well with Bob and perhaps twenty of the residents of Sachem Wood, as the barracks were called. A few of the students who, I think, were naturally outgoing, sought me out for casual conversations. My race was never a topic of those conversations. As to the Sachem Wood residents I never met, I have always assumed that the reason I did not meet them was that they had other things on their minds. I didn't seek them out and they didn't seek me out. As I look back, it seems that most of my non-black friends were Jews and Italians.

There Is Black Life at Yale!

It took me a week to learn that there were other blacks on campus. There were three others in the class of 1952 and they had been assigned to room together on Old Campus: Charles Payne, the son of a dentist, was from Charleston, West Virginia; John Richard Cooper, the son of a postman, was from Cincinnati, Ohio and Jack Harris, the son of a chemist, was from New Haven. They did not know one another before they were assigned to room together and I wondered what happened to me. Why hadn't I been put with them? Most of the housing on Old Campus accommodated four men. There were only three of them.

So there were four of us in a class of 1,500. The class of 1952 was, I was told by a white classmate who had a job in admissions, the largest class of blacks ever recruited to Yale.

Soon after meeting Charles, Dick and Jack I learned there were others: two black sophomores, Sidney Clark and Enoch Woodhouse - both from Boston; two juniors, Byrd Brown from Pittsburgh and Robert Rivers from New York; and one senior, Levi Jackson, the star football running back.

So there were nine of us in the undergraduate school (Yale College) of around 6,000.

Still later I met the remaining three black students: one, a law school junior, Charles Fielding from Arkansas; two, a divinity school student, Emanuel Branch from New Haven and three, a woman in the graduate school of drama whose name I do not recall because I seldom saw her.

So there were twelve of us in the University population of around 11,000.

Charles, Dick, Jack and I got to be very good friends. The most valuable member of the foursome was Jack because he was our avenue to the New Haven women. We got a lot of special treatment from the women and a lot of grief from the New Haven men.

At the end of the first semester there had been enough attrition to make room on Old Campus for some of us who were in the barracks. I was one of the lucky ones. So four of us shared two rooms and a bath in Wright Hall: Bob Ward, Ray McElligott (the son of a naval officer from Chevy Chase, Maryland), and Carl McMillan (the son of a diplomat and also from Chevy Chase but who had lived in Lima, Peru with his father).

A week into the second semester I discovered that another black, John Johnston, from Connecticut had transferred to Yale as a sophomore for the spring semester and was living in a single in Wright Hall.

So now there were thirteen.

Racial Attitudes

The blacks got together regularly to share stories about our girlfriends, homes and relatives and to talk about our experiences at Yale with faculty and with other students. We had friends among the white students, but we preferred one another for "family" talk.

The faculty seemed more curious about us than the students were. It was not unusual for a faculty member to pull one of us aside and inquire about our academic and personal lives before Yale. None of us felt that the faculty graded or treated us differently. Students, on the other hand, seemed generally not to care about our backgrounds. Occasionally, the topic of race would come up with those whites with whom I had established friendship. I would ask questions and so would they.

The students who were merely acquaintances rather than friends, sometimes were patronizing.

I recall only one instance of what I considered racist behavior. One evening after dinner, I was playing ping-pong with a white student who was about as good as I was. The game was tight and we both were making spectacular shots. A crowd began to watch and then two or three of them decided to make bets on which of us would be the ultimate winner. One of them announced he was betting on me and declared he would take bets from anyone who favored my opponent. The minimum bets were $20. To me, $20 was an obscene amount to bet on anything. I won the game and the student who backed me was calling for a second game with new bets. It made me feel like a prized nigger that the master was having sport with. I slammed my paddle down, congratulated my opponent for a good game, stared at my backer and walked out. Was he racist? Was I super-sensitive? I'll never know.

Bird Brown, the junior from Pittsburgh, was the most vocal on race. He often said that his blackness was the major trauma of his life. I think what he meant was that he wanted to be white. I never felt that way. Yes, I wanted the treatment accorded to whites in our society, but I never wanted to be white. I never accepted the idea that blacks were inherently inferior to whites, though

I had heard it thousands of times. People, I thought, are gifted in different ways regardless of race. I liked my blackness. I was proud of my ancestors. I knew I was as good as anyone of any race.

And then I had a conversation that shook me to the core. I was told by my white friend who had a student job in admissions that my application to Yale was accepted, not because of my high school performance and the results on the College Board examination, but because of my race. I knew I was the best student at Hillside. But I had never compared my scholastic performance to anyone who was not black. I did not know how I did on the College Boards compared to the white students coming from the segregated schools near Durham who took the examination with me. Were my results far below theirs? Could it be that I was, in fact, inferior to all these white people?

At the end of our freshman year, eight of the nine blacks were inducted into the Alpha Phi Alpha Fraternity, the oldest of the college-based, black Greek-letter fraternities. It was established in 1906 at Cornell University by a small group of black undergraduates who felt the need to be supported by one another and felt the desire to be supportive of new arrivals on that campus who were also black. None of the fraternities on the Yale campus had ever had a black member as far as we knew. They functioned primarily to have a good time and as a means of business networking after college. Alpha and the other black Greek-letter fraternities and sororities, on the other hand, were created to serve our communities, encourage academic achievement and to provide cultural and social outlets. Charles Fielding, the student in law school, was already an Alpha and served as Dean of Pledgees. Zeta Chapter had been established at Yale much earlier, but because there had not been enough blacks on campus at the same time to meet the minimum membership requirement of the Alpha constitution as it had been amended, its charter should have been withdrawn. However, somehow, the Alphas of New Haven who had joined at black colleges in various parts of the country, managed to keep the charter alive by becoming members of Zeta. Actually, the men should have formed a graduate chapter for the City of New Haven, but there weren't enough to do that either. They welcomed the new recruits with open arms, but they didn't slack off on the hazing that is part of the requirements to "cross the burning sands" into Alpha.

So Many New Things

My freshman year was an explosion of learning that had little to do with the classes. Jack's father was a chemist in an industrial firm in New Haven. I had never met a black chemist who was not a teacher. Jack introduced me to a black engineer who lived in New Haven, but before that introduction,

I had no idea that there were any blacks in that profession. I met a beautiful black/Puerto Rican high school girl who was Catholic. I had never met either a Puerto Rican or a black Catholic. I had never met a Jew or an Italian and I learned to enjoy corned beef and pizza, neither of which had I tasted before Yale. The wealth of some of the students was unbelievable. The buildings, library, equipment and landscaping were all much more impressive than I had seen at North Carolina College and Duke University back home. And the Payne Whitney Gymnasium! I marveled at all that it had to offer: swimming pools on one of the top floors, a tennis court, the varsity basketball arena, polo practice facilities, weight rooms, track and about any kind of equipment made. I had never heard of a field house where you could enjoy outdoor sports inside. I didn't know there were such sports as ice hockey, lacrosse, soccer and crew racing. I had entered a world that I never knew existed.

I also got my first opportunity to confirm what I had been told about the uniqueness of Durham. Blacks in New Haven did not own businesses at anything like the rate in Durham. The largest enterprise was Key's Funeral Home. No financial institutions, manufacturers, schools or developers, and very few professionals and retail establishments.

Good News on Grades

At the end of my first year I came home and learned that my grades had been sent to the principal at Hillside. I had compiled a B average. My old teachers were so proud. I was the first ever to go from Hillside High to an Ivy League school. And I was making good grades to boot! This validated my former teacher's skills. At the advice of counselors at Yale, I had taken only four courses for my first semester. But my Hillside background had prepared me well. Actually, I was disappointed to fall from being an "A" student at Hillside to being a "B" student at Yale. I thought I would do better in the ensuing years, but I did worse.

The Benefits of Diversity

For my sophomore year, Charles, Dick and I decided to room together and selected Pierson, one of the seven residential colleges. Jack didn't move with us because he failed two courses as a freshman and his parents required him to move back home. He continued his enrollment at Yale, however.

I sometimes wonder how the university felt about our decisions to room together. Were they counting on us to seek or allow ourselves to be absorbed into the culture(s) of the white students? Today, much is said about the importance of diversity on college campuses. The argument is that, exposing students to people who are different - racially, culturally, geographically, economically - is an essential part of creating an educated man or woman. I firmly believe this is true. I have heard a law professor at another school talk about one of his experiences. His class was discussing the intentional tort of "assault," which is defined as an intentional act that places another in fear of an imminent, uninvited touching. The professor posed the hypothetical: if a man comes toward you holding a pistol that you know is not loaded, is that an assault? The white members of the class stated that it was not, because knowing the pistol was not loaded meant you need not fear the uninvited touching. But a black student countered that analysis by saying that in his community, if a man comes toward you holding a pistol, you can expect at least to be pistol-whipped.

In addition to points of view that may be discussed in classrooms or conversations, partying together, teaming up in sports activity and sharing living quarters are elements of the diversity experience. I recall a conversation between Dick Cooper and a well-to-do white student who grew up in Pennsylvania. They were talking about foreign travel and the white student said that he had made the Atlantic crossing thirteen times. To which Dick, the down to earth and very smart product of a black family of modest means, smiled and said, in intentional dialect: "Hmm. According to dat my friend, you is still over dere." We all cracked up, including the white student, at Dick's blackened humor and put-down.

I don't know how much the 11,000 students at Yale learned from the thirteen of us, however, I know we learned a lot about them. But by coming together as we did in the fraternity, in rooming and in our activities off campus, we denied the whites an opportunity to learn more about our race than they had through all their interactions with blacks before college. To many of them, blacks were contented and uncomplicated servants at home, porters in train stations, mail carriers, low level employees in their father's businesses, sports figures, entertainers and welfare sponges. But we blacks at Yale had a strong need to come together. The slang, the music, the knowledge of black heroes, the devotion to uplifting our fellow blacks and the memories of racial injustice and violence all compelled us to come together.

Life In Pierson College

In addition to rooms for students, each college had its own dining room, a small library, and recreation space for handball and squash. Each was built around a central courtyard. Most of the sleeping rooms were actually four-men suites with two bedrooms and a study. There were usually two such suites on each of the four floors, served by a common entry. Each floor had a bath that was shared by the occupants of the suites on that floor. The rooms were paneled and either painted white or left in wood tones. There were also offices for a few faculty members who often took their meals in the dining room with the students - an excellent way to interact informally with us. Each college had a Master who had an apartment within the complex. Gordon Haight was the Pierson Master. His job was to have oversight of the dining hall, the grounds, the library, the sports facilities, the snack bar operation, the cultural programs and the conduct of the students. This latter duty primarily was to help curb too much revelry, especially on weekends when drinking got to be very heavy. I was a disappointment to Gordon Haight in two ways.

First, I became the editor of the *Pierson Slave* and when Robert Frost came and read his poetry to us at a gathering in the dining hall I wrote the article for the newsletter. My story must have reflected the fact that I, personally, had not been all that impressed with Frost's performance, much to the chagrin of the Master.

The second involved the snack-bar in the Pierson basement. The snack-bar equipment was owned by whatever student operated the business. I worked in the snackbar during my Junior year and bought it from the owner (who was graduating) at the end of that year. With all my experience at dad's drugstore back home, it was a natural thing for me to do. I hired Bruce Balaban and one or two others to make the sandwiches and to cover some of the hours of operation for me. They were also supposed to clean up at the end of their shifts, but didn't always. Therefore, true to Dad's teaching, I often had to do the cleaning. But, unlike Dad, my standards were not the highest. I think one of my customers complained to Gordon Haight about sanitation. Haight inspected and gave me a well-deserved lecture about the condition of the place.

Girls, Grades and Summer School

Together, Charles, Dick and I discovered Smith College, Vassar, Wellesley and Holyoke. These four were part of the group called the seven sisters - prestigious New England schools for women. At the undergraduate level they and Yale were not co-educational at that time. There were just enough black students at those schools to make the trips to those campuses worthwhile. That source plus the selections in New Haven provided all the diversion we could handle. In fact, *more* than *I* could handle. My grades suffered badly and I flunked a course in chemistry during the sophomore year. This meant that I had to go to summer school. Dad and Mother sent me to Cambridge to spend that summer with Mother's cousins, the Cottens, as my brother Oliver had done. I enrolled at Harvard for summer school, took and passed the chemistry course and a course in English composition. Since I had only taken the four courses for the first freshman semester I needed the composition course credit.

Poker Buddies

For my junior and senior years I decided to take a single room. Charlie and Dick were able to enjoy college life and also maintain a good grade point average. I, however, had slipped badly. I reasoned that a private room might help me to take my studies more seriously.

The room I took was in a section of Pierson that was next to a small enclave of white brick buildings referred to as the "Slave Quarters." I thought the name was unfortunate, but it didn't bother me any more than the name of the college newspaper, *The Slave.* In fact, I sometimes joked that I was an overseer of the Slave Quarters,

I developed several additional friends - all white - during my final two years. One particular group was my Thursday night poker buddies: Bruce Balaban, whose father owned theaters; Bill Trent, whose mother was Hannah Troy, the fashion designer and Joe Giantonio. One weekend, the four of us went to New York for poker at Hannah Troy's apartment (she was away for the weekend). Bill had arranged another new experience for me - the opera. It was *Tristan Und Isolde* performed at the Metropolitan Opera House. That weekend was also my introduction to the Stage Delicatessen and those gigantic sandwiches named after famous people. The Stage Deli was on 7th Avenue, a block or two from the Troy apartment. Even today, each visit to New York, has to include getting a sandwich at The Stage.

I Meet Joyce and Get Introduced to the Numbers Racket

Between the poker games, the girls off campus and forays to Smith College in Northampton, Massachusetts, I was still having a great life outside the classroom during my junior year. Charlie's folks were friends of a family from Atlanta who had a daughter, Eleanor, at Smith. I went with Charlie to Northampton to meet her and to be introduced to her friend, Joyce Finley from Cleveland and Detroit. She was a sophomore.

Joyce's father lived in Cleveland but was divorced from her mother. The mother had remarried and was living in Detroit. Her biological father's family made their money primarily from the numbers racket. Her father's sister was married to a man who was one of the top numbers figures in Cleveland. He didn't go around collecting bets. Instead, he was a banker for several small businessmen and women in the racket who, themselves, hired the number writers, bagmen and clerks. Her stepfather, who lived in Detroit, was also in the numbers business as the head of his own organization.

Joyce and I hit it off very well. She was attractive, a good dresser and academically talented. At spring break during my junior year, she came to Durham for a visit to meet my family and friends. That summer, Billy Marsh, one of my friends, and I borrowed Dad's Lincoln Continental and drove to Cleveland and Detroit to meet her family and friends.

Her family in both towns lived very well. Her uncle and aunt in Cleveland had a very fine apartment in a building overlooking a park. The square footage of the apartment was greater than our house at 1502. Her stepfather and mother lived in a beautiful home in one of Detroit's best neighborhoods - a two-story brick home with a recreation room in the basement. Both families were very nice and very hospitable. Though none of them had college educations, and some butchered the English language, there was nothing about their deportment that suggested that they were anything other than law abiding, upper-middle income people.

Joyce took her junior year abroad in France, near the Swiss border, so my senior year I did less romancing and a lot more studying. With the help of a summer school session at Boston University between my junior and senior years, I graduated on time with the class of 1952. I was not far from the bottom of the class, but I made it. an A.B. in psychology.

Graduation

Graduation services for Yale College were held on Old Campus in the middle of June. A pipe with a very long stem and a generous bowl was packed with tobacco, lighted, and passed among the 1,500 students. We all took a pull. Don't think that would happen today.

Mother came to the graduation; Dad stayed at the store, as usual.

What Did It All Mean To Me

I have had many great opportunities in life since Yale and I credit Yale for a lot of them. It wasn't that I mastered more knowledge at Yale than I could have at a less prestigious school, black schools included. It is true that the competition is keen, but at the undergraduate level, a serious student under a decent faculty almost anywhere will learn. The faculty was good, but not clearly superior to professors that can be found on hundreds of campuses all over this country. There were many professors who were on the cutting edge in their fields - great researchers, philosophers, and writers. But at the undergraduate level, we saw very few of them. Instead, graduate students taught many of the classes. I honestly think that it was much harder to get *into* Yale than to get out of it with a degree. Once there, if you applied yourself at all, you could be sure to graduate.

So it wasn't the knowledge I gained, but the diploma, itself, that caused opportunities to open for me. In most instances, except for my job-seeking experiences three years later in Detroit, once I told a prospective employer or client that I graduated from Yale, I was given the benefit of the doubt. I was given a chance to show what I could do. Of course, I had to perform when the doors were opened to me, but I don't credit the Yale experience for the way I have performed. I know of many talented people - both black and white - who had abilities equal to or better than mine who were not given a chance at a position because the schools they attended were not of Yale's caliber.

I don't know how they managed the $5,000 per year it cost, but by sending me to Yale, Mother and Dad went a long way toward assuring my success in life.

Photo # 9. Graduating seniors who lived in Pierson College, 1952. Top row, 3rd from left is me, 8th from left is Charles Payne (room mate). Second row 6th and 7th from left are poker buddies Bruce Balaban and Joe Giantonio, 9th from left is Richard Cooper (room mate). Bottom row, center is Gordon Haight, Head Master.

CHAPTER FIVE

The Military Years

These were two years of new experiences and new relationships that have impacted my life ever since.

During my four years of college, I was not subject to the draft. All college kids who were making progress in school got a draft deferment. I hadn't been accepted to medical school and had made no applications for graduate school, so I fully expected to be drafted soon after my mid- June 1952 graduation; I wasn't. There was no point looking for a job because I knew the Army would be sending for me soon, so I resumed my work behind the counter at the drugstore.

July passed, then August. Finally, in October I went to the Draft Board and asked to be drafted. They granted my request and took me in November.

Fort Jackson

I was sent to Fort Jackson, South Carolina, just outside of Columbia, the South Carolina capital.

I had never seen an army installation of any kind before. The buildings were light green, all of wood and not more than two stories high. There were but very few patches of grass, though I learned later that there was a golf course on the base. The rest of the landscape was strips of pavement wide enough for two cars to pass each other, scrub oak trees that didn't grow more than five feet high, and sand. Sand in the streets in front of the barracks, sand between the barracks, sand walkways and sand in the training areas.

I had boarded the bus with only a kit of toiletries. The only clothing I took was what I wore. We would be issued everything else: two sets of underwear, two sets of cotton twill fatigues, boots, steel helmet, plastic helmet liner, a wool dress uniform, a dress trench coat and an M-1 rifle. We also were issued a duffle bag and a footlocker.

I was assigned to take 16 weeks of basic training that would lead to a specialty in heavy infantry weapons.

Military Training

The first part of training focused on getting us into shape and learning the military organization, military justice, how to salute, how to march, how to take care of our hygienic and medical needs in the field, how to protect ourselves in cold weather, and how to read a map. There were also "Information and Education" lectures that acquainted us with what was going on in the world outside the base, always with a slant toward patriotism or the Army's point of view.

In addition to learning to fire and clean the M-1 rifle and how to throw hand grenades and launch them using the M-1, we learned to use infantry weapons that could kill more than a few people at a time, disable enemy equipment or destroy structures. These weapons were heavy mortars, the Bazooka, the Recoilless Rifle, the Browning Automatic Rifle and the 50 Caliber Machine Gun.

Mortars are essentially a tube of steel with one end open and a firing pin at the closed end. The tube is placed on a steel pad and is held in an upright position by two adjustable legs. You fire the thing by dropping a shell into the open end. The shell has a cartridge on the bottom that explodes when it contacts the firing pin. The explosion lobs the warhead portion of the shell toward the target. The thrust out of the tube arms the warhead so that it explodes on contact with a surface. The distance the shell travels is controlled by the elevation the operator chooses and/ or by the size of the shell. Mortars come in several sizes. The smallest is light enough for one man to carry and operate. The larger ones, which have greater range, require two or more men to operate.

The Bazooka is used to launch a rocket that travels more or less parallel to the ground and is used to penetrate armor such as on a tank or to break through the side of a structure. This weapon is a metal cylinder, open on both ends with a grip, battery, wires and a trigger about one-third of the length from the rear. The shell is inserted in the rear. When the trigger is pulled a current from the battery explodes the cartridge and sends the shell toward the target. There is no recoil because the backward force of the cartridge explosion flows freely out the open rear end. There are different warheads depending on what the target is.

The Recoilless Rifle can send a bigger shell to a much greater distance than could be reached by either the mortar or the Bazooka. Compared to the heavy guns, which of course are for shooting even larger shells longer distances, the recoil is fairly small. This gun is mounted on wheels and can be moved around in battle by a team of three or four infantrymen, depending on the terrain.

The Browning Automatic Rifle is a machine gun that, although much heavier than the nine- pound M-1 rifle, can be handled by an infantryman of average strength. The 50-Caliber Machine Gun, however, requires two men. The 50-caliber ammunition can penetrate light armor such as is found on trucks.

The Training Unit; the Men; Leadership

Because our specialty was heavy infantry weapons, our group of around 150 men was called a battery rather than a company. We were "B" Battery, 43rd Field Artillery Battalion, 101st Airborne Division, Third Army.

Our Battery was located on a street of sand that ran between two narrow paved roads. We were on a hill at the top of which was a water tank. Thus the name, "Tank Hill." There were 16 Batteries running from the top to the bottom of Tank Hill. Each Battery had six buildings: three two-story barracks, each housing 50 men who slept on two rows of double-decker beds; a building that housed the 1st Lieutenant, the "top" sergeant and the supply room; a "day-room" with a few armchair, a ping-pong table, a library-like table and a radio; and a "mess" hall for eating.

The men in my Battery ranged in age from 18 to around 30. Most had come from Alabama and the hills of North Carolina, Tennessee and Kentucky. Three of us were college graduates. One or two were high school graduates. The rest had less than high school educations. About half were black and half were white. With such a group, I thought, surely there was going to be racial tension and perhaps even violence.

Surprise: I personally never experienced a moment of racial tension, probably because of an unexpected development.

This was November 1952 and the Korean conflict was in full-bore. After the first week of our training, the sergeants who were in charge of our barracks were all sent to Korea. So, they made the three college graduates "acting cadres," one in charge of each barrack. One had graduated from Auburn, another from The University of Tennessee and I from Yale.

Being cadres meant that we were responsible to see that the men cleaned their areas and the barracks as a whole, cleaned their rifles, shined their boots, wore uniforms correctly, were lined up for inspection each morning on time, and respected the curfew and the "lights out" commands. When we left our barracks for training, we were responsible for marching the men and for supervising them during breaks. Any problems that came up, we had to handle. If a soldier broke the rules or disobeyed an order from one of us, we could punish him by assigning extra duty such as kitchen, grounds or toilet (latrine) cleanup, or even guard duty. We were in charge. We were acting sergeants, noncommissioned officers. The men did what we said. Nobody ever challenged my authority. If they might have had problems with my race or what I did, I never heard it from anyone.

Some Bad, Some Good Experiences

Of course we, the acting cadre, had to be trained right along with the other soldiers, though sometimes we were used by the trainers as aids. At one training station I almost lost my life.

On that day we were to learn how to use the rifle grenade launcher. In order to launch the grenade, we had a special attachment that we placed on the barrel of the rifle. We loaded a blank cartridge with more explosive power than the normal M-1 bullet and placed a grenade on the attachment. This type of grenade had a warhead similar to that used for mortar shells. It would arm itself from the thrust of the launch and would explode upon impact with the target.

The training plan was for each man to enter a bunker made of sandbags with a roof and a window, attach the launcher to his rifle, load the blank, fix the grenade in place, lean through the window and fire at a target some 100 yards away. We were using live ammunition. After the trainer taught me how to do it, I was assigned to a bunker to train 20 other men. Prentiss, a black recruit from Kentucky, was the third man in line and watched as the rifle's stronger-than-usual recoil pounded the shoulders of the two men in front of him. They were good-sized guys and the recoil obviously hurt them. Prentiss was short and slight of build. When it came Prentiss' turn, I showed him what to do and told him to lean way out the window, aim and fire. But anticipating the recoil, Prentiss began to pull back from the rifle. In doing so he also pulled the rifle and grenade inside the bunker. Somewhere I got the strength and speed to grab him and push him and his weapon halfway out the window as he pulled the trigger. Had I been a moment late, the grenade would have hit the inside wall or ceiling of the bunker, exploded and we both would have been dead.

Most of my experiences were good, however; often even fun.

There was this black guy in my barracks named Clampton. Clampton was from a rural area near Chattanooga Tennessee and had only gone through the 8th grade in school. He was about five feet four inches tall and had a terrible limp. He said every step was a painful one. It hurt inside his right leg, but the doctors could never find anything. He always claimed he should not have passed the induction physical, but the Army was hungry for manpower.

Clampton was a nice enough guy and we all took turns trying to help him when we could. In return, he would make sure that he crammed as much candy into his backpack as he could when we went to the field for training. He would buy Baby Ruths and Butter Fingers from the canteen at seven cents a bar and sell them for ten cents each or two for a quarter. I tried to tell him that the logic was bad but he never changed his price. Surprisingly, he made a lot of two-for-a- quarter sales.

One of the soldiers in our battery was a professional singer: Bobby "Blue" Bland, also from Tennessee. When we took field breaks, he often entertained us *a cappella*. The guys raved about him. I had not heard of him before then, but became something of a fan for several years after.

During some of the training sessions, I enjoyed showing off my smarts. It reinforced my leadership position with the others and sometimes resulted in less hardship on me. I recall once when we were being trained on map reading, after listening carefully to the instructor the first time he went through the procedures, I became bored during his second and third repetitions. When he spotted me looking off and disinterested, he challenged me as to whether I had learned anything. I was a little cocky and told him I remembered everything he had said. He then called me up front and ordered me to go through the lesson for the entire group. I did a better job of explaining it than he had done, initially. He congratulated me, got my name, gave me a cigarette and let me have the next hour on break.

Our training went well. It was strenuous. I was in the best shape of my life. I had learned a lot about the lives of the other two acting sergeants and about the schools they attended. In my youth, Auburn and University of Tennessee were not available to me, so I knew nothing of them except that they had football teams. As a Yalie, the only schools we had an interest in were the other Ivy League campuses and, of course, the girl schools such as Vassar, Smith and Holyoke.

I also had learned about people, black and white, who had grown up in rural, mountainous areas. As a rule, I found them either completely and passively accepting of authority or rebellious of authority without any attempt to understand why the rules and requirements they were to satisfy had been established in the first place. They all knew much more than I did about the outdoors, farming, hunting and how to protect yourself from the elements. I got to know them well enough to be able to tell whether they were from North Carolina, Tennessee or Kentucky by the differences in their drawls.

Perhaps most importantly, I had learned a lot about myself; what I could take and what I could do without.

Maneuvers Brought About a Change

Near the end of the 16 weeks, we were to go on maneuvers for four days. It was mid-February and, even in South Carolina, uncomfortably cold at night. Maneuvers meant four days of living in a tent, eating mostly cold canned food, lugging around the heavy infantry weapons we had learned to use, and marching 20 miles a day. I wasn't for that. I had never slept outdoors, nor had I ever taken anything like a one day, 20 mile hike with or without a 50-pound back pack. The toughest thing I had ever gone through was a little football practice in high school. The intramural football I played at Yale was only for laughs. I wanted out of maneuvers! I found a way.

I had gotten to know Corporal Corning, who ran the supply room, fairly well because I would requisition cleaning and toilet supplies for my barrack and the oil and patches the men used to clean their M-1s. Corporal Corning would also meet with the three acting sergeants about what time the troops should line up to get the items they would need for a training assignment: canteens for days when we would be sweating a lot, compasses for map reading, ponchos for rainy days, etc.

Since, as a teenager my Dad had made me the manager of the "front end" of the drugstore, I had to learn about inventory control: what, when and how much to order. I, therefore, was more familiar than anyone in my Battery, other than Corporal Corning, with the procedures for maintaining the proper amount of goods on hand to avoid running out of inventory.

I was curious and asked the supply Corporal Corning how he determined how much cleaning supplies and paper goods to keep in stock. He told me that he didn't determine it; the Army had standards based on consumption at all Army installations worldwide. By way of an example, he told me that toilet paper is supposed to be consumed at the rate of two sheets per day per male and four sheets per day for females.

Amazing!

Near the end of our training cycle, but before we went on maneuvers, Corporal Corning told me he would like to request that I be reassigned to help him. The maneuvers were going to require him to issue a lot more equipment and supplies and to deliver a lot of the heavier items to the field. He had to take such things as large Lister bags for water, radios, tents to house the officers, communications equipment, and the implements needed by the crew that would prepare an occasional warm meal for the troops. He needed help and wanted me.

Perfect! I readily agreed and was relieved of my "command" duties.

The End of Basic; Shipping Orders

Our 16 weeks of training ended a few days after maneuvers and everyone was sweating out what the assignments would be. I thought we were all bound for Korea. I had been offered an opportunity to go to Officer Training School based on the intelligence tests that were administered to us at the very beginning of our training. I had scored high enough to be a Certified Public Accountant, something I had never heard of. I refused the offer because that would have meant at least a four-year stay in the Army versus the two that were required as a draftee. I didn't want Korea, but I also didn't want those extra two years.

I was shocked when the orders came down. Every white soldier was assigned to duty in Korea and every black soldier, except me, was assigned to Germany. The Third Army had placed a hold on me and I was to stay at Fort Jackson. The supply room would be my duty for the foreseeable future. When I got the news, I was pissed at myself. Had I not agreed to take the supply room job before the end of basic training, I could have spent the rest of my service time in Europe.

On that same day, as I was standing in the street in front of the supply room talking to Corporal Corning, I saw Clampton, the crippled guy who limped for the full 16 weeks. Clampton was running wildly down the street and shouting. His orders were in his hand. He was going to Germany and his limp was gone! It was a miracle.

Life After Basic; Marriage

From the end of our training to the start of the next training group, life was easy. I was given housing near the B Battery location and I walked to work at 8:00 A.M. and back to my quarters at 5:00 P.M. with an hour for lunch. But when the new recruits arrived in early April, my hours changed. I had to be at the supply room before the men fell in for inspection, which could range from four to six A.M. depending on what training had been scheduled. I was off duty after the men returned from training. My job included checking in any training items the men had been issued that morning. This meant leaving my job between seven and ten P.M. Not as easy as before, but during the hours the men were away training, I could read, sleep atop the pile of blankets we had in inventory or chat with the lieutenant, top sergeant and the Corporal Corning. Life wasn't so bad.

During all of my training time, I had kept in touch with Joyce. We had agreed to get married in June of 1953, shortly after her graduation from Smith College.

A wife meant that I needed an apartment in Columbia, so I found one on Gadsden Street near downtown Columbia in the black section of town. The apartment wasn't much, but after months of barracks living, it looked pretty good to me: second story with a living room flanked by a bedroom and a very small kitchen. The property was owned by an elderly couple who lived downstairs. They had converted the second floor into two apartments that shared a bath. Nearly everybody on that street had done about the same thing. Soldiers at Fort Jackson who had families created a brisk demand for such space. The landlord provided the furnishings.

Three days before the scheduled marriage date, I got a ride to Durham, borrowed my sister's car and drove to New York. My mother, my sister Gloria and my best man, Billy Marsh, drove Dad's car. We all stayed at a prestigious East Side hotel. It was a formal wedding at St. Patrick's Cathedral on Fifth Avenue. Everything was elegant and expensive.

There was no honeymoon except for two days in a Manhattan hotel. I had to get back to Fort Jackson. We broke the trip in Durham and covered the final four hours to Columbia the next day, arriving around 1:00 P.M. on Friday. We drove straight to my new apartment and when I ushered my bride in, she walked the three rooms and said we needed to go to the paint store. On the way to get paint we stopped at a market for fruit. By the time we got to the paint store, Joyce had decided that the living room and bedroom walls would be painted a deep purple, the color of some grapes we had gotten at the fruit stand. The ceilings and woodwork would be white. I had never seen anything painted purple, but what the hell. By the time I left for Fort Jackson on Monday morning at 4:00 A.M., the painting was done.

When I got home at 9:30 that evening, Joyce had decided that we needed to renovate the tiny kitchen. The little table supplied by the landlord took care of our dining space needs, but you couldn't move around in the kitchen without bumping into it. Also, Joyce refused to use the living room or bedroom for ironing. She wanted to be able to do it in the kitchen. The solution was that I had to make a drop tabletop that was hinged to the kitchen wall. The table was a two feet wide and two and one half feet long piece of plywood. I glued linoleum to the top side of it and screwed an eye screw in the end of it. Beneath was a narrow piece of plywood attached to the table with a hinge. When not in use, we folded it up against the wall and secured it with a screen door hook that had been attached to the wall two and one half feet above the table. I had learned a little about carpentry work in high school but hadn't used the skill at all for six years. Nevertheless, by the end of the second weekend we had a fold-up-and-down dining table and, therefore, room for an ironing board in the kitchen.

The next weekend we drove the car back to Durham and Mother drove us back to Columbia. We bought a car in Columbia, courtesy of Joyce's parents.

By July, I was nearly dead. Monday through Friday and some weekends I was leaving the apartment at 4:00 A.M. to take a 40 minute bus ride to the supply room at B Battery. Joyce kept the car. To save money, I often skipped lunch. I got back to the apartment each night around 9:30 or 10.00 in time for a late supper and sex. When I had lost 30 pounds I decided something had to change.

One day during idle time at the supply room I got permission from Corporal Corning to be absent for a few hours. I went to the building where the training instructors were housed and applied for a job. Fortunately, several of the instructors remembered me, especially Sergeant Shorkey from Pittsburgh, who had taught us map reading.

I got the job and saved my life. I was assigned to give the Information and Education lectures and to teach map reading, field sanitation and cold weather indoctrination. The earliest any of my classes started was 9:00 A.M. and the latest was around 4:00 in the afternoon. This meant getting on the base by 8:30 and leaving by 5:30. Absolute heaven.

Meanwhile, Joyce had applied for a teaching position at Booker T. Washington High School. She had majored in Political Science and though she had no courses or experience in education, she got a job starting in September. Now, together, we had decent income and we both had decent working hours. Life was perfect!

By the end of March 1954 we were pregnant. Joyce finished out the school year and we agreed that since I would be getting out that November there was no point in her applying to teach beginning in September. At that time teachers had no tenure and were hired and fired at the will of the school principal.

By the middle of July school was out, the heat was awful and Joyce was four months into her term. We agreed that she should stay with Mother and Dad in Durham and I would visit when I could on weekends.

George Jones and the Final Months

I gave up the apartment and arranged for it to be rented by my best friend, George Jones, who had recently married Mary Case. He finished North Carolina College for Negroes in Durham in 1953 and had been inducted into the Army shortly thereafter. He, also, went through basic training at Fort Jackson and I stumbled into him in the summer of 1953 near the start of his training cycle. The Third Army put a hold on him as they had on me and, after basic training, he was assigned to work as a company clerk. He and Mary, his sweetheart from Hampton, Virginia, had married in the summer of 1954.

After the army, George and Mary moved back to Washington, D.C. where he entered medical school at Howard University. Following Howard, George did a residency at Sloan Kettering in New York and became an internationally known urologist. He and Mary had three children: Randolph, Carlton and Janet who live in Massachusetts. Randolph had a career as an officer in the army. Carlton and Janet served in executive capacities with the City of Boston. George and Mary divorced for reasons I did not inquire into and she moved back to Hampton. Several years after the divorce, George met and married Edna Robinson from Manassas, Virginia. Edna was an expert in clothing design and was a buyer for the downtown Washington location of the fashionable Garfinkles emporium. Edna was a Catholic and George an Episcopalian, so they arranged to do whatever Catholics do about George's first marriage so they could wed. When George brought Edna to Durham for our approval a group of us went from a really good party to midnight mass at the downtown white Catholic Church. I, however, missed a portion of the service because I went outside with George so that we could pee. We didn't know where the toilets were and were too much in a hurry to ask for directions. A bush outside was convenient. We laughed as the act reminded us of our high school days. George and Edna had two children: George Bladen and Adria Teresa, both creative producers of art products. Edna became, and remains, our very good friend. The four us went back and forth to our respective homes in Durham and Washington and enjoyed other vacation spots together, especially on Martha's Vineyard in Massachusetts and at Pinehurst here in North Carolina. When George's health declined, including his memory, she was as supportive as a spouse could be. She cared for him lovingly until his death.

I moved back on the base and focused on my work. My promotions from Private to Private First Class (one stripe) and then to Corporal (two stripes) came faster than they did for most. I enjoyed teaching and was good at it. I was considered one of the top three instructors in the training group.

Joyce moved back to live with her parents in Detroit in September, so when I was discharged in November I headed straight to Michigan. I had given the Army my best and it had served me well. I had matured, was healthier than I had ever been, had gained in my respect for people of both races regardless of their backgrounds, and was now free to pursue life at age 23 with a wife and a baby on the way.

CHAPTER SIX

Detroit

I arrived in Detroit with few clothes, even less money, but with great hope for the future. The plan was to get a good job, live with Joyce's mother and stepfather in their home on Boston Blvd for a few months and then find an apartment or a small house of our own. I didn't know just what I wanted to work at, but I was confident that several of the major corporations in that city would want me.

Wrong!

Job Searching

Chrysler was my first stop. I was granted an interview during which I was asked what the company needed to do to get its own employees to buy Chrysler vehicles. Knowing nothing about the industry and never having driven a Chrysler automobile, I stumbled badly. I talked about financial incentives and programs to help the workers feel a sense of pride in the company history. It never occurred to me to say: "design and build a better car." I never got a call back.

Michigan Bell, the telephone company, was my second try. The interviewer gave me a test that had questions totally unrelated to the communications industry, except for one: "How many newspapers are published in the United States?" I hadn't a clue. I must have flunked both the interview and the test. I never got a call back.

The story was the same at a half dozen other companies and, finally, a friend of Joyce's suggested I go to the Detroit Urban League for help. The Urban League is a national organization devoted to opening up employment opportunities for blacks in metropolitan areas with a substantial black population. The head of the local Urban League office was John Dancy who had family connections back in Tarboro where I was born.

Dancy was not surprised to hear my stories about rejections. None of those companies, he said, had black people doing anything other than working on the assembly line or doing low-level clerical jobs. However, he had been working with several retail firms to hire black sales people. Luckily, he said, the J. L. Hudson Company, Detroit's largest and finest emporium, had committed to him that they would hire a black sales clerk if Dancy could find the right kind of person for them. Dancy said: "You are it." I got the job in December, in time for the Christmas rush. It was in the sporting goods department on the second floor. All the other blacks either ran the elevators or cleaned up.

A few weeks later on December 27th our daughter, Andrea Fleming Garrett was born. Joyce selected the name: Andrea, from the beautiful and ill-fated ship, the Andrea Doria, and Fleming, the last name of her stepfather. Everybody was happy in the house on Boston Blvd.

I stayed on at Hudson's after the Christmas holidays. The money wasn't good, but at least it was a job. The Flemings flatly refused to let me pay for meals or help with the utilities. They insisted that they considered me as one of the family.

After several months Joyce got a job as a management-training aide with the City of Detroit. She was making much more money than I and that spurred me on to try to get into the executive training program at Hudson's. Their reply was: "The company is not now ready to take that step." Shortly after that rejection I quit Hudson's to sell sickness and accident (S & A) policies with a Mutual of Omaha Agency headed by Malcolm Byrd. I had enjoyed clerking at Hudson's just as I had at the Biltmore. I became a specialist in selling two products I had never used: bowling balls and ice skates. But if there was no future, I had to go.

In 1958, a few years after leaving Hudson's, I attended a Yale alumni gathering at the Grosse Point Country club. The pattern was that you introduced yourself to someone and inquired about when they graduated and what work they were doing. One of my encounters went like this:

"High I'm Nathan, class of 1952."

"Nice to meet you, Nathan, I'm Joe, class of 1953."

"What do you do, Joe?"

"I'm a vice president of the Joseph L. Hudson Company."

"Wow" I said, "you moved up fast. I used to work at Hudson's, but I found out there was no future there for me. What's your full name, Joe?

"Joseph L. Hudson Jr." was his reply.

We smiled at each other briefly and quickly moved off to greet other people.

I started with Mutual of Omaha in June 1955. I learned to deliver the sales track extremely well, but my heart wasn't in it and, as a result, I was awful at selling. The people I approached needed a lot of things more than sickness & accident insurance. A part of the sales pitch was to point out how much the prospect would earn in a lifetime at his present salary. I then asked what would he do if his earnings capacity was lost due to an illness or accident. "Sick leave and personal savings would be quickly exhausted, family help would have to be only for a short period of time and, of course, welfare, was unthinkable," according to the sales track. The answer? A Mutual of Omaha policy.

Not really. Most of the people I prospected were close to needing welfare. They were working full time but, with low wages, they were unable to save for emergencies. Fitting premium payments for S&A policies into their budgets would have been impossible. It was not unusual for them to turn to public assistance of some sort when their income streams were interrupted.

I sold very few policies. Two of the few were to people who did not qualify. They were ostensibly unemployed alcoholics who were writing numbers. Joyce's stepfather referred them to me. The company promptly returned to them the premiums they paid me.

While Joyce and I were working, the baby was cared for by Joyce's mother and grandmother.

The grandmother, Mary "Nonnie" Griffin, was a beautiful woman with a strong will, great energy and fantastic love for her two daughters and sole grandchild, Joyce. That love easily stretched to her great granddaughter, Andrea. In fact, it seemed that as each new generation began to mature, her love shifted slightly from the older in favor of the younger. She was a native of Sumpter, South Carolina near Augusta, Georgia. Her maiden name was Chavous. She was light brown in complexion with high cheekbones, probably one quarter Indian blood. Nonnie did whatever it took to make a living. She sewed for others, did laundry and maid service, catered parties, kept foster children, and had a small numbers route. "Dad" Griffin, her third husband, helped out by doing whatever Nonnie told him to do.

Wayne State University

Although my relationship with the Flemings was good, things were going poorly between Joyce and me. My inability to find decent employment was a major, but not the only, cause of our problems. It was clear that an AB in psychology from Yale was not getting me anywhere in Detroit. I looked back over my life and concluded that I had been happiest when involved in business in some way - the drugstore, the snack bar at Yale and the supply room in the Army. So I decided to enroll at Wayne State on the GI Bill to earn a Master's in Business Administration. The Bill would provide about as much money for living expenses as I was making selling insurance. I stayed in the insurance business part time and devoted nearly full time to my studies at Wayne State, starting in September 1955.

Wayne State is in the heart of Detroit, about two miles north of downtown and the Detroit River. The university serves the needs of the residents of the city. There was only one dormitory and it housed from two to three hundred. The rest of the student body lived and worked in and around the city.

Because Yale offered no business courses in its undergraduate school, and because I had not taken a course in economics, I could not start on an MBA right away. I became a "post-baccalaureate" student in order to earn the credits in the introductory courses needed for admission to the MBA program. The first semester, I took the beginning courses in economics, management, marketing and accounting.

My first course in economics was wonderful. I fell in love with the subject. I soon realized, however, that to make good money in economics, one needed a PhD. With a wife and child, I could not delay making good money for that long.

My second love was management, and I was a good student in that course. However, my professor counseled me that there were no jobs in the Detroit area for African-Americans in management. Of course, I had already discovered that fact.

Next, I considered marketing. I liked it, too. However, my professor counseled that although I was one of his top students in that class, there were no marketing jobs for African-Americans in Detroit.

Finally, after finding that accounting was easy for me, I thought about becoming a certified public accountant. However, my professor counseled that I was not likely to achieve certification because, in addition to the requirement to pass the Uniform CPA Examination, there was a requirement that a person gain two years of experience in a CPA firm. None of the CPA firms he and his colleagues on the faculty knew of in Detroit hired African-Americans. I knew that if I couldn't get a job in a CPA firm in Detroit it would be sheer folly to think of getting one back home in Durham. Without the experience, no certificate. But, I decided, I wanted a career in business and I had learned that the decisions and transactions made by the management and marketing executives eventually had to flow through accounting. Accounting, therefore, was a window on the entire enterprise. If you understood the numbers, I thought, you could understand the business and perhaps work your way into the executive level. This mode of thinking was reinforced by the fact that Lynn Townsend, a CPA whose firm had been the auditors for Chrysler, had been tapped as the Chrysler president and CEO.

Uncertainties about becoming a CPA notwithstanding, I decided to stick with accounting. There seemed to be no other route to a business career.

The Family Business

Joyce, the baby and I were still living with Joyce's parents in November 1955 when Bill, the step-father, asked me if I could give him a little help in his business. He needed someone he could trust to work for him in the office. He said that the accounting I was learning at Wayne State would be a really big help to him.

By this time, he had provided major support for my family and me for just over a year. He was someone I liked and trusted. I had met many of his employees at parties at the house on Boston Blvd. and on other social occasions. They were all really nice people, I thought. I was a curiosity for them - all that education, but without a decent job. After only a little thought, I agreed to learn the numbers business and work for my father-in-law.

Bill's numbers business had three classifications of employees: numbers writers, bagmen and office clerks.

The writers would visit the barber shops, beauty parlors, automobile service stations and residences in their territories daily. The customer placed his bets on the numbers he wanted to play and the writer gave him a receipt showing the writer's number, the customer's name (often in code), the date, the numbers he was betting on, and the amount bet on each. The writer kept one copy of the receipt and turned in the original and the money to the bag man whom the writer met at a designated location at a designated time. The bagman was responsible for sometimes as many as eight writers. Bill's business had three or four bagmen, each with his own group of writers. The bagmen took the receipts to the office where they, the clerk (me), and Bill would total the amounts bet for each writer's route and reconcile the money to that total. We then waited until we got a phone call to tell us the numbers for the day. The office, usually somebody's basement, was changed often.

There were two three-digit numbers each day, Monday through Friday. The numbers were derived from the Parimutuel bets on five races at a specific track somewhere in the Eastern Time Zone. At the designated race track, when the betting windows are closed, the totals bet on each horse and for all horses for the race are posted for the racing fans to see. The last number for the amount shown for the total of the race was the important digit. If the total bet on the first race was $25,324 for example, the first number for the day was 4. An agent at the designated race track would call someone and report the last digit for the totals for the first two races. That person then called a network of people and, within an hour, all numbers offices in the time zone were notified. After the third race, the process was repeated and the first three-digit winning number was determined. The digit from the third race was also was used as the first number for the day's second winning number. The fourth and fifth races provided the final two digits for the second winning number.

The office crew then checked all of the betting slips for winners. The amount of money needed to pay the winners on each writer's route was then packaged and dispatched via the bag men to the writers who paid their customers within hours of the time the final winning numbers were known. The odds were 1,000 to one, but the payoff was 500 to one. A dollar bet on one of the two winning numbers paid $500.

On occasion, the winning number was one on which there was heavy betting. On such occasions, if Bill did not have enough money to pay off, he would borrow the money from his "banker." A single banker, depending on his cash resources, might serve the needs of ten or more businesses such as Bill's.

Joyce's uncle in Cleveland had worked himself up from writer to bag man to owner of a business and to banker. He invested his earnings in a variety of legitimate business and real estate ventures that produced considerable wealth for him, thus enabling him to get away from the risks of getting caught by the police in the numbers operations.

Bill had done pretty much the same, but had not amassed the wealth it took to become a banker as the uncle had done. He had invested in several retail enterprises but they had met with only modest success. However, the businesses were important because through them he was able to report at least some of his income from the numbers business. The retail enterprises might have been doing poorly in actual sales, but Bill could produce whatever profit he wanted to show, and pay federal and state income taxes on that profit merely by puffing up the sales figures. This arrangement allowed him to have regular bank accounts for some of his money, to buy and furnish his home, and to own late model (but not too fancy) automobiles.

In 1957, Congress passed the Money Laundering Control act that makes what Bill was doing a criminal offense.

All the principles for business success were incorporated into Bill's operations. He recruited, screened and trained the writers, bagmen and clerks. He made customer service a priority and insisted on prompt payoffs. He kept accurate records of income and commissions earned by the writers. He maintained a system of checks and balances to assure accuracy. If a writer was caught by the police, Bill made sure the family was taken care of. He gave incentive bonuses and had parties on many holidays. He was careful to maintain sufficient working capital for normal operations and kept the cash in a safe place - a compartment beneath the bar and the floor in his basement recreation room. He negotiated lines of credit with his banker to get him through the times when unusually large payoffs were necessary. Working for him was almost like taking a course in management.

Years later, the State of Michigan, legalized betting on the numbers and created a state agency to handle it. They, also, paid 500 to 1 odds. This disrupted the private operators for a short while, but they came back in strength and paid 600 to 1 in order to beat the competition from the State.

The Marriage Deteriorates

Between the GI Bill, the insurance commissions and my work with Bill, my income was more than I had ever made in life to that point. But that wasn't enough to save my marriage. Working two jobs and taking nearly a full load at Wayne State left me little time for Joyce and the baby. The difficulty I had in finding prestigious and good-paying employment was a second major factor. Though she never said it, I also think it bothered her that I had become involved in the numbers racket.

In December 1955 I found a job as a housing aide at one of the public housing projects. My job was to investigate tenant complaints and to resolve issues between tenants and the Housing Authority. It paid decently, so I quit the insurance business and cut back on my course work for the spring semester hoping those adjustments would make a difference to Joyce. I did not stop working for Bill, however, because he needed my help. I should have quit, but I felt I owed him. And besides, by that time, it seemed like just another job.

In February, Joyce told me that she had fallen in love with a young man who worked in her department at the city. He was white. I argued that things would get better for us soon primarily because of my new job at the housing authority. But as I think back on it, she probably thought there was nothing prestigious about the housing project job and she probably felt that job prospects in Detroit for me would not be good even after I earned my MBA. She rejected my argument. Her love for the other man was too strong; he had prospects for the future that I did not have and, according to Joyce, he had physical qualities that I did not have.

That knocked all the underpinnings out from under me. It wasn't bad enough that white business managers and owners felt I wasn't good enough to be given a job with a real future to it. Now, my wife tells me that she preferred this white guy to me.

Two days later, I moved into an apartment in a respectable neighborhood. It was a third floor walk-up with a kitchen, a sort of porch with windows that were opened with a crank, and a room that could serve as either a living room or a sleeping room. The connection between that room and the porch was an open portal that once accommodated French doors.

I consulted a decorator at one of the better stores and furnished the apartment stylishly with Danish sofa, chairs and lamps, oiled walnut end tables and cocktail tables, and an ottoman that converted to a bed. A week later I bought a new Desoto - a white two-door sedan with leather seats and gold trim. It cost $2,000. The cash I was earning by working with Bill afforded me the necessary down payments for all of this. But my credit limitations forced me to stop short of getting a television set and a stereophonic music system. So, I bought a decent radio. I set up the furniture payments for a six-month payout and financed the car for three years. I was deeply in debt, but I had pretty good income, a fancy car, a radio and a great bachelor pad.

I am almost ashamed to say that it took me only two weeks to get over Joyce. She got a lawyer and instituted divorce proceedings. I made no objections whatsoever. But in order to have access to my daughter, Andrea, I resolved to maintain good surface relationships with her.

I told Bill I was quitting, but he begged me to stay. He said there was no one else he could trust to handle things when he had to be out for some reason. I knew where he kept the records and the stash of cash. I had to stay with him, he said. Against my better judgment, I agreed. Loyalty. Bill even insisted that I keep a key to the house so that I could get to the records and cash if he needed me to.

Life as a bachelor was very good. I continued my studies at Wayne State in the evenings and earned the respect of the managers and my co-workers at the Housing Authority. I met lots of new people at work and at school. One of the new people was Elbert Nance. Elbert was from Greensboro, North Carolina, 55 miles from Durham. He had graduated from the historically black Johnson C. Smith University in Charlotte and was enrolled in Wayne State's law school. Elbert was my height, slight of build and a good dresser. We liked many of the same things - mostly pretty women, good liquor and Rhythm and Blues music. We each had an apartment. He had a stereo and TV but no car. I had a car but no stereo or TV. We decided to join forces, share an apartment and be God's gift to the women of Detroit. That never happened for several reasons, but it was a good idea.

Several times during the rest of 1955 and most of 1956 Joyce made overtures about a possible reconciliation, even though she continued to see the white boy. I said *no* each time. I gave her the argument that we should go ahead and get the divorce and, after that, decide whether or not we ought to remarry. It was a weak argument, but it was all I could think of at the time. I reasoned that by holding out the prospect of getting back together at some time in the future, I could maintain at least a cordial relationship resulting in access to my daughter. Later, when the affair with the white boy ended, Joyce became unstable. In 1956 I received at least three calls from her in which she threatened suicide.

In the fall of 1956 my lawyer received a call from Joyce's lawyer. Through Elbert Nance I had gotten to know Joyce's lawyer and her husband very well. We liked one another and I was often in their home by invitation from the husband. On some weekends we would play tennis, have a beer, listen to music and discuss a variety of topics, but never the divorce.

The message my lawyer received was that Joyce's lawyer had concluded that Joyce had no grounds for divorce under Michigan law. Apparently, Joyce had been delaying going to trial. She was basing her suit on extreme and repeated mental cruelty. Usually, if the divorce is not contested, the testimony of almost any witness as to observed acts of cruelty is enough for the judge to grant the divorce. But in this case, Joyce either did not try or was unable to find a witness who would testify on her behalf. Because of the family business, her relatives wanted to stay away from court and none of her friends were willing to go to court and lie about my treatment of her. My lawyer then advised me, if I wanted a divorce, I would have to bring the action.

I signed the papers, found two of Joyce's friends who were willing to testify as to her treatment of me, and the divorce was granted in late 1956.

No More Numbers; Resigned the Housing Authority; Full Time Student

Before I signed the papers to bring the divorce action, I told Bill that I absolutely was quitting my work with him. A month later the police raided his operation and his entire office crew was arrested. I had barely missed being one of them. What an absolutely stupid fool I had been! What if I hadn't quit? I vowed never again to become so beholden to anyone that I would be willing to do anything that might cause me to lose more than I was willing to lose. I had done that with Bill and, as a result, I had come close to losing my future. It wasn't Bill's fault. The fault was all mine.

Bill was back in business within a week. I rarely saw him after that episode.

I had paid off the debts for my furniture, and with my savings and the

GI Bill money, I could pay off the car and handle the rent and most of my personal expenditures. It was time to get back to my studies at Wayne State on a full time basis. All I needed was a part-time job.

By mid December I was working at the Canada Dry bottling plant as a dispatcher. My job was to tally the orders received from the various retail outlets served by that plant so that the trucks could be loaded overnight and made ready for the next day's deliveries. It didn't pay much, but enough to take care of my needs.

Wonderful Wanda June Dianne Jones Wofford

In August 1957 I was asked by my then girlfriend to pick her up at a women's card party at the home of her friends, Darwin and Dolores Davis. The home was in a fashionable, predominantly black, community. The girl and I had been dating since January. I showed up as requested, but she wasn't quite ready, so Darwin, the man of the house, invited me to come in and have a drink. We chatted for a while and he showed me around his home, including the living room where the young ladies were finishing up.

When I entered the room, my girl friend greeted me warmly and introduced me around. I had never met any of them before. They were all in their early to mid 20s, well dressed and good looking. As I approached the table where Wanda sat, I heard a woman at her table lean toward Wanda and say: "Girl, you ought to hit on him."

Wanda was slightly shorter that I am, with long dark blow-hair and a medium-brown complexion with a tinge of red. Brown eyes, soft voice, small waist, large hips, modest bosom, pretty legs. Very fine, I thought. I agreed ... she "*ought* to hit on me."

As the girls were wrapping up, I paid special attention to Wanda, staying close enough to her to make it easier for her to "hit on me." Wanda had removed her earrings and had placed them on the bridge table. They were the clip-on type that can sometimes pinch. After about ten minutes of hanging around her, it was clear that she wasn't going to take her friend's advice, either because she was too shy or because I didn't interest her. It couldn't have been the latter, I thought, so I decided to help her overcome her shyness. When she wasn't looking, I picked up her earrings and slipped them into my pocket. By that time, my girl friend was ready to go, so we drove off.

Once alone in my apartment, I put the earrings on the mantle to the fireplace and decided I was going to call her. But I didn't act right away, partially because I didn't have her number. I couldn't have asked for her phone number on our first meeting and in front of my girl friend. Also, money and time were tight, I was finishing up the second session of summer school and my job at Canada Dry required me to work until 1:00 A.M. Sunday through Friday.

I maintained my contact with Darwin and one day in early October he dropped by my apartment. He was teaching in the Detroit Public Schools at the time and wanted my help finding an evening part-time job at Canada Dry. He asked me about the earrings on the mantle and I said they were Wanda's. I learned from Darwin that he and she had graduated from Arkansas AM& N, a black school in Pine Bluff, Arkansas. Wanda had married William Wofford, her college sweetheart, and William had died in 1955. The couple had a son, Devron Marc, who was just under a year old when his father died. She was a native Detroiter and her parents lived on what was called the North End of town. Wanda taught at a junior high school on the lower east side. Darwin encouraged me to call her and promised to get the number for me.

I called her in late October and she agreed to dinner and a movie on a Saturday night. Darwin had already joked with her that he had seen her earrings in my apartment, asking how they had gotten there. We had Chinese and cocktails at Victor Lim's downtown and caught the movie (*The Pajama Game*) at a nearby theater. From our conversation at dinner I learned that she was the youngest of six; three brothers and two sisters, all married with three or more children, each. Her college majors had been speech and drama. She had gone to Arkansas because her mother's family was from Wabbaseka, a tiny settlement not far from Pine Bluff. The college had a total enrollment of around 1,500. Wanda had won a scholarship for cheerleading, an activity in which she excelled at Northern High School in Detroit. She had compiled a very good record in college; entered in 1949 at age 16 and graduated right on time in 1953. She married during her senior year and her son was born February 17, 1954. Her husband was a native of Arkansas but they left Pine Bluff for Detroit so that he could pursue his aspirations to become a medical doctor. They were living in the same housing project where I had worked when he contracted a fatal pulmonary disorder. When I asked about her coloring and hair she told me that her grandmother, Katie Rainwater Hockenhull, was a full-blooded Native American, probably Cherokee.

When our first date ended, I decided that if I ever married again, Wanda would be the one. I arranged a final date with my then girlfriend to break up with her. She didn't take it well. Her final words to me were shouted up from the foot of the stairs in my apartment building: "You big-eared nigger, I hate your butt."

From that night I dated no one else. Wanda didn't reciprocate, however. There were several guys who also thought she was special, so I had to compete. Except for Joyce's paramour, I had never before competed for a woman. I had lost out to Joyce's lover, but I was not going to lose to any of Wanda's suitors.

A Job in Public Accounting

Since I was scheduled to finish the course work for the MBA in December, I had started looking for jobs with accounting firms in the fall of 1957. My professors had been right. I went to the Detroit offices of all of the "Big 8" national CPA firms and two regional ones. The message was always the same. Even though I had compiled a straight "A" average at locally prestigious Wayne State and had a degree from an Ivy League school, the firms could not hire me. The explanation was that their clients would object to having a black man come into their offices to work as a professional. *They* didn't object, they said, but they couldn't risk offending the clients.

However, I learned from my interviews at the regional firms that there were two black CPA firms in Detroit. Milton Monjoy had a one-man operation on the lower east side of town and Richard H. Austin had a firm with two partners and several employees located on Woodward Avenue, a major thoroughfare near a solid middle to upper- middle class neighborhood. I gave Richard Austin a try.

Austin had been Michigan's first black CPA and the 11th in the nation. He was 18 years older than I. He was born in Alabama, but Austin's mother moved the family to Detroit after the father, an itinerant coal minor, died. Austin learned bookkeeping in high school and established his own accounting practice serving a few clients. He had been able to get the required experience to become a CPA by working out a deal with a CPA who had been his instructor at the Detroit Institute of Technology. Austin turned his clients over to his former teacher's firm and the teacher then supervised Austin in providing service to those same clients. Austin also did tax and accounting work for the teacher's clients, but always in the teacher's office, never the clients' offices. When he satisfied the experience requirement and passed the CPA examination, he took his clients back and set up his own firm.

Austin provided the needed experience for Milton Monjoy who got his certificate in 1949, George Washington who was certified in 1950 and Ernest Davenport who got his in 1956. Monjoy had established his own firm, but Austin formed a partnership with Washington and Davenport under the name of Richard H. Austin and Company, CPAs.

The firm did not need any new employees, but I impressed them in the interview. As we sat and talked in the firm's library, where the tax reference books were kept, a client called for advice on a tax problem. Davenport had taken the call and immediately after Davenport hung up he told Austin what the client wanted. Neither man knew the answer without research, but it was a question that I had recently researched for my tax class at Wayne State. I inserted myself into the conversation and told them what I thought the answer was. Luckily, I remembered the code and regulation references to support my answer. They looked them up, concluded that I was right and then looked at each other. At that point, I knew I had a job!

The pay, because they really did not need another staff member, was $15.00 per week I would have to work six days a week, but there was the chance of a bonus at the end of tax season if the profits were good. I was elated. Actually, if they had said *no*, I was prepared to work for nothing or even pay them for the opportunity to work. If I was going to become a CPA, this was my only shot. I started January 2, 1958.

The staff accountants were Otis Washington (no relation to George Washington), Ethel Madison and Dewitt Sullivan. The receptionist-statistical typist was Martha Woods. The office manager-bookkeeper was Marion Nathaniel.

Otis had graduated from Wayne State with a major in accounting and had been at the firm for three years. His job was to assist George Washington on audits. Audits are accounting engagements in which the CPA examines the transactions and management estimates that have been used to produce financial statements. The CPA then renders an opinion as to whether or not the statements are presented fairly (reasonably accurate) and in accordance with generally accepted accounting principles. Otis and I became friends, but we didn't socialize much. He was married and always went straight home from work on his motorized bicycle, which he rode year round. I never understood how he did that during Detroit's brutal winters wearing only his business suit and a light raincoat without a lining. At any rate, he had no time to hang out with a bachelor.

Ethel Madison had been with the firm for many years and did most of the write-up work. Write-up work consists of creating the accounting records and producing financial statements for clients unable to do it for themselves. She worked primarily under Austin's supervision, though she needed no supervision at all. Ethel was much older than I and had a son, Mizel Washington, who was my age. She was a pleasure to work with. She freely gave me tips on what to do and not do. She was a stickler for having the male employees act like gentlemen at all times and the females to be ladies.

Dewitt had preceded me at the firm by a couple of years. He, too, was a Wayne State graduate, but he had started college at Alcorn State, a black college in his native Mississippi. His accounting instructor at Alcorn, Polly Anne White, advised him that he was smart enough to become a CPA but that Alcorn did not teach enough accounting courses to constitute a major.

She urged him to go north to Wayne State where he could get the courses he needed.

Initially, I was assigned to work under Dewitt. He and I mostly assisted George Washington, the partner in charge of the firm's audit clients. All of us were assigned to work under Davenport, the tax partner, as needed.

Dewitt and I became fast friends. Although he had a wife and child, he found time on occasion to have a beer with me after work. On one of those occasions we selected the wrong place to get the beer. It was a bar on Woodward Avenue, four blocks north of our office. It was 5:30 and we sat and ordered two Stroh's. Stroh's Beer was made in Detroit and was very popular. The bar tender said he didn't have Stroh's. We thought that was unusual, but said, OK, give us a couple of "Buds", the top selling national brand. The response was that there were no "Buds" either. We got suspicious and asked for any beer the guy had, to which he replied that they had no beer. We quietly got up and left. We two southern boys had gotten good old-fashioned southern treatment in this northern city across the river from Canada. I had suffered employment discrimination but had never before been denied public accommodations in Detroit. I had heard a story about a white waitress at a diner near the Wayne State campus who deliberately and publicly broke a glass that had been used by an unwelcome black customer as the customer was leaving the eatery. Before my experience in that bar, I had not believed the story.

At the end of tax season I got a $400 dollar bonus and a raise to $75 a week! This accounting business might pay off down the line, I thought. I quit Canada Dry.

The Question is Popped

My other fast friend, Elbert Nance, and I continued to pal around, but instead of becoming God's gift to the women of Detroit, we had fallen in love. He had fallen for Marcella Langley and I for Wanda.

Elbert had met Marcie at a Kappa Conclave in Buffalo, New York, during the summer of 1957. It must have been love at first sight for both of them, because she found a teaching job in Detroit that September. By spring, 1958 they were married.

Elbert was married and Dewitt was married, so, I thought, I guess I'll put on a major campaign to win Wanda.

By August I had out maneuvered all of the competition and felt that I had a good chance of getting a *yes* when I asked Wanda to marry me.

Wanda and I had dated heavily starting at the end of tax season. I had brought Andrea along on several outings so that I was sure that the chemistry was right for the prospective family of four: Wanda, her son Marc, Andrea and me. I spent time with Wanda's family. Went to church with them, had dinner with them and partied with them. They were really a great group.

Georgia and Will Jones, the parents, lived near the CPA office. Her Dad (usually referred to as "Brother Willie") had a career at the Chevrolet plant and was near retirement. He was from St. Louis. Mother (Ga Ga) had done a variety of things, including running grocery stores and selling insurance for Great Lakes Life Insurance, a black owned Michigan company. While she lived in Arkansas, she had been the first black woman to be a Post Mistress. She, naturally, looked more Native American than Wanda because she was the daughter of Katie Rainwater. She was a serious student of the bible and earned a degree in bible studies at the Detroit Bible College. When she met me and heard that I was a divorcee, she encouraged Wanda to help me to reconcile with my former wife, the Christian thing to do.

Lois Valeria was Ga Ga's oldest living child and was from her first marriage. Lois was married to Fred Peoples, a great guy from South Carolina who was a long-time assembly line worker for Chrysler. Fred was also a Jack-of-all-trades who was constantly on the go fixing things for his neighbors. They lived in a neat middle-income neighborhood in Conant Gardens in northeastern Detroit. Before marrying Fred, Lois had had three children - Gwendolyn, Geraldine and Constance Jenkins - by her former husband, Lloyd Jenkins.

Therland Melrose Jones was the oldest boy. He thought he was, and I thought he was, the smartest of a very smart family. His attitude about his own intellect and his opinion of the intellects of his brothers and brothers-in-law were the source of many moments of friction and laughter within the family. Until I realized what was going on, I was wary. When I got to know them all better, it got to be funny to me. Melrose had a career as a postal supervisor. Although he went to college, he never finished. In those days it was accepted as fact that if you did not become a medical doctor or preacher in Detroit, a job with the Postal Service was the best a black man could do, both in terms of income and job security. Most of the blacks he worked with in the Service were college graduates. Melrose, a Mensa, had passed the civil service exam for the job without earning a college degree. He and his wife, Daisy, lived in northwest Detroit with their five sons and daughter: Frank, Brent, Michael, Daryl, Glenn and Carole.

Sydney Menro Jones was the next oldest. He had served in the Army as a first lieutenant and had careers in Detroit as a heating specialist for the Housing Authority and as a photographer on his own account. Sydney and his musically talented wife, Eilene, had four children - Adrian, Sydney Derrick (Rickie), Claudia and Jeffrey - and lived in northeast Detroit not far from

Lois and Fred. Sydney's garage was the Saturday afternoon hangout of six or seven guys for beer, bourbon and bluster.

Across the driveway from Sydney was the home of Howard Elroy Jones, the fourth oldest. Each brother had a garage, but they shared the driveway. Howard was among Detroit's oldest and finest police officers and had been the first black officer assigned to a beat downtown. Not many blacks had been able to join the force during his day. He and his wife, Delphie, had three children: Marlene, Elroy and Edgar.

Sybil Esther was the next child. She had earned her baccalaureate and master's degrees at University of Detroit, a Jesuit school, and she taught in the Detroit schools. She played the piano exceptionally well and had an outstanding voice. Her husband, Aubrey, was a painting contractor who was born in Tennessee. Though skinny as a rail, Aubrey drank at least two jumbo beers (32 ounces each) every day. They had three children of their own - Gregory, Lynette and Stephan - and later adopted two more - Audrey and Bronson. They lived in northwest Detroit not far from Boston Blvd.

Melrose, Howard, Sydney and Lois's husband, Fred, often bragged, justifiably, about the fact that, together, they had built their four homes. They separately learned enough about plumbing, carpentry, electricals and heating to be able to do all the work. Melrose was the first black in Detroit to get a license as a building contractor. They were good houses that have already lasted 65 years or more. Of course, the best house was the last one built and the other three never let Melrose forget it. It was built for him.

In addition to spending quality time with her family I found other ways to discourage Wanda's two other active suitors during the spring and summer of 1958.

Bill R. was tall, dark, good-looking and had a good job. He got out of the picture when I dropped by Wanda's apartment one day without notice and discovered that she was entertaining Bill R. I apologized and said to her - in Bill's presence - that I had just come by to get my comb. Wanda, Marc, Andrea and I had been to the beach three days earlier and I had left my comb in Wanda's beach bag. I told Wanda not to bother, I knew exactly where I had left it and marched myself back to her bedroom where I guessed she kept the beach bag. Fortunately it was there but I didn't find the comb. But I had a spare comb in my pocket so I emerged from her bedroom holding it and exited, again apologizing for the interruption. Bill R. was no longer in the contest.

Karl G. was a tougher competitor. He was my height and was about at the mid-point in his studies to earn a PhD in economics. But because of his studies, he had even less income than I did, so I was able to out spend him on dates. He had not been married and had no children, so he could not demonstrate his capacity to be a good father for Marc. Also, he had not taken the time, as I had, to get to know the Jones family. Little by little I impressed Wanda with these distinctions between Karl and me. Another blow against Karl was happenstance.

On one Saturday, Wanda and I had scheduled to be together during the afternoon at Darwin and Dolores Davis' home and for a party that evening. Marc was visiting with some of his cousins. A few hours before I was to pick up Wanda to take her to the Davis', I received a call from Joyce saying that Andrea had been crying for permission to spend the night with me that night. "Could you possibly pick her up around 6:00 today?" she asked. I suspected that the real reason for the request was that Joyce had plans for the evening, but I agreed because I had not been spending as much time with Andrea as I felt I should have. But that meant breaking the date with Wanda for that evening.

I called Wanda with the news an hour or so before we were to be at the afternoon party. She was disappointed, but said she understood and decided we should each drive and meet at the Davis home, which we did. The party was for Malcolm (Bunny) Hemphill, a dear college friend who was visiting from Chicago. Bunny was married to the daughter of track great, Jesse Owens. After a very pleasant afternoon I left to pick up Andrea at 6:00. When I got back, Andrea and I visited with the group for a while. Around 7:00, since Wanda was not going to be able to go to the evening party and since it was getting dark, I insisted that I trail her to her apartment. When we got to Wanda's apartment, Andrea announced she had to go to the toilet, so, instead of driving on, we went in. While Andrea was in the bathroom, the doorbell rang. It was Karl. He and Wanda had arranged for Karl to substitute for me at the party that evening. This must have been done right after my call to Wanda about breaking our date. Anyway, Andrea and I left shortly after Karl came in. Karl later told Wanda: "I didn't know you knew them." His confidence was badly shaken by the incident. It has never been made clear to me whether Wanda called Karl or Karl just happened to call her after Wanda and I talked that morning. As I was writing this story, I asked Wanda again who called whom. She still won't say, but she did tell me that a day or two earlier she had driven past Joyce's new apartment on her way to visit her brother. The apartment was a block from her brother's house. She said she just happened to look through the bare windows and saw me painting the walls. I then concluded that Wanda called Karl. First I got mad, then I had to laugh at myself for getting mad at something that happened over 50 years ago.

The foregoing stories about Bill and Karl might not be what actually transpired, but at the end of August Wanda said *yes* to my proposal.

The only mishap during this period of courtship was around my efforts to finish doing a practice set for my auditing class and also to finish my master's essay.

I had an "A" in the auditing class pending completion of the practice set. A practice set involves the creation of a complete set of working papers for a make-believe audit. The exercise was going to take almost a week to complete and I thought it was a silly requirement. Clearly, I had demonstrated my knowledge of auditing principles through my class participation and examinations. Why do a practice set?

As to the essay, I had done the research and had submitted the paper to my professor in late April. I thought it was pretty good, however the professor returned it to me so heavily edited that I hardly recognized it. His line-throughs and added language were all over the document. But he told me to re-type the paper using all of his edits, and he would accept it.

Pride can be a terrible thing. My feelings were that if I submitted the paper as edited it would be *his* paper, not mine. I decided not to submit his version. Since I was not going to re-submit the paper, there was no point in doing the practice set for the auditing class. I had to complete both in order to get my master's degree.

I talked my decision over with Wanda and she advised me that to do as I had decided would be stupid. During our discussion I asked her: "If I change my mind, will you help me by typing the edited version of the paper while I work on the practice set?" She said: "I don't type." I didn't believe her. Every college graduate had to learn to type. I had learned in high school. She just doesn't want to be my secretary, I thought. Quite a few talented women back then had started resisting the roles of secretary or assistant that many men forced them into. But, she'll type this thing for me because of our relationship, I thought.

When I finally agreed to do the practice set and resubmit the paper I had only a week to beat the deadlines. Plenty of time, I thought. She could come over for three evenings and type while I finished the practice set.

She dutifully came over as I had requested, but still insisted that she could not type. I told her that although she might be a little slow, her help was essential if I was going to beat the deadlines. She stared at me, sat down at the typewriter that I had placed on my kitchen table and proceeded to peck out the work at the rate of about one line every three minutes.

"Jesus Christ," I thought. "She really *can't* type!"

The paper didn't get finished, I abandoned the work on the practice set, and I never got my master's degree.

We eloped to Toledo Ohio on September 6th. Between her *yes* and the elopement, Wanda got her hair cut very short and bought a sharp velvet suit with a blue pattern on a white background. I wore my blue suit. As we approached the courthouse for a license, a man came up to us and identified himself as Marrying Sam. It was obvious to him that we were there to take advantage of Ohio's laws allowing marriages without any delay at all. He told us that he could help us through the licensing process and take us to a preacher. There were other people hanging around who offered the same service. We agreed to pay his small fee and he took us to the home of Preacher Joe Smith who did the ceremony *in his church* at Wanda's insistence.

Our witnesses were Teola and Bobby Gragg. Teola had been Wanda's life-long friend; they considered themselves chosen sisters. She had attended Arkansas AM&N, also. It had been Teola who whispered to Wanda, "You ought to hit on him" at the card party. As it turned out, she hadn't been talking about me at all. She was referring to a medical doctor who was, at that time, a bachelor. As fate would have it, a few years later Teola divorced Bobby and married that doctor.

We surrendered our respective apartments and found a flat on Elmhurst Street near Sybil and her family. We occupied the ground floor and the owners, who were Jews who had fled Poland during the Second World War, occupied the second floor. They were a nice couple in their early 60s who spoke with heavy accents. I recall Mrs. Klar telling us that Johnny *Mathews* (Mathis) was her favorite singer.

I adopted Marc soon after we were married and he and Andrea got along quite well. Andrea spent the night with us frequently and the two of them explored the neighborhood together, especially the alleys, where they often found and brought home what they called "good stuff."

Wanda and me at the Copacabana night club in New York City, 1959

One Saturday morning Wanda and I awakened to find the children sailing our record collection from the dust porch into the alley behind. Marc was four and Andrea was three when Wanda and I married. Though ten months younger, Andrea tended to be bossy where Marc was concerned. Once, while they were playing with a blanket, Marc kept referring to the blanket as a "blinket." Andrea decided to correct him. "No Marc," she said in a tone befitting a parent or a teacher, "the word is not *blinket*, it's ... *blanklet*."

Marc was a happy and mischievous boy. He sincerely loved his grandparents, his aunts and uncles and his many cousins.

The CPA Examination

Otis Washington and Dewitt Sullivan, my co-workers at Austin and Company, had been taking the CPA examination. It was a two and one-half day examination that was offered in April and November. Otis, especially, studied hard for the test, but neither man had had success with it. There were five parts to it and candidates had to pass at least two of the parts at the same sitting and get at least a 50 on the other three parts in order to get partial credit. For example, if a candidate passed the auditing and law sections but got less than 50 on the accounting theory and the two accounting practice sections, he or she was not given credit for the sections passed. Also, once the candidate had received credit for two sections, he could get credit for passing an additional section only if he scored at least 50 on the remaining two sections. The average candidate took the exam three or more times in order to pass all sections. Only around 15% of the first time candidates passed the whole thing in one sitting. Fewer than half of the people who took the exam ever passed it. There was no shame in not passing the exam, but your way up in the world of accounting was barred if you didn't pass it. I have met many people who were better than I on tax or auditing or accounting theory but, because they had not passed the examination, they could not become partners in CPA firms or did not get the higher salary jobs in industry or government.

Each state has its own rules and regulations for granting the CPA designation. All states require that candidates pass The Uniform CPA Examination that is prepared and scored by the American Institute of Certified Public Accountants. Until 2004, the examinations were given on the same series of days all across the country under very tight security. In 1958, most states, Michigan included, required that before taking the examination, the candidate had to get two years of experience working under a CPA. However, Michigan had a provision that if a candidate passed a special examination he or she could take The Uniform CPA Examination after only one year of experience. The special examination, called the Certificate of Examination, consisted of the auditing, law and accounting theory sections of The Uniform CPA Examination. If you passed all three, you were given a Certificate of Examination and the second year of experience was waived. This meant that you could take the full examination without further delay.

At the end of my first three months at Austin and Company, I was encouraged to apply to take the Certificate of Examination, but I decided not to. I reasoned that since Otis and Dewitt knew a lot more than I did, and since they had not earned any credit on the examination, it was pointless for me to try. So I waited another nine months before applying.

What Some Friends Will Do To You

Wanda and I moved from our apartment on Elmhurst St. to a duplex on Ewald Circle in 1960. The house cost $10,000 and the down payment was $300. We didn't have the $300, so we borrowed it from Wanda's brother Melrose.

The house was on a small corner lot with a front yard and a fenced-in rear yard with a tree or two. This was great for Marc. Downstairs were the living room, dining room, a toilet and the kitchen. There were three bedrooms upstairs and a full bath. There was also a basement. The house was brick and covered with ivy. We were three blocks from Richard Austin's home on Oakman Blvd. The houses on Oakman were much grander than those on Ewald Circle, but we were really happy with our neighborhood.

I let the office crew know about the purchase, but we didn't have the funds to have a house-warming party. That, however, didn't bother my good friend, Dewitt Sullivan. He told me that I needed to invite him and his wife Kaye for a chitterlings dinner. I immediately accepted his invitation to dine at our house. I had enjoyed chitterlings at many of the get-togethers with Wanda's family, so I knew she must know how to cook them. As it turns out, I should have asked first. The dinner invitation was fine with her, but she had to get instructions and close supervision from several relatives for the chitterlings.

The dinner party was a great success. Wanda, Kaye Sullivan, Dewanda Sullivan (daughter) and Marc all got along just as well as Dewitt and I did. Kaye was medium brown with big eyes, a pretty face and a dancer's figure. She was trained as a modern dancer and was very good at it. The four of us became lifelong good friends.

On another occasion in 1960 I was asked by Dewitt to host a meeting at our house with Richard Austin and the staff accountants. By that time, the staff included Otis Washington, Ralph Richardson, Ethel Madison, Dewitt and me. Dewitt and the others had been talking about the firm's policy of having office hours on Saturday morning. They concluded that a meeting away from the office in a pleasant setting was the best strategy to discuss the issue with Austin. Dewitt decided that my house was a pleasant setting; I guess because we had a new couch and enough chairs to accommodate everyone.

Again, I said *yes* to Dewitt's second invitation to my house.

I wasn't sure how I felt about the office-hours policy, but I thought it was worth discussing. I could see both sides of the issue. The staff agreed with the requirement to work Saturdays during tax season, but felt that Saturday work for the rest of the year interfered with time for family and friends. But from my conversations with Austin, I knew that many of our clients were retail establishments that were open on Saturday, and that Austin wanted them to feel that they could call on us on Saturday, if needed. Austin's policy of being accessible to clients was the same as my father's policy about store hours and being accessible to customers. Both men had built their businesses by catering to the needs of their clients/customers. It was easy for me to understand Austin's point of view.

I told Dewitt that he or someone else would have to do the talking. I was only providing the place and ice water to drink.

Dewitt had spearheaded the meeting, but when all were assembled, neither he nor anyone on the staff would say a word about why we had gathered. Finally, after ten minutes of meaningless pleasantries, Austin turned to *me* to ask why I had hosted the gathering. He assumed I was the leader. I was trapped. It was clear that the staff was afraid to speak and I didn't want to look like a fool for hosting a meeting without a purpose. Reluctantly, I began to explain how the staff felt, but I also let Austin know that I understood his reasons for having us work on Saturdays. I said I hoped we could come to some middle ground, such as having one member of the staff assigned to work on each of the Saturdays of the month.

Austin stated that he considered the discussions to be labor-management negotiations. At first, I was uneasy about his assertion and thought that he was miss-characterizing the talks. But then I remembered that labor unions are a big thing in Detroit. Naturally, he would think in those terms. The staff didn't have a union, but in effect, this was bargaining between the workers and the owners. There were no unions in Durham that I knew of, and, of course, although I worked as a clerk in Dad's store, I always identified with Dad, the owner.

The meeting resulted in precisely the compromise that I recommended as a middle ground. Both sides had given a little. From that evening on, the staff and the partners viewed me in a different light. I was someone whom the staff could trust as a spokesman, and the partners saw me as someone who understood what it took to run a business.

Another Lesson About Service to Clients

At the Austin firm, Dewitt and I learned lessons about building a practice that guided us for many years. One of the lessons was to give every client your very best service. This was brought home very strongly by the following story.

Among the firm's clients was a man who had tried several business ventures and had failed at each. As you would expect, when the businesses failed, the firm did not collect for the services we had performed. But with each succeeding venture, this particular client was able to talk Austin into keeping his books and doing his taxes.

The last venture the man started had to do with promoting local musical groups. He even rented a building and was trying to record some of the groups. Although Austin did not refuse to serve the guy, he assigned the newest and weakest accountant in the office to work with him (not me), and did not stay on top of the service as he did with his other clients. I assume he thought that he needed to spend his time where there was a strong likelihood of getting paid for his work. Of course, the weakest accountant did a sorry job. If the client did not provide good information on revenues and expenditures, or was slow in providing the data, the accountant Austin assigned didn't bother to follow up.

After around nine months, the client got some financial backers who concluded that the Austin firm was not providing the quality of work needed for them to assess how the business was doing. They insisted that another CPA be engaged to do the work. Austin gladly relinquished the client, thinking that the man would probably fail yet again.

The man was Barry Gordy and the business was Motown.

We Leave Detroit

I passed all three parts of the Certificate of Examination (CE) in May,1960 and became eligible to take the full CPA examination in November. The rule was that those who passed the CE were given credit for the law and theory sections. However, you had to retake the auditing section and the two practice sections in order to be eligible for licensure. On the November examination, I passed auditing again but only one of the two practice sections. In May 1961 I passed the second practice section.

My certificate was awarded in August 1961. I became the fifth black CPA in Michigan and something like the 65th in the United States.

The people in Durham heard about my certificate through a news article in the Carolina Times and my parents. I began to get calls from business people I knew about returning home - H. M. Michaux, Sr., who owned Washington Terrace Apartments, and Asa Spaulding, Jr. who was a junior executive at North Carolina Mutual. Those people informed me that there was only one black CPA in the state and he was teaching at North Carolina College for Negroes, not practicing. That CPA was Joseph Norman from Oklahoma.

By this time, Wanda and Marc were not strangers to Durham. We had driven the 700 miles to Durham for Thanksgiving in1958 so my parents could meet Wanda and Marc. Andrea was with us. For Christmas, 1960, we took a 23 hour train ride with the children so we could enjoy the holidays with Mother and Dad, Yorkie, Oliver and Doris and their two children, Tommy and Yvonne.

During the eleven months following the receipt of my certificate, Wanda and I had serious discussions on the negatives and positives of moving to Durham. She made more as a teacher in Detroit than she would in Durham. Building a practice would probably mean several years of low earnings from my efforts. If I stayed in Detroit, it was clear that I would become a partner in the Austin firm. We would see a lot less of Andrea if we moved. (Joyce had bought a home for herself and Andrea less than a block from us on Ewald Circle.) All of Wanda's family and friends were in Detroit. Although there was racial discrimination in Detroit, it was much worse in the South. As I recall, the major positive was that we felt Durham would be a safer environment for rearing Marc. I had great hope, though little confidence, that because of the number of black-owned businesses in Durham, I could succeed in building a lucrative practice there.

With her brothers and sisters counseling her against going behind the "cotton curtain" (as they referred to the South), and with all of the negatives we had identified, Wanda showed more faith in me than anyone had ever done. She said, *"Yes, we should move!"*

I was scared to death, but we relocated in August 1962.

CHAPTER SEVEN

Back Behind the Cotton Curtain

The Move

In early May we left Marc with his grandparents and drove to Durham to find housing. On the way, we stopped overnight at a Holiday Inn at the Breezewood exit on the Pennsylvania Turnpike. Once in Durham, we found a new three-bedroom house that was available for rent located on Fayetteville Road across from Beechwood Cemetery a mile and a half south of 1502. The house had been built by a family that once had lived in Durham. They planned to return to Durham to retire within a year or so.

We returned to Detroit, sold the house and packed up our things by the end of July. We then discovered that the overnight stop in Breezewood not only gave us a night's rest, but also a much desired pregnancy. Wanda, Marc and the baby-to-be flew to Durham. I stayed behind to pack the remaining clothing and the fragile things in our 1962 six-cylinder Ford and our used, four-cylinder, Simca (The Desoto had fallen apart). I hitched the Simca to the Ford and set out for Durham in early August.

Victoria McCants, had decided to ride down with me to visit her parents. She was the daughter of Dr. and Mrs. Cordice who lived across the street from 1502. Near Pittsburgh on the Pennsylvania Turnpike, Victoria lost control of the car when a truck cut in front of us. She braked and turned the wheel sharply to avoid a collision, but the quick movement caused the Simca to whip to the left when she turned the Ford to the right. Victoria kept trying to make quick adjustments to counter the whipping action of the Simca, but the situation kept getting worse. Finally, she lost control and the right front headlight of the Ford hit the highway's center railing. We might have been badly hurt but for the fact that the Simca whipped in the other direction and pulled us off the railing. We were very lucky that the cars behind us had slowed.

We spent the night in Pittsburgh, had enough work done on the cars so we could drive them and limped the remaining 500 miles into Durham.

After a few days I drove the Simca back to Detroit, sold it and rented a U-haul truck for the furniture. Elbert Nance joined me on that trip. This was a chance for him to visit his parents in Greensboro, some 55 miles from Durham. Since Greensboro is west of Durham, we decided to drive through West Virginia instead of Pennsylvania. The West Virginia route enters North Carolina 140 miles northwest of Durham and the road from that point to Durham goes through Greensboro. The Pennsylvania route goes near Washington, D. C. and then down US 1, entering North Carolina east of Durham.

But the mountains were too much for our U-haul and we had transmission problems at 10:00 at night on a lonely stretch on a West Virginia highway. We found and awakened a shade tree mechanic who knew what to do, but he did not have the power equipment needed to get the job done. So, Elbert and I had to help by grabbing hold of the truck's gear lever to keep the engine from falling on the mechanic while he disconnected and reconnected whatever he needed to do to get us moving again. I am not a big guy and Elbert is even smaller than I. The mechanic had more faith in us than I would have had.

Once we were settled in our new home, good old Dad offered to buy us a car to replace the Simca. I hated to accept, but I had to. At that point neither Wanda nor I had income and, therefore, no credit. I selected a six-cylinder Dodge Dart with a stick shift, trying to keep the purchase price to Dad as low as possible. Dad was willing to pay for a more expensive car with automatic transmission but I decided against it for the additional reason of wanting to keep down my operating costs. The automatic transmissions burned more gas and were more expensive to repair.

Wanda didn't like that car from the start because she hadn't mastered the art of shifting gears. Eight months later she grew to absolutely *hate* the car. She had our then three months old baby in the back seat and was driving up a steep hill on Roxboro Street. The traffic light caught the car in front of her and she stopped. When the light changed, she put the car in low gear but could not execute the required simultaneous action of easing off the clutch while lightly increasing the pressure on the accelerator. The result was that the car stalled, the engine stopped and the Dodge began to roll back down hill. By this time, other cars were coming up the hill behind her. She jammed on the foot brake! But now she had to execute an even more complicated maneuver that required keeping her right foot on the brake, her left foot on the clutch, re-starting the engine with her right hand and then quickly moving her right foot off the brake and gently onto the accelerator while easing off the clutch. If she didn't do it correctly, the car would either lurch forward, roll back down the hill into oncoming traffic or stall again. She never told me how long it took her to get off that hill. Even today she gets mad at me when she thinks of that little coffee colored Dodge Dart.

My First Office

By the middle of August I had found office space. It was a room within Attorney Floyd McKissick's office suite. The suite was a second floor walk- up at 213 ½ West Main Street, above Rosenberg's Jewelry store. Twenty-seven steps as I recall. There were four rooms that surrounded a large reception area. Three of the rooms were used as offices and one as Floyd's library and conference room. A hallway led to the rear of the building where there was storage and a break room with a table, chairs, a sink, a refrigerator and a hot plate.

McKissick let me use his office furniture but I had to buy an adding machine, a cardboard filing cabinet and a used typewriter. With almost no money coming in and Wanda being uncertain whether and when she could begin teaching, frugality in all things was the rule. Lunches came out of paper bags brought from home. Parking was five blocks away across from Dad's drugstore where it was free. Adding machine tape was saved and re-used on the reverse side.

I put in phones that rang on my desk and on the receptionist's desk. The receptionist, Liz Cofer, worked for Floyd, but he expanded her duties to include answering my phone when I was out. This was not much of an expansion in work, since I had only three clients: Hillside Taxi/Associated Cab owned by James T. Hawkins, Washington Terrace Apartments owned by H. M. Michaux and Garrett's Biltmore Drugstore owned by guess who.

Building a Practice - Lessons Learned

James T. Hawkins needed my help to compute payroll withholdings and payroll reporting forms for his drivers and switchboard operators. His cab company had grown to the point that he could no longer do those things himself and still have time to manage the business. He did not want financial statements or income tax preparation work from me. Hawkins had been the head of the local Elks when, as a young boy, I entered that oratorical contest. He personally escorted me to the finals in Fort Lauderdale, Florida.

H. M. Michaux headed several enterprises. His insurance and real estate company and his cemetery were located in Durham. His apartment complex was located in Raleigh. His two sons, H. M. Jr. (Mickey) and Eric, worked with him in various capacities.

Both sons became attorneys and formed a firm. They still operate the enterprises started by their father as well as others they, themselves, developed. Mickey is also a very influential state legislator. Eric has served the State on the Board of Transportation and as chairman of the Bar Examiners.

The apartment complex had to have annual audits due to having been financed largely through a below-market-rate-interest loan from a federal housing program. It had been the Michaux family that contacted me to take over the audit in 1961 when I got my CPA license in Michigan. Therefore, they were a client before I relocated to Durham.

Dad wanted me for payroll tax as well as income tax work. He recorded his sales and expenditures daily and I classified and totaled his entries monthly. He did not permit me to do his sales tax reports or to reconcile his bank account. The agreed fee for the work was $40.00 per month

When my practice had grown to the point where I had eight partners, eight office locations and had stopped almost all of my personal client services to focus on firm management, I continued to serve Dad, personally, in the same way. The fee remained at $40.00 per month for 36 years from 1962 to 1998.

Gaining other clients was painfully slow. My biggest competitor for tax and bookkeeping work was John Payne, an old friend of Dad's and my Alpha Phi Alpha Fraternity brother. It had been John Payne who had congratulated me after my first year at Yale when he learned that I had become an Alpha. I told him that since Dad was a member of the rival Omega Psi Phi fraternity, Dad was not happy about my choice. Mr. Payne then shocked me with some history. Dad, he said, had joined Alpha at Howard, but since there were no Alpha graduate chapters in Tarboro or in Durham before 1935 he was not associated with the fraternity. When the Durham Omegas approached him, thinking he was unaffiliated, Dad said *yes*, he would like to join. Most of the business and professional men in Durham at that time were Omegas. No one in Durham, other than John Payne, knew Dad's dark secret. I never told, but it came out when a member of the Durham Clement family, who was living in South Carolina, returned to Durham to attend the funeral of a friend who was a member of Omega. When he saw Dad participating in the Omega rites for their deceased fraternity brother, the man said to Dad, audibly, "What are you doing in that Omega line?" He then announced within my hearing and others that he and Dad had "crossed the burning sands" into Alpha *together* at Howard.

Fraternity members just don't do what Dad did, but I guess business is business.

But John Payne's competition was not the primary cause of the difficulty I had in building a practice. I gained, and then lost, several clients who didn't want to tell the truth on their income and sales tax forms. One client who had a grocery store came to me for tax work. He had been doing his own income tax returns. After I had started work on his records I asked him to show me his tax returns for the last three years. Those documents showed that he had lost money each year. In fact, his cost of goods sold *exceeded* his sales each year. This would mean that he sold merchandise for less than he paid for it. Expenses such as rent, utilities, phone and transportation added significantly to the negative income figure. When I asked about inventory, he said he had never taken one, but he assured me that the dollar value was under $500. This did not make sense to me because his shelves were well stocked and he was purchasing merchandise at the rate of nearly $1,500 a week. But despite losses for the last three years and no family income from any other source, the man had bought new cars for his wife and older daughter and was paying tuition and board for a younger daughter in an out-of-state private college. I remember thinking: was this how Dad had been able to pay the $5,000 a year that it took to get me through Yale? I declined to keep the man as a client.

Another client, also with a grocery store, gave me an income and expense summary that showed sales numbers that were almost ten times his purchases. The usual practice for small grocers was to mark up purchases by around 50% so that something bought for a dollar would sell for a dollar fifty. If sales were ten times purchases, the storeowner would have to have a policy of buying for a dollar and selling for ten dollars. When I discussed this unusual pricing policy with the client, he admitted that he had income from money lending and other illegal activity and he needed to show (through the store) enough income to the taxing authorities to justify his luxurious home and life style. My thoughts went immediately to my former numbers-business father in law, Bill Fleming, and the 1957 money laundering law. I declined to serve that client also.

A CPA's ethics require that if you associate yourself with a financial statement or report of any kind you must use professional care and reasonable diligence to determine that the numbers are realistic. The clients I referred to above were both very nice people, but I simply could not produce (and thereby associate myself with) tax returns or reports that I knew or strongly suspected would be untrue. When word got around that I was good, but would insist on honesty, some would-be clients decided they did not need a CPA to do their work.

John Wheeler and Mechanics & Farmers Bank

John Wheeler, the president of the black-controlled Mechanics & Farmers Bank gave me invaluable support. The bank had opened in 1908 under the leadership of John Fitzgerald (the brick manufacturer), W. G. Pearson (the educator), John Merrick (white-trade barber and N. C. Mutual Founder) and C. C. Spaulding (N. C. Mutual President). Wheeler, who was born in a small town in eastern North Carolina and who had been educated at Morehouse College in Atlanta, had been named president of the bank several years before I returned to Durham.

Although M& F was the smallest bank in town, it was financially strong. In fact, it was the first bank in Durham to reopen after the 1933 National Bank Holiday when all banks were forced to close for a time by order of President Roosevelt. The purpose of the closures was to provide a cooling off period for those depositors who were withdrawing their money in fear of losing it and to give Congress time to pass legislation to strengthen the banking system. During the year before Roosevelt's inauguration, 5,000 banks had closed.

Banks make their money by using the deposits they receive from *all* customers to make loans to *some* customers. As long as the interest received on the loans is greater than the interest the bank has to pay on the depositors' savings and checking accounts, the bank should prosper. For instance, if you deposit $5,000 in a savings account, your bank might lend $4,000 of your deposit to another customer. If the bank pays you 2% interest ($100 per year) on your savings account but earns 6% on the loan ($240 per year), the bank would have net interest income of $140.

But when the funds are loaned it means that only $1,000 of your $5,000 deposit is still in the bank. This is OK, however, so long as the loan customers pay the principal and interest on their loans and you and the other depositors don't all come in all at once demanding a return of your deposits. The banking crisis occurred because, during the early years of the Great Depression, some banks had made too many loans on which the borrowers were not paying the interest and principal. Also, because money was circulating at a slow rate, deposit customers were maintaining lower balances in their bank accounts. When banks began to lose money, many depositors panicked and decided to withdraw all of their funds. Since the banks did not have enough cash on hand to take care of massive withdrawal requests (primarily because they had loaned the money to others), many banks were forced to close. The more the closures, the greater the panic, resulting in a rising number of closures.

Once John Wheeler was convinced of my intention to remain in Durham and work seriously at building a practice, he became a source of steady referrals.

One of the first of Wheeler's referrals was Service Printing Company, owned by Nat White, his brother George and Day Reid. All were Hampton University graduates. Service Printing had printed the high school paper when I was its editor and was the firm black Durham went to for wedding announcements, stationery, posters, souvenir programs, funeral programs, etc If you wanted the printing to look better than what a stencil and Mimeograph machine could produce, you took the job to Service.

Type was set at the Linotype machine. The machine had a keyboard similar to a typewriter and it produced letter and numeric characters in metal in various sizes and in whatever line length was desired. The type was then placed in a metal frame and a page proof was made of the material by inking it, placing a piece of blank paper over it and rolling over it with an instrument that looked something like a rolling pin. When the proof was ready, the customer came in to approve the printing before copies were made. Service had an array of designs on dies from which to select for decoration. Photographs to be included in the material were sent to a vendor who specialized in engraving. The frame was then locked into one of three presses, depending on the size of the job, and copies were made.

Wheeler recommended that the president of Service see me because the bookkeeper at Service had fraudulently signed or otherwise issued thousands of dollars of checks on the bank account at M & F. My job was to determine the extent of the fraud. There were two complicating factors: The first was that the bookkeeper had learned to forge the president's signature so well that it was very similar to the president's signature. The second was that the president trusted the bookkeeper so much that he would often sign checks made to vendors without insisting that the supporting document for the check be presented when the check was being signed. On occasion, if he was not going to be available at the shop for a day or so, the president would even sign blank checks and leave them with the bookkeeper.

I had to review all of the expenditures for the period in question to determine if the payments made were correct and related to the operation of the company. I found checks payable to clothing stores that were entered in the books as payments for printing supplies. I found checks to Duke Power Company and the phone company for more than the amounts shown on their bills to Service. I found checks made to "Petty Cash" for which I could not find documents to show that the cash had been spent for company operations. The total of both clearly fraudulent and suspicious payments over a period of six months came to over $6,000.

For protection against forgery, a small business owner should receive the bank statements from the bank <u>unopened</u> and should leaf through the checks to satisfy himself that the signatures are genuine. For protection against improper payments to vendors or to replenish petty cash, the owner should insist on seeing the documentation that supports the payments. The documentation should be cancelled by the owner at the time the check is signed. And of course, <u>never</u> sign a blank check.

Of the roughly $6,000 in forgeries and questionable payments, Service recovered only around $300 from the bank, the amount of the forged checks that were returned with the bank statement for the first month in which the forgeries started. Subsequent months showed larger amounts because the bookkeeper got bolder as he saw how easy it was to get away with his theft, but, because of the law, the bank was only liable for the first batch of forgeries.

Under the laws governing banking transactions, the organization or person who owns the bank account must notify the bank of any forged checks within two weeks of receiving the bank statement and canceled checks. If the depositor fails to do that, the bank will only reimburse for those forged checks that came back with the first bank statement following the date when the forgeries began. The bank is not required to reimburse for forged checks that are charged to your account in subsequent months.

The bookkeeper was not bonded, so there was no recovery from insurance. Even had there been a fidelity bond, the laxness of controls on the part of the company might have precluded payment under the bond. The bonding companies have a right to expect reasonable efforts to deter theft and fraud.

This was the first of many instances where I saw weak internal controls that allowed, and sometimes even encouraged, people to commit fraudulent acts. When a business owner makes it too easy to commit fraud, sometimes even an honest person finds the temptation too great.

Another referral from Wheeler was *The Carolina Times*, a black weekly newspaper edited by Louis Alston. Service Printing was next door and printed the paper.

The Times needed to borrow money from M& F and Wheeler wanted me to compile financial statements that he could have as part of his decision-making and documentation for the loan.

The paper's accounting journals showed cash receipts and disbursements, but there was no general ledger showing assets, liabilities and equity. Therefore, I had to produce a balance sheet by making inquiries of the editor. Assets were not significant but I discovered that liabilities were fairly large. The paper had been losing money for a long time and was delinquent in paying some of its suppliers. But the largest liability was for pre-paid advertising. As it turned out, two of Durham's three black-controlled financial institutions - North Carolina Mutual Life and Mutual Savings and Loan - in order to keep the paper afloat, had paid for advertising for several years in advance. They could not legally lend money to the paper, but they did not want it to fail. *The Times* was much too important to the black community to be allowed to fail.

I was to learn over the years, that all three financial institutions would, from time to time, bend the rules or become creative in order to support an important segment of the black community. They were not reckless in doing this. The amounts of money risked were usually small compared to the income and assets of the financial institutions. But they did take risks that no white institution would have considered doing even for a moment.

Many would-be borrowers from M&F Bank felt that the bank's loan policies were anything but lenient. My father told me the story about a black fellow who went to talk to R. L. McDougald, a top executive at the bank who preceded Wheeler by several years. The story goes that McDougald asked the fellow a lot of questions: what collateral? what is your income? why do you need the money? who else do you owe? how much do you owe? are you married?, etc. After a few minutes of this, the fellow leaned back in his chair and asked McDougald: "Do you have a bathroom in your house?" After McDougald replied that he did, the fellow asked: "Do you have a bathtub in your bathroom and if you do, did you take a bath this morning?" *Yes* was McDougald's reply to both those questions. Whereupon the fellow leaned forward in his chair and said: "I'm glad to hear that because apparently I'm going to have to kiss your ass to get this loan!"

Based on my work, Wheeler's faith in Alston and the desire of the M&F loan committee to help the paper to continue, the loan was made. The paper is still published today. Alston's daughter served as editor for many years after his death.

Wheeler also arranged to have me added to the group of men who performed the annual audit of the bank for the bank's Board of Directors. Jay Walker, J. W. McClinton and "Bro" Edwards had been doing the work for years. All three were trained as accountants, though they were not Certified Public Accountants. At that time, the bank was not-required to have an audit performed by a Certified Public Accountant. All three worked at North Carolina Mutual Life or one of its subsidiary companies. I became the fourth member of the team under Jay Walker's leadership. It was a great learning experience for me in that I had never before known anything about the accounting for the banking industry. In fact, the only black bank I had ever entered was M&F. Detroit had a black savings and loan, but no bank. And the savings and loan in Detroit did not use the services of Richard Austin and Company where I had worked.

An Unexpected Involvement in the Civil Rights Movement

After a year and a half of practice building, I was asked by Maggie Dent, a white woman, to do the accounting and tax work for her movie theater. Up to that point I had never talked to a prospective business client who wasn't black. Maggie was from New York but had roots in North Carolina and had decided that Durham would be a good place to open an arts-film theater because of the two colleges in Durham and the one some thirteen miles away in Chapel Hill. She had made friends among the faculty and administrators at the colleges - both black and white - and with a few other white people who were moderate to liberal on racial issues. I assume her black friends referred her to me.

Her theater was downtown on Main Street and was segregated, as were the Carolina and Center Theaters, also downtown. By custom, those theaters maintained separate seating areas for blacks and whites. There was no local or state law on this. The black-owned and operated Regal Theater on Pettigrew Street next to the Biltmore never maintained separate areas for the few whites who went to shows there.

Maggie leased the theater building from one person and the vending machines, counters, cash register, the screen and the projection equipment from another. Although she wanted to integrate the theater she was unable to do so because of a clause in the equipment lease that allowed the owner to repossess the equipment at any time. The equipment lessor controlled the Carolina Theater and had been resisting pressure from the black community to integrate it. He told Maggie that the provision in the lease allowing him to repossess the equipment was put in to prevent her from integrating, thus putting more pressure on him. If she integrated, he could remove the equipment.

Floyd McKissick had been a strong supporter of civil rights plaintiffs all over the state. He and his wife had filed suit in the late 1950s to win the right for their daughter to be admitted to the all-white Durham High School. Floyd, himself, had been admitted to the University of Chapel Hill Law School as the result of a court order won by Conrad Pearson, a crusading black lawyer in Durham. Floyd was also an advisor to the local organization of Commandos, a youth group sponsored by the National Association for the Advancement of Colored People. These young people were trained in using non-violent protest methods to help break down segregation and had been picketing the Carolina and Center Theaters. When they decided to also picket my client's theater, I asked for a conference.

The meeting was held in Floyd's conference room, a room that he and I used in common (since I was his tenant). On one side of the table were Floyd and two leaders of the Commandos, and on the other side, my client and I.

I argued that the pickets were hurting my client's business and that her heart was in the right place. She wanted to integrate but was prevented from doing so because of the lease terms. Floyd and the Commandos understood my argument but concluded that the most important fact was that she was operating a segregated movie house. They decided to continue the picketing.

Since continuation of the picketing was going to hurt my client's fledgling business seriously, she and I developed a plan. She went to some of her white and black friends and got written pledges from them to lend her $10,000 to buy new equipment in the event the equipment owner invoked the clause allowing repossession if she integrated the theater. She then went to the equipment owner and announced that she was going to integrate and showed him the pledges of $10,000 in support to buy replacement equipment. The equipment owner capitulated. He did not want to incur the expense of removing and storing the old equipment. He would also lose the rent income. He probably also concluded that integration was going to come eventually anyway, so why suffer a significant financial loss on the matter at hand? The Woolworths in downtown Durham had already begun to serve blacks at its lunch counter due to sit-ins and boycotts.

Maggie integrated the Rialto and a few months later the other theater owners and several other merchants in downtown Durham decided to end the denial of public accommodations for black people. "Colored" and "White" signs on restroom and theater doors came down as did the restrictive signs over water fountains and in busses. Restaurants downtown agreed to serve black patrons the same as white ones.

This episode reaffirmed the old adage that when faced with a chain of opposition, it is wise to attack the weakest link. My client was the weak link in this case. She didn't want to be a part of the chain and, to remove herself from it, she took action. The action she took helped greatly in breaking the chain of public accommodation denial to black people in downtown Durham.

Anti-Poverty Work

John Wheeler also introduced me to the North Carolina Fund. The Fund had been started by then-governor Terry Sanford with a mission to "Break the Cycle of Poverty" in North Carolina. Through the efforts of John Ehle,

Sanford's trusted advisor, the Ford Foundation in New York and the Z. Smith Reynolds and Mary Reynolds Babcock foundations in North Carolina had awarded grants to the North Carolina Fund totaling over six million dollars to underwrite experimental programs for a five year period.

Sanford had assembled a group of distinguished men and women from all over North Carolina to serve as the board of directors, one of whom was John Wheeler. The foundation grants were made in 1963. In April 1964, as Treasurer, Wheeler recommended me to George H. Esser, Jr., the Executive Director, to oversee the accounting. Esser was a graduate of Virginia Military Institute and Harvard Law. He had worked for many years at the Institute of Government at the University of North Carolina at Chapel Hill. In that capacity he had provided research and training in support of governmental entities statewide.

The interview with Esser went well. He had assembled a small staff of fairly young people to work with him. Mike Brooks was in charge of research. Jack Mansfield was to develop volunteer programs. Billy Barnes was the publicist. William Darity was working on health care delivery problems that contributed to poverty conditions. Sue Graham was the bookkeeper. Burnella Burke was the secretary. Darity and Burke were black.

The office was located at 107 ½ East Parrish Street, just down the street from M&F Bank and not far from my office on Main St. It was above an office supply store that I swore I would never enter again. A few months earlier, a white woman who was a member of the owner's family, had called me "uppity" when I insisted on getting the exact office supplies I had requested.

Initially, I took on the North Carolina Fund as a client, but after a short while I concluded two things. The first was that the amount of work that needed to be done demanded my services full time. The second was that the mission of the Fund was one that I supported absolutely; I had to do whatever I could to make sure it succeeded. Therefore, I put further practice development on hold and became a full time employee at the Fund. I moved the accounting office into my home where I could continue to serve the few clients I had by working nights, holidays and weekends.

1814 Cecil Street

By this time, Nathan, Jr. had been born and Wanda had started teaching at Hillside High School. I had also started teaching a course in the business school at North Carolina Central University to provide a little extra money. Therefore, shortly after I began working at the Fund, we were able to buy a home at 1814 Cecil Street where we lived for 30 years.

The house cost $36,000 and was financed by Mutual Savings and Loan.

It was located on a hill at the end of Cecil Street in southeast Durham. It was about a mile from 1502. The surrounding community was all black, mature and stable. Our house was the newest in the community, having been built two years earlier in 1962 by James Tucker, economics professor at North Carolina Central University. The house was less than half a mile from the university and from Hillside High School where Wanda was teaching. Spaulding Elementary School was just two blocks away. Across the street was the home of Booth and Cynthia Smith. Their's was an attractive home on a deep and heavily wooded lot. Booth was a college graduate and a postman. Cynthia had been one of my English teachers at Hillside. Her mother had been a pharmacist in Durham before we came and her uncle was W. G. Pearson, the well respected educator who had co-founded North Carolina Mutual. The west side overlooked a large wooded lot and home owned by William J. Kennedy, III, who later became president of North Carolina Mutual Life. His father, William J. Kennedy, Jr., had also been president of the company. The others on our block of Cecil Street were mostly middle-income folk, some of whom were in business, some were employees at the university, and some were public school teachers. Nelson Street, which dead ended into Cecil Street, was the home of several more teachers, college professors and professional people.

The house was of brick with four bedrooms, a living room, dining room, kitchen, family room, two full and one half baths and laundry room on the entrance level comprising 2,000 square feet. The lot sloped from front to rear so that we had a 1,000 square foot basement with a tile floor, an additional half bath and painted cinder block walls. A sliding glass door led to the heavily wooded rear yard and railroad tracks that were traveled once or twice a day to carry tobacco and other freight to and from the cigarette factories downtown. We built an L shaped swimming pool - 40 by 20 feet with a 16 by 16 foot diving area - out back and added a huge deck that was accessed through the basement sliding door. I never liked gardening, and neither Wanda nor I had time for it, so when we were having an "important" group of visitors in the pool area, Wanda transformed the area instantly into a beautiful flower garden by buying whatever she thought was appropriate for the season. We also renovated the basement by paneling it, building a raised platform area for entertaining smaller groups, building a large bar that was put on rollers so that we could re-position it as needed and by adding a full Pullman kitchen. The setting was great for Wanda's "summer camp" when our four Detroit grandchildren: Dorian, Sulaiman, Rashid and Malik would spend two to three weeks with us. We drove to Detroit to get them and drove back to return them. The four boys were sometimes joined by Audriana, Christina and Sophia, my brother Oliver's grandchildren, and by Sarah Grace Parker, Yip's youngest daughter. Nathan III, Nathan Jr's. oldest child, learned to swim, at least a little, in that pool. Lalia Corinne and Dalton Myles came along too late to have that experience. The pool and house were great attractions for the kids all over the neighborhood. They were welcomed to swim so long as a parent or guardian accompanied them. It is not unusual for successful young men and women who grew up near our house to tell us about the times they visited our home to swim or play with our children. Durham's former Chief of Police was one such person.

> *We moved from that house in 1994 to the fashionable New Hope Valley development in Southwest Durham. At the time we moved, there were three black couples living here that we knew of: Doctors Anne and Onye Akwari, Doctors George and Elaine Brothers and Attorney Floyd and Rhonda Lewis. The decision to move was a difficult one for us. We had been a source of inspiration and recreation for some of the families from across the railroad tracks from us and most of our friends were within a two-mile radius. But when we borrowed money to make additional improvements on Cecil Street, the bankers told us that the $75,000 we intended to put into the house would not increase the market value as much as a nickel. We had already invested nearly $100,000 in improvements and it had become, arguably, the finest home in the entire area. After a lot of searching, Wanda found this location that had nearly 5,000 square feet, four bedrooms, three full baths, two rooms downstairs with a nearby ½ bath that I could use for my office, a parlor, dining room, family room, butler's pantry and a huge deck out back. The market value of this home, for which we have made but few improvements, has increased two times what we paid. The Cecil Street house, on the other hand, has only increased by 10% during that same 15-year period. If we, or our family members, need capital for a new entrepreneurial venture, the equity in this house is a source that would not be available if we still lived in our old neighborhood.*

Social Life

Durham offered the kind of social life we had wanted for ourselves and the children. First, there were Mother, Dad and Yorkie with whom we spent most Thursday afternoons from 3:00 to 4:30 having one of Mother's great fish dinners. Usually, Doris, Tommy and Yvonne were also at dinner. Oliver was not at those meals because he substituted for Dad at the store during Dad's meal break from 3:00 to 6:00. Mother seemed always willing to have Marc and Nathan, Jr. for evening or overnight stays when Wanda and I wanted privacy or a night out. As often as not, Tommy and Yvonne were there, too.

As soon as she joined the faculty at Hillside High, Wanda made many friends. Two of the best ones were Jeannie Lucas and Tiny Burgess. Their husbands, Bill and Tom became good friends of mine. The Lucases, who lived a few miles out of town, had a lake for fishing and raised a few farm animals. We spent many Saturday afternoons with the children at the Lucas home. The Burgesses lived close by us and had two girls, Tamara and Tonya. We played pinochle with the Burgesses and often planned joint meals on weekends.

Wanda joined two ladies-only card clubs and a study club: Elhconips (pinochle backwards) Cardettes and the Congenials Bridge Club. The card clubs had eight to twelve members each, though there were several who were members of both. Each met once per month on different Saturday afternoons or evenings. The Tuesday Morning Study Club consisted of a small group of women who were very influential in civic, business and political affairs in Durham. Wanda also became active with the local Delta Sigma Theta Sorority which she had joined as a charter member during her college days at Arkansas Agricultural, Mechanical and Normal in Pine Bluff.

Shortly after a group of women called the Skoals was formed, Wanda was asked to join. They met on Wednesday evenings for parlor games and talk. A few years after the club started, they became the local chapter of the National Smart Set, a women's organization with some30 chapters nationwide. Wanda served at different times as the local president and the national president.

Durham has an interracial organization of approximately thirty influential men and women who meet once a month to learn about and discuss issues that are, or may become, important to our community. The members are expected to use the insights gained from their meetings in their corporate, nonprofit and governmental executive capacities. Wanda is a member.

The local chapter of Links, Incorporated invited Wanda to join. The Links is a national service club of very prominent black women. Wanda served the local chapter as its president.

Initially, my principal social outlets among men were my fraternity, Alpha Phi Alpha, and a pinochle club called the Saturday Night Therapeutics. The pinochle club was, and is, a very diverse group who meet at someone's home every week. Age, education, wealth and religion don't matter for membership. Slamming cards, drinking beer, eating soul food and talking bullshit are our hallmarks. Some of the current members are:

Val Atkinson (radio talk show host and political analyst)

Bill Bunch (retired stock broker)

Charles Cook (MD)

Larry Dark (landscaper)

Tom Evans (retired sports official and avid fisherman)

Tom Holmes (retired Social Security Administration executive)

Murphy Jenkins (retired pharmacist)

Ted Johnson (former computer programmer and now owns a maintenance company

Roy Jones (chef)

Ralph Joynes (accountant)

Scott Kincaid (postal worker)

Wilbert King (registered nurse and retired military)

Nate Mclaughlin (retired maintenance supervisor at NCCU)

Louis Perkins (development officer at St. Augustine's College)

Bobby Rigsbee (restaurant owner)

William Robinson (retired from the NC Department of Transportation)

Don Scott (college professor and former livery business owner)

Thurman Spicer (auto and retail salesman)

Lewin Warren (retired CIA employee)

Lester Woody (long distance truck driver)

The club has been in continuous operation for fifty years or so. We have rules that are unique to us. Any pinochle player outside the club would say we were cheating, but we don't care. The club was started by a woman, Mary Young, but the men put her out after the first year. Mary is a good friend and an expert Bridge player. She often reminds me and others that she was the inspiration behind the Therapeutics.

Some 13 years after we moved to Durham, I was inducted into Sigma Pi Phi. This is the oldest Greek letter fraternity for blacks. It was formed in 1904 in Philadelphia for men who had finished college and who had distinguished themselves in their careers or communities. This organization with 6,000 or so members is much smaller than the better known college fraternities (Alpha Phi Alpha, Omega Psi Phi, Kappa Alpha Psi and Phi Beta Sigma), each of which may have well over 100,000 members. The local bodies of Sigma Pi Phi are known as Subordinate or Local Boules which meet once a month, usually for dinner, discussion of serious topics and often a well-researched and delivered lecture. Members are referred to as Archons and their spouses as Archousae. The leader of the local group is called the Sire Archon in which capacity I served for two years. I am now inactive with Sigma Pi Phi but some of the local former and continuing members are:

F. V. (Pete) Allison (former CEO of Mutual Savings & Loan), Franklin

Anderson (former owner of a plastic molding company), Charles
Becton (managing partner of a major law firm), William (Bill) Bell
(executive of a local development company and Durham's Mayor),
George Brothers, Jr. (Physician), Walter Brown (PhD historian), Joseph
Campbell (dentist), A. J. H. Clement (former insurance executive and
Durham City Councilman), Bert Collins (CPA, JD, former president
and CEO of NC Mutual Life Insurance Co.), Willie Covington
(Durham Recorder of Deeds), John Daniel (physician), Wendell Davis
(County executive), Robert Dawson (physician and former president of
the National Medical Association), Stanley Fleming (dentist and former
chair of the NC Board of Dental Examiners), John Hope Franklin (PhD,
perhaps the pre-eminent historian in this country, Medal of Freedom
awardee), Philip Freelon (owner of a major architectural firm), Ralph
Hunt (convenience stores, former state senator and member of the NC
Utilities Commission), Ron Hunter (hotel manager), Charles Johnson
(physician and former head of the National Medical Association), James
Johnson (PhD, Distinguished Professor of Management, Keenan-
Flager Business School), Eric Michaux (attorney and former chair of the
North Carolina State Bar Examiners), Lew Myers (business executive),
Charlie Nelms (university chancellor), Michael Palmer (CPA, Director
of Community Affairs, Duke University), Wade Wayne Perry (attorney
and former legal counsel for NC Mutual Life Insurance Co.), George
Quick (county executive), John C. Scarborough, III (owner of a major
funeral home in Durham), Maceo K. Sloan (attorney and CEO of a
major investment management firm), Leon Stanback (Superior Court
Judge), Richmond E. Stewart (CEO of a major community development
firm), Leroy Walker (PhD, former head of the US Olympic Committee
and college chancellor), Charles D. Watts (physician, former chief
medical officer of NC Mutual Life Insurance and member of its board
and executive committee), Albert Whiting (PhD and former president
of NCCU), George Williams (architect and president of G. H. Williams
Collaborative, PA), and Phail Wynn, Jr. (PhD, former president of
Durham Technical and Community College, and currently Vice
President for Community Affairs for Duke University)

Some 15 years after we moved, I was voted to membership in the North
Carolina Association of Guardsmen, a chapter of the National Guardsmen.
At various times Wanda and I had attended Guardsmen social functions as
the guests of local Guardsmen members, Dr. Leroy Swift, Dr. Robert Dawson
and Alex Rivera (a renowned photographer and journalist). The criteria for
membership include: are you fun-loving?; do you enjoy sports?; do you not
have bad character?; can you afford it?; do you have a good-looking wife

or girl friend (not both) who knows how to dress? The Guardsmen were started in 1932 in Brooklyn. Now there are 18 chapters: Boston, Connecticut, Manhattan, Brooklyn, New Jersey, Baltimore, Philadelphia, Washington D.C., Richmond, Norfolk, North Carolina, Atlanta, Savannah, Florida, Detroit, Chicago, St. Louis and Los Angeles. Whether a chapter covers a city or an entire state, membership is limited to 30 men. The organization doesn't have any purpose other than to have fun. Although as an organization, we do no good for anyone, our members usually have fantastic records of public service. There are three national meetings per year, hosted by one of the chapters. The host chapter pays for all food, beverage and entertainment for a weekend that normally starts on Thursday evening with a reception, golf and tennis on Friday morning, a late luncheon on Friday, a dinner dance on Friday night, a luncheon on Saturday, a dinner dance (usually formal) on Saturday night and a brunch on Sunday morning. Friday and Saturday following the dinner dances there is additional hospitality in two or more hotel suites until three or four in the morning with live entertainment and food. The host chapter provides open bars for all events. Members are expected to bring their wives to these gatherings. No other guests are permitted. Attendance at these "weekends" ranges from 350 to 700 people. The chapters may entertain the group wherever they wish. Most do so at their home site but chapters have entertained in the Bahamas, Puerto Rico, Mexico, Montreal, Quebec City (Canada), Bermuda, New Orleans, Hilton Head, Boca Raton, and resorts in Southern California and Western North Carolina. For the Guardsmen I have served as both North Carolina and national president. I have now been granted emeritus status, but the current eight local members are:

Bert Collins (CPA, MBA, JD, chairman of the board and former president and CEO of NC Mutual Life Insurance), Walter Davenport (CPA former head of Garrett and Davenport CPAs and partner of Cherry Bekaert and Holland, CPAs), Stanley Fleming (dentist), Eric Michaux (attorney), Eric Rivera (periodondist), James Speed, Jr. (CPA, MBA, president and CEO of NC Mutual Life Insurance), Leon Stanback (Superior Court Judge) and Charles D. Watts (attorney and former senior vice president of NC Mutual Life Insurance),

My cousins Hobart Price and his son Mark are members of the Manhattan chapter. Fletcher Wiley of Brookline, Massachusetts, who is married to my sister Gloria's stepdaughter, is a member of the Boston Chapter.

Almost immediately after we relocated to Durham we joined a couples club called *Raison D'etre*. These were all young and upwardly mobile couples who had a party every month, hosted by a member. Members included:

Howard (insurance executive and city councilman) and Dolores (administrator) Clement, Richmond E. (educator and developer) and Eunice (insurance and real estate) Stewart, Randal (real estate agency) and Gracie (dietician) Rogers, Frank (state corrections executive) and Veatrice (secretary) Bright, Dewitt (CPA) and Marcella Kaye (dance school owner) Sullivan, Lindsey (educator) and Betty (educator) Merritt, James (dentist) and Juanita (accountant) Pilgrim, Larkin (insurance executive) and Violet Teasley, Thomas and Zenobia Jefferson, F. V. (Pete) (savings & loan executive) and Lavonia (PhD in physical fitness) Allison, Asa (insurance executive) and Shirley Spaulding, Jr., Jessie and Constance Allen (educators), Bert (CPA, attorney, insurance executive) and Carolyn (artist) Collins, Bill (tobacco worker) and Jeannie (educator and later state senator) Lucas, Tom (state corrections employee) and Tiny (educator) Burgess, William (PhD sociologist) and Juanita (educator) Howell, Walter Hugh (PhD biologist) and Constance (educator) Pattillo, J. C. (funeral home executive) and Clara (personal shopper) Scarborough, James (PhD economist) and Caroline (home maker) Tucker, Marion (PhD psychologist and college president) and Lula (health care manager) Thorpe, Theodore (business) and Carolyn (mental health therapist) Thornton, Wayne (attorney and insurance executive) and Patsy (PhD English) Perry, H. M. (developer, attorney and state legislator) and Joyce (management worker) Michaux, Donald (M. D.) and Barbara (health care manager) Moore, Charles (M. D.) and Carolyn (attorney and judge) Johnson, and Albert (association executive) and Janice (educator) Fisher.

Wanda and I had friends in each of the fraternities and sororities and were invited to their annual events - usually formal at the city-maintained facility called The Armory. The facility was used for basketball, meetings, high school graduation exercises, concerts and balls. The affairs had catered food and we brought our own liquor either in a case that carried one to three bottles or in the brown paper bag it was placed in by the clerk in the liquor store. At that time there were no sales of "liquor by the drink" in public places anywhere in North Carolina. Some counties had state-controlled ABC stores for the purchase of liquor, others prohibited the sale of alcohol completely. We were one of the "brown-bagging" counties. You could take your "brown bag" with you to dances and restaurants where you could purchase "set ups" of ice, cups, mixes, lemons and limes. Visitors from the north and mid west were shocked at the practice at first, but then, invariably, fell in love with it. When the proposition to have bars came to a vote in Durham, Wanda and I voted against it. Fortunately for the hospitality industry, the measure passed, however.

Currently, the organization to which Wanda and I both belong is the College View Duplicate Bridge Club. The club is affiliated with the predominantly black American Bridge Association. I resisted joining because, unlike my pinochle club, the duplicate Bridge games are serious and players must maintain proper decorum. Talking trash, beer, and even slamming cards are forbidden. But, for reasons of her own, Wanda persuaded me to join. I must admit that I now enjoy our sessions except when an opponent wants to be overbearing about something. The members are mostly senior citizens and the current long-term members are:

Harold and Laverne Burch, Carolyn Thornton, Constance Pattillo, Thelma Lee, Louis Perkins, James Forde, Sandra Shuler, Alicia Jones, Esther Bivins, Francine Blackwell, Ida Dark, Joyce Scott, Billie Jones, Eldee Brown, Margo Harris, William Haynes, Anita Smith, Linda Harris, Ernestine Goods, Carol Bond, Dianne Crawford, Frank Hurd, Heddy Echard, Harlan and Helen Burgess, Addie Marshall, Julia Bon Smith, Irene Williams and Randolph and Mary Young

Mary is the Director for our club and is in charge of setting up the games and dispute resolution.

Because of Wanda's strong belief in family and higher education, we have helped when we could. Two nieces, three nephews and two grandsons, all from Detroit, came to college in North Carolina and lived with us either all of the time or some of the time. The first was Constance Jenkins Stephenson, the second was Lynette French, the third was Stephan French, the fourth was James Gooden, the fifth was Bronson French (actually, he spent a year at Virginia State in Petersburg) and the sixth and seventh were grandsons Sulaiman and Malik Mausi.

Tennis remained my first sports love for many years. Although Wanda had played a little tennis long before we married, she took it up again in the mid to late '70s and developed a great forehand. When we played singles, she got two bounces by which to return my drop shots. On one occasion, she and I won the *men's* winners trophy at a National Guardsmen weekend at Virginia Beach. Wanda's good friends whom she met in college, Rufus McKinney and Frank Hollis, came to Durham along with their wives, Dorothy Ann and Jan, a few times to play.

When Achilles' tendonitis forced me out of tennis, I went to golf, but with much less success. Rufus McKinney, a retired lawyer and lobbyist from D.C., James Harrington, a retired postal worker, retired Air Force Colonel Wes Brown from Roxboro, retired Army General Harold Burch, Walter Davenport and my son, Nathan Jr., are my mainstays in golf. Rufus and his present wife, Glendonia (who is a retired corporate banker and terrific golfer herself), are members of Congressional just outside of D.C. and it has been my privilege to hack through that course several times. Unfortunately, James may have to quit golf at least temporarily due to his decision to have hip-replacement surgery. I have only been able to play golf once with my new son-in-law (Shahida's husband), Ray Johnson who is an expert on learning environments for high school students, especially in urban areas. Ray might have been put off when we played a round at Pinehurst here in North Carolina and I tried to help him with his game and to warn him about peeing either uphill or against the wind while on the golf course.

"Girl's Camp" is a group of close women friends who gathered initially in Detroit, but when Wanda invited them to Durham at our current home on two occasions, she expanded the group to include participants from New York, D.C., Florida and of course, Durham. On these two gatherings in Durham I found long golf weekends to go while over fifty "girls" camped in and did "their thing." Detroit participants were Teola Hunter, Sylvia Muthleb, Ruth Johnson, Betty Bennett, Marcella Nance, Hermonce Lassiter, Joyce Gallant, Ester Allen, Clara Butler, Martha Vaughn, Ada Halloway, Willa Darque, Marjorie Patton, Shirley Patton, Delores D. Brown, Roberta Hinton, Corine Young and Valerie Johnston. Gloria D. Davis and Bernice Moore came up from Florida. Our cousin, Ernestine Price came down from New York and Edna Jones and Glendonia McKinney drove down from D.C. Local partyers included our cousin, Mariah (Popsie) Creed, Betty Blackmon, Betty Perkins Jones, Patsy Perry, Joyce Patton (co-host), Beatrice V. Allen, Marion Thorne, Amelia Powell, Connie Pattillo, Kaye Sullivan, Helen Garner, Faye Rivera, Carolyn Thornton, Carolyn Collins, Judge Carolyn Johnson, Lula Thorpe, Edna Harrington, Della Michaux, Meredythe Holmes, Joyce O'Rourke, LaVerne Burch, Billy Jones, Mary Young, Edith Johnson, Gwen Jones Parham, Dolores Clement, Eunice Stewart, Veatrice Bright and State Senator Jeanne Lucas.

Wanda and I really enjoy traveling. So far, we have visited 44 of the fifty states and 36 countries. When possible, we have traveled with family and close friends. We and Ernestine and Hobart Price have been together in resorts in many parts of this country as well as in Mexico and Spain. We have taken Gail and Nathan Jr's children by car to Detroit, Tennessee, Kentucky, New England, Windsor and Montreal. Those children, their parents, Wanda and I went to Paris, London and the Baltic Sea capital cities plus St. Petersburg in Russia. We went to South Africa, Turkey, Greece, Egypt, Cyprus, Italy, and Spain with Carolyn and Bert Collins. Wanda and I went to Beijing and Shanghai with the Collinses, Shahida and Ray Johnson, and Connie Jenkins Stephenson. On a trip to Chile, Argentina and Brazil we were with both the Collinses and LaVerne and Harold Burch.

I now turn from social life to social engineering.

CHAPTER EIGHT

Social Engineering

From 1964 to 1967 I was employed at The North Carolina Fund. From 1967 to 1972 I was employed at The Foundation For Community Development. Both organizations were formed to address poverty in North Carolina. Both organizations worked to "Break the Cycle of Poverty" by encouraging the State of North Carolina, local government units and private enterprise to provide early childhood education, adult basic education, housing, health care, transportation and other services to help enable people to climb out of poverty. The Fund's basic approach was to work with elected officials and others in power to show them how to improve these services and how to deliver them to the poor. The approach of the Foundation For Community Development was to help poor people form organizations through which they could effectively bring pressure on those in power to improve the quality of services and to eliminate discriminatory treatment. The Foundation also promoted the formation of corporations owned or influenced by low-wealth citizens to pursue housing and commercial developments in their communities.

The North Carolina Fund

The story of the North Carolina Fund has been told amply in film documentaries, papers and chapters authored by several people and through its archives located at the University of North Carolina. The following pages are meant to describe my experiences and to introduce some of the people with whom I worked.

I started work in the Spring of 1964 as the controller. The address was 107 ½ East Parrish Street, a walk-up second floor location. Mechanics &

131

Farmers Bank, Mutual Savings & Loan and North Carolina Mutual were a block away to the west.

Susan B. Graham, who was already working there as secretary to the Executive Director and as bookkeeper, was my assistant. Sue was a tall, attractive redhead with two children. She had learned bookkeeping in high school and had taken a few accounting courses at University of North Carolina at Chapel Hill, though she did not have a college degree. She was an extremely capable assistant and we became good friends almost immediately.

By the time I arrived, the Fund had chosen eleven nonprofit organizations located in four different sections of the state to receive grants for staffing and program support. The boards of those organizations were drawn from a cross section of citizens of the cities or counties they were to serve. The organizations were strongly encouraged to include among the board members people who understood the problems of the poor and could speak for them. This meant that, for the first time in many parts of North Carolina, blacks, Indians and whites came together to make decisions to govern the personnel and program policies for organizations dedicated to anti-poverty work.

One of the first things I urged George Esser (the Executive Director) to do was to allow me to attend the board meetings to report on fiscal affairs. By being at their meetings, the board members could ask me questions and could indicate their concerns about our finances to me directly rather than have them filtered to me through Esser. Also, it was important to me for those board members to see that a black man could handle the job. After all, except for John Wheeler, none knew that black CPAs existed.

In addition to Governor Terry Sanford, board members were: Dallas Herring the Chairman of the State Board of Education; Pete McKnight, the editor of the Charlotte Observer; Gerald Cowan, a retired Wachovia Bank executive from Asheville; Ann Forsyth, a member of the Reynolds (cigarettes) family; Tom Pearsall, a farmer/business man and powerful legislator from eastern North Carolina who had called for converting the public schools to private schools to avoid the impact of the *Brown V. Board of Education* decision; Sam Duncan a black PhD who was the president of Livingstone (a black private college); Hollis Edens the former president of Duke University and at the time, the top executive of the Babcock Foundation; John Wheeler, the president of the black-owned Mechanics & Farmers Bank; Rosa Parker, the sister in law of Luther Hodges who preceded Sanford as Governor; Wallace Murchison, a Harvard lawyer in Wilmington North Carolina; and Hargrove Bowles, a successful business man and politician from Greensboro North Carolina. This was, indeed, a power group and I felt good about getting to know them and getting them to know me.

After a few months we were offered a large building near downtown rent free. It had been occupied by North Carolina Blue Cross-Blue Shield and they had not been able to sell it when they moved to new quarters. The building contained roughly fifteen thousand square feet, around five times the space we were occupying. The move allowed for the hiring of staff to support the executives who were in charge of volunteers, training, publicity, research, technical assistance and, of course, accounting. The jobs of planning for space allocation, renovations and coordination of the move itself were given to me.

Puerto Rico Meeting of Ford Foundation Grey Areas Projects

After six months on the job I learned that the Ford Foundation was convening a meeting of selected board members and the top staff of a group of its grantees from different parts of the country. These were referred to as the "grey areas" projects because all of us were working on means of changing state and local practices to relieve some of the burdens of poverty. The projects were located in Oakland, New Haven, Boston, Washington, D.C., Pittsburgh and Chicago. I always thought it was interesting that, despite the missions of the organizations represented, the meeting was convened in San Juan Puerto Rico.

The purpose of the meeting was to share information among the grantees on program problems and progress. Esser, Bill Koch and Jack Mansfield were the Fund executives slated to go, along with three board members. I went to George Esser and told him that I needed to go to the meeting, even if I had to pay my own way. I explained that my role as controller was not only to keep track of expenditures and manage risk, but also to help with budgeting and to find ways to achieve the Fund's objectives in a manner that did not violate the law and the contractual agreements with the supporting foundations and governmental agencies from which our funds came. Esser finally agreed that I should attend. When I learned that some attendees were bringing spouses, I decided that Wanda should attend, also.

The meeting was held at El Convento, a very stylish hotel located in the heart of Old San Juan. I was in meetings all day every day and some evenings. When we were meeting, Wanda went on tours and socialized with the spouses. There were two social events at which the entire group was present: one was a visit to a night club that included limbo stick dancing; the other was a reception hosted by the Puerto Rican Governor at a castle overlooking the sea. Wanda and I were the only blacks in attendance. We made strongly positive impressions on both the Ford staff and the Fund delegation. Tom Pearsall, the Fund board member who had advocated closing the public schools to avoid integration, very respectfully asked me, and then

Wanda, for permission to dance with her. The Ford Foundation people were both surprised and delighted with my knowledge of financial affairs and the role of the fiscal officer in achieving program objectives. The credibility and upward mobility I enjoyed at the Fund was aided by our attendance at the meeting in Puerto Rico.

Federal War on Poverty Starts

President Lyndon Johnson's War on Poverty was launched in 1964 through several federal agencies, including the Office of Economic Opportunity (OEO)

(OEO's first director was Sargent Shriver, President Kennedy's brother-in-law, former director of the Peace Corps, and later, vice presidential candidate with George McGovern. Beginning in 1969 and under President Nixon, Don Rumsfeld was the OEO director and Dick Cheney was a staff member.)

The approach for the federal War on Poverty and the Fund's plans to Break the Cycle of Poverty fit very well. The eleven Fund-supported organizations were among the first in the nation to be designated Community Action Agencies (CAAs) under the War on Poverty. As CAAs they became eligible for federal grants for administration and support for service programs such as early childhood education, adult basic education, counseling, day care, and health care. The federal grants required that the CAAs provide local matching for the federal money and, since the agencies had foundation funds through the Fund, the matching requirement was satisfied.

The Fund, itself, also became a federal grantee for programs to train volunteers and staff for CAAs, to experiment with effective means of recruiting and relocating people from high unemployment areas of the state to the more prosperous Piedmont area, to provide job training and supportive services for the unemployed and underemployed and to develop ways of producing housing that could be purchased by low wealth families.

With all the new money and activity, I was swamped. I was traveling heavily to provide training for the staffs of the eleven CAAs to help them avoid mistakes in handling fiscal affairs. I had to study the requirements that came with the federal grants to the Fund to make sure the money was used properly. I had to provide current information on expenditures compared to budget and expenditure forecasts to Esser, the Fund board and our department heads. Much of what was done during the War on Poverty was not politically popular, especially in the rural areas of the state. I concluded that one of the easiest ways of shutting down an unpopular program would be to find fraud, improper spending or poor fiscal reporting. One could argue forever about whether or not a particular program was effective, but if the accounting was bad, there was no defense. I was determined that neither the Fund nor the eleven CAAs would fail to maintain their fiscal affairs in top-notch condition. When the auditors came, the Fund and its grantees always had good reports.

Nonprofit Accounting - Innovations

Although at that time there was substantial professional guidance for accounting and reporting for business organizations and governments, there was very little for community-based nonprofits. I had to create - by myself - some of the accounting treatment for matching funds, capital assets, restrictions on fund balances and financial statement preparation for multiple grants from several different federal, state and private sources. When the auditors came to do their audit, I had to explain and justify my accounting procedures to them.

When I told Clifton Campbell (a black man retained by the Ford Foundation to conduct periodic reviews of the Fund's activities) about the fact that no one (including the auditors) completely understood what I was doing, the result was a two-week visit by a retired Price Waterhouse partner to see if *I*, in fact, knew what *I* was doing. The Price Waterhouse man was so impressed that he recommended that Ford use me to review the accounting work of some of their grantees in Louisiana, Los Angeles and Maui. Wanda and I made those trips together. They were first-time exposures to those places for us and we learned a great deal.

No Sponsors for Joining the North Carolina Association of CPAs

I had been licensed initially in Michigan and had been a member of the Michigan Association of Certified Public Accountants. Within six months of my arrival in North Carolina I made application to the North Carolina Association but was turned down because they required me to have two sponsors who were members of the Association. Bill Gantt, a white CPA who had Tarboro connections, was willing to be one of my sponsors, however, I had not been able to find a second one. Every CPA I had asked told me that the Association was mostly social and that there was no reason for me to join. Joe Norman, the only other black CPA in the state could not help because he, also, had not been able to become a member. I was told by the top staff person at the Association that they would allow me to attend the education courses without being a member, though I had to pay a higher fee than members paid. After two clean opinion audits by our local auditing firm I asked the partner in charge of the audits if he would be my second sponsor for membership in the North Carolina Association. I had worked closely with that partner for two years as his firm did the audit work. He had learned a lot about nonprofit accounting from me. I expected him to say *yes*. But instead, he told me to send him a resume and he would think about it. I took that to mean that he did not want to sponsor me so I didn't raise the matter again.

Promotions at The Fund - Enter Dewitt Sullivan

I got along very well with George Esser and the rest of the staff. Esser's confidence in me grew to the point that when he needed someone to relieve him of his general administrative duties he named me as Deputy Director for Finance and Administration. Sue Graham and I had been handling the accounting work, but because of the growth in the size and complexity of the Fund's operations we had hired Juanita Pilgrim, a recent graduate in accounting from North Carolina College in Durham. However, it became clear that I needed more strength in the accounting area than Graham and Pilgrim could provide. I turned to my old friend in Detroit, Dewitt Sullivan.

Dewitt had left the Austin & Company firm at which we had worked when I was in Detroit and was the controller at one of Detroit's black-owned private hospitals. When I asked him to consider the job of controller at the Fund and told him what it paid, his response was that he was making more than that at the hospital. My only come back was "Dewitt, I need you." He, Kaye and the children, Dewanda and Dwight, moved to Durham two months later. It turned out to be a great decision for both of us. He handled the job superbly.

Ford Foundation Program Evaluation

With Dewitt taking care of the controllership function, I was able to get more involved in other aspects of the Fund's operations. When the time came for Ford to perform a formal evaluation of the Fund using its own staff and volunteers, the Fund was asked to develop a plan for the evaluators to follow. After the research department and the top program staff failed to produce a document that all could agree upon, I asked Esser to let me try. The major problem was that it was not possible to evaluate the programs using only statistical data. For example, the *number* of enrollees in day care or adult basic education was not as important as the impact of their participation on their lives. Only by following the participants for many years could you assess the impact. Since the Fund was then only in its third year, there was no way to know whether or not the programs had resulted in lasting benefits.

The evaluation plan I designed focused on the structure, policies and capacity of the Fund and its grantee agencies. The evaluation teams would be asked to determine whether or not the boards were comprised of people with the needed knowledge and skills. Were the top staff people capable? Was there adequate training and support for staff? Did the personnel policies and practices provide for non-discriminatory hiring and firing? Were fiscal controls and financial reporting adequate?

The staff found my approach acceptable with but few modifications. I completed the document and it was used to conduct the evaluation.

As a result of my work on the evaluation and other activities, Esser promoted me to Deputy for Finance, Administration <u>and Program</u>, making me the second person in the line of authority. We conferred closely on all important matters. We attended important meetings as a team. When he was unable to make a speech or visit one of the grantee agencies, I handled it for him.

Near Lynching

One such visit was traumatic. It was a trip to the little Appalachian Mountain town of Franklin in Macon County, the western part of the state near the Tennessee and Georgia lines. Billy Barnes, the Fund's brilliant public relations director, and I drove together. Our mission was to represent Esser to discuss a funding request we had received from our Macon County grantee.

We were on a mountain road near Sylva, some 30 miles east of Franklin when we decided to stop for a bite to eat at a roadside restaurant. We pulled into the nearly empty parking lot, went in and had an early dinner. As we exited the restaurant, we noticed that the parking lot was virtually full of cars with drivers in them. As we started toward our car two Highway Patrol cruisers came speeding into the lot and came to a screeching halt near us. The troopers rushed over and told us that they would escort us out of the lot and follow us for a spell to make sure we reached our destination safely. Unknown to me and to Billy, who is white, some of the patrons had called friends to notify them that a black man was eating at the restaurant. When the owner of the restaurant saw what was happening, he called the Highway Patrol. That episode could have resulted in a lynching, and as I think back on it, I am appalled that Billy and I could have forgotten that in 1967 there was still fierce resistance to public accommodations for black people in western and eastern North Carolina. I suppose the relationships we enjoyed with the black, white and Indian employees at the Fund had lured us into a false perception of racial attitudes in our state. When we ate together in Durham or in the grantee organization's areas, the white people always selected restaurants they knew had no objection to serving blacks so I had not had a bad experience as a Fund employee. The Sylva incident impacts me even today. I don't patronize any establishments where I think my money isn't welcome. There are a lot of them.

A Visit to Yale

In June 1967 Wanda and I went to my 15th reunion at Yale. I had not been to New Haven since I graduated. I enjoyed showing her around campus and introducing her to the few classmates I remembered and who remembered me. Mostly, however, we spent time in light chatter with people during breaks and receptions. The conversations usually revolved around vocational activities. All were doing very well, indeed. They were professionals of all sorts, especially in finance. Very few were in politics. None were in the ministry or social action work of any kind. When the first dozen people asked what I did, my response was that I worked for the North Carolina Fund. That usually resulted in a second question: "Is that a mutual fund?" When I responded that our mission involved promoting institutional change, they responded with the question, "Why would you want to change anything?" For them, I guess, everything was just fine the way it was.

The Beginning of Direct Funding for Grass Roots
Organizations in Black Communities

The Fund was in the middle of North Carolina's Civil Rights Struggle. Clearly, racial discrimination was the leading contributor to the depth of poverty blacks endured. Denial of equal rights to jobs, education, health-care, decent housing, paved streets and public transportation almost assured that black adults would be poor and that their offspring would be poor for generations. However, the Fund's strategy, as I have said, was to *influence* change, not demand it. The insistence that the CAAs have board members who were black and could represent the poor was a part of that strategy. But those representatives of the poor were always in the minority on the boards. Usually they were ministers, educators, professionals of various kinds or small business owners. Their ability to understand and speak for the poor was limited because, with the possible exception of churches, the Elks and the NAACP, there were no organizations in which the poor were in control and where there was discussion on the issues that affected the poor. Certainly, those who sat on those boards to "speak for the poor" were not poor themselves and had not been asked to serve in that capacity by the poor. Also, it was often true that those representatives were constrained in their conduct by the knowledge that they could incur economic reprisals if they spoke of racism or advocated measures that were outside the mainstream of the social and economic thinking of the white community. Teachers and other employees could lose their jobs; business owners and churches could lose access to capital from white financial institutions, and so on.

The staff of the Fund of all races seemed to agree on this point. With Esser's permission, efforts were launched to encourage the CAAs to support the creation of neighborhood organizations to work on problems faced by the poor themselves. The leaders who emerged from the neighborhoods were to be taught leadership skills. They were to learn how to conduct meetings, how to build consensus, how to make an effective speech, how to negotiate, etc. The groups were to get heavy doses of civics lessons so that they could understand the workings of local government. Arrangements were made to make telephones, copiers, office supplies and office equipment available to the groups. Although such activity was encouraged in each of the eleven CAAs, the most successful work was done in Durham and in a four county rural area in the north central part of the state referred to as the Choanoke area.

In Durham the work with neighborhood organizations was spearheaded by Howard Fuller, a staffer at Operation Breakthrough (OBT). Fuller came to Durham from work and school in Cleveland where he had earned a master's in social work. His work at OBT resulted in the creation of nine neighborhood organizations, each with its own set of priorities for addressing the problems of poverty. These nine neighborhoods ultimately were pulled together into an organization named United Organizations for Community Improvement (UOCI). UOCI then began to bring pressure on elected and appointed officials, and employers for better treatment for black and poor people. The board and staff of OBT were heavily criticized by those in Durham who opposed the changes that were being asked for by Fuller and UOCI. Ultimately, that criticism led to an agreement for Fuller to leave OBT and come to work for the Fund. But at the Fund, with Esser's blessing, Fuller continued his work with UOCI and, since he no longer worked for OBT, the criticism was deflected to the Fund.

While Fuller was still at OBT, Fund staffers under the leadership of Jim McDonald began to use the Fuller approach in Northampton, Halifax, Hertford and Bertie counties. The Fund grantee in that area was The Choanoke Area Development Association (CADA). However, unlike OBT, the CADA board and top staff strongly opposed the creation of the grass roots organizations. Nevertheless, the organizing proceeded and the four county rural area created Peoples Program on Poverty (PPOP).

Both UOCI and PPOP, with the encouragement of Fund staff, sought grants from the Fund. Although OBT indicated it favored a direct grant to UOCI, CADA strongly opposed such action for PPOP. Independent funding was acceptable to Esser personally but CADA's resistence and his reading of the Fund Board's probable reaction caused him to propose a compromise arrangement. The compromise was for the funding for the two organizations to flow through the respective CAAs. Although I understood and empathized with Esser's conflict, I, and the rest of the black staff members, felt that the time had come for the Fund to support independent organizations of the poor such as UOCI and PPOP where responsible leadership had developed.

All of the black staff members at the Fund tendered resignations to be effective immediately on the evening before the day Esser was to drive to CADA to offer the compromise.

Esser relented and agreed to allow me to make the case for independent funding at the Fund board meeting that was scheduled within two weeks. In exchange, the black staffers agreed to stay on. When Esser announced his decision he was actually applauded by the full staff.

At the board meeting, I did my best, but Esser could sense that the votes in favor of the funding were not there. He asked if I would object to him speaking to the board. I readily agreed. There was no doubt that the board's respect for Esser's judgment was many levels higher than for any other members of the staff.

The board members reminded Esser of the mission of the Fund: to promote change within the public and private sector organizations through well reasoned arguments and by demonstrating the impact that innovative approaches to education and new supportive services had on helping people to rise above the poverty level. Changes in society, they felt, would be at the margins and necessarily slow, because the minds and hearts of those who ran institutions had to be won over. They feared that independent organizations of the poor would result in confrontation rather than verbal persuasion. They wanted evolution, not chaos and revolution.

Esser was masterful in addressing the concerns of the Board. He pointed out that though the organizations would protest the status quo, because of the support of Fund staff and the development of responsible indigenous leadership within the group, the organizations would follow the paths that civic organizations all over the state had followed in advocating for community improvements. Why shouldn't these organizations be given the opportunity to try to change the institutions in their communities that impacted the lives of the poor?

Finally, the Board made two decisions. First, that funds would be granted to UOCI immediately and to PPOP when they were administratively ready to receive them; second that future grants to organizations of the poor would be channeled through an intermediary organization that would be responsible for providing close monitoring and continued technical assistance.

The Beginnings of The Foundation for Community Development

As a result of the Board's action, I was invited to write a proposal for the establishment of a new organization that would be a Fund grantee. I did so. I then called a meeting of a racially mixed group of people from across the State to discuss, amend, and endorse the proposal. It was submitted to the Fund Board in September 1967. The "theory section" of the proposal contained the following language.

All poverty in this nation results from the decisions made by those persons who exercise varying degrees of control over the creation and/ or distribution of our financial resources. This is not to imply that this group has made poor decisions in the majority of instances. On the contrary, this large group of decision-makers has constructed and is maintaining a socio-economic system which in 1966 produced personal incomes of approximately six hundred billion dollars, equivalent to three thousand dollars for every man, woman and child in our country. Their decisions on the creation of wealth have been fantastically successful; however, the decisions on the distribution of that wealth have left between forty and fifty million people in this nation without the ability to acquire a sufficient supply of the various goods and services our nation produces.

An uncomfortably large segment of Americans proclaim and believe that drive and initiative on the part of the poor, when coupled with what our society now offers, can eliminate most of the poverty which now exists. It is true that social security, Medicare, welfare, public health, free schools, unemployment insurance and many other human services enable some individuals to escape poverty and others to avoid outright starvation. The existence of these services is partially responsible for the fact that the size of the poverty group remains relatively stable, or at best, decreases slightly each year. However, the pace of the decrease demonstrates that both the *amount* of resources allocated to these programs and the *deployment* of these resources are inadequate to do the job; the pace of the decrease requires that better decisions concerning the amount and deployment of resources be made in the future

The composition of the poverty group remains consistent from generation to generation. The overwhelming evidence is that the poor are born poor and do not fall into poverty from some higher station in life. This means that the individual decisions they have made with respect to their lives have not played as important a role in determining their economic status as the decisions made by others in shaping the philosophy and structure of our economy. The farm youth who misses school in North Carolina in order to help his family in the tobacco field is absent with the blessings of the school attendance laws of the state, which provide that a child may be absent to perform work under the supervision of the parent. The social system, which for centuries has denied an entire race the opportunity to work at a level commensurate with ability, crushes the initiative of that group to acquire training. The denial of birth control assistance to an unmarried mother is based upon a kind of morality and logic which is more suited to life styles of fifty years ago than today. The unmarried mother is more the victim of that logic than of her natural emotional and biological urges.

If the composition of the poverty group remains consistent (with the exception of the relatively few who break out and become part of the upper strata), then so does the composition of the decision-making group. The requirements for membership call for a level of knowledge and an outlook on life which the poor do not have. But a way must be found to introduce the point of view of the poor into the decision-making councils, because the amount of allocation and the manner of deployment of the resources appropriated to benefit the poor must become consistent with the problems the poor face.

The reasons for the poor quality of decisions in the past range from outright prejudice on one extreme, to indifference, to inadequate information on the needs of the poor (both extent and nature), to improper interpretation of what might be considered adequate information. A former sharecropper, Negro, migrates to the city; he finds that most jobs are closed to him because of his race. The few jobs which might have been open, despite his color, require skills he does not have. The plants he checks provide no on-the-job training and he is not referred to the pre-vocational and vocational classes being offered locally. Eventually he finds a job paying $30.00 a week, working ten hours a day, and then happens to hear about the vocational classes. After he has spent five months on the waiting list, the classes begin, but now he finds that he cannot attend because the class hours conflict with his job, his only source of support. Even if his employer changed his schedule, and reduced his hours, the fact that the courses are held at the Industrial Education Center located miles out of town means he has no way of getting there. Since this man, and others like him, do not use up the class slots available, or enter only to drop out later due to difficulties such as these; and since it is not economical to offer classes with fewer than twenty trainees in attendance, the board of the

Industrial Education Center decides not to offer the class again because of lack of sufficient local interest

In seeking more voice for the poor in the decisions made, the aim is not to replace those who either have inadequate information or who improperly interpret the information they have, but rather for the poor to join them in decision making to help improve the quality of their joint decisions. Representation of the poor on the board of the Industrial Education Center described above would probably have resulted in different decisions on the hours and location of the classes and on what action to take about continuation of the course.

Since this nation has the wealth to wipe out poverty, any anti-poverty effort *must* have as its basic aim the improvement of the decision-making process. Peter Maris and Martin Rein in *Dilemmas of Social Reform: Poverty and Community Action in the United States* state it this way: "Reform cannot succeed by appeal to institutions themselves. It must rescue them from dependence on middle-class approval or influence the criteria by which performance is judged and resources distributed." (Atherton Press: New York, 1967, p. 47.).

This, of course, is not a simple task. Access to the decision-making councils is not freely given; even when the access is accomplished, articulation of the needs and point of view of the poor, under circumstances which will result in maximum impact, is a problem of gigantic proportions.

The remaining sections of the proposal described the nature of the organizations to be formed, the requirements for organizational stability and strategies to be employed to create the organizations

The grant was approved and the Foundation for Community Development (FCD) was incorporated in October 1967 as a private, nonprofit corporation. The incorporators were a former domestic, a minister, a savings and loan executive and an Appalachian Mountains craftswoman.

George Esser and Howard Fuller, circa 2006. Courtesy of Rah Bickley

The Foundation for Community Development

FCD opened operations in a third floor walk-up office building near downtown Durham on the southeast corner or Main and Gregson Streets. I was named executive director by the board. The charter and by-laws provided that representatives of low-income people were to have 51% of the seats on the board. Other board positions were reserved for representatives of education, labor, civil rights, The Governor of North Carolina and FCD staff. Some of the initial board were: William Holloman of Ahoskie; Nathaniel White, a business owner from Durham; J. W. Thomas, a Lumbee Indian and business man from Lumberton; Eva Griffin from Rocky Mount; J. Archie Hargraves, a minister and educator from Raleigh; Rubye Gattis of Durham, James Pierce, a labor leader from Charlotte; Louise Jenkins of Fayetteville; A. C. Cofield of Weldon; Alice Ballance of Windsor; Fannie Corbett of Wilson; Eva Clayton (who later became a Congresswoman) from Warrenton; Julius Chambers, a civil rights attorney from Charlotte; Howard Miller, a professor at North Carolina State University in Raleigh; E. B. Palmer, an educator from Raleigh; Aggie Lowrance, a white craftswoman from Valley Crucis and Marion Thorpe, a psychology professor and administrator at North Carolina College at Durham. The Governor never named a representative.

The first chairman of the board was John S. Stewart, president of the black-controlled Mutual Savings & Loan in Durham.

The initial staff of FCD came with me from the Fund. Howard Fuller was named by me as director of training. I placed Susan Graham in charge of fiscal affairs and John Justice, who had worked under Billy Barnes, directed public relations.

The training department developed curricular and methodologies for training indigenous persons with leadership potential, the staff and boards of OEO community action agencies and college students who were willing to volunteer for community work. The goal of the training was to develop neighborhood-based, issue-oriented groups of the poor across the state.

Staff members in the training department initially were Thelma Miller, Arch Foster, Pauline Bowman, Reginald Durante, and Linda Sauls. Later additions/replacements included Gloria Evans, Tempie Poteat, Levi Smalls, Ray Spain, Cynthia Ruffin, Jose Goodson, Sandra Philpott, Joyce Ruffin, James Lee and Vaughn Glapion.

Typically, our staff would spend time in a community, meeting with whoever would talk to them about their problems. These interviewees would then be brought together for a general discussion about creating a community-wide organization. If agreement was reached on the community-wide organization, a mass meeting would then be arranged at which local leaders and Howard Fuller would speak. Howard was always the main speaker and he was always effective. Howard was striking in both appearance and rhetoric. He was over six feet tall, dark and athletic. He knew how to deliver a speech as well as anyone I have ever heard. He never exhorted the audience to violence, but he always urged them to act with vigor and determination to demand fair treatment. There was never a crowd that was calm after a Fuller speech.

In almost every instance, these mass meetings were given sensational coverage in the local press and Howard was labeled as an outside agitator. Editorials followed within a few days and all decried the need for such meetings because they usually led to local unrest.

This was the process through which eight groups were formed, including the initial two – UOCI in Durham and PPOP in Bertie, Halifax, Northampton and Hertford Counties. They applied for grants and, if approved, we and they collaborated in selecting a person who would be trained by us to be the paid staff person to perfect the organization, train other leaders and plan strategies. The six that came into being after FCD commenced operations were:

Consolidated Councils for Improvement in the eastern town of Rocky Mount

Greensboro Association for Poor People in the Piedmont section

Wilson Community Improvement Association in the Coastal Plains section

Fayetteville Area Poor People's Organization in the sand hills section to the south

United Poor Peoples' Organization in Raleigh

HOPE, Inc. in the Lumbee Indian Territory in Pembroke

Issues and achievements varied from community to community. However, with each of the groups, the strategy was to focus first on an activity which had a very high probability of success so as to reinforce the idea that group action was more beneficial than individual action. After the initial success, typical activities of these groups included negotiations with local government for improved city services, amendment and enforcement of housing codes, representation on boards and commissions, and redress of welfare grievances. . When negotiations failed, the organizations began to use public demonstrations, picketing and selective buying campaigns to achieve their objectives.

UOCI, under the leadership of Benjamin Ruffin as master organizer, was clearly the most successful of the eight community organizations. Ruffin helped 23 neighborhood councils with a total membership of 5,000 to sponsor cleanup campaigns and helped them start a food cooperative. They helped black businesses that were forced to move by Urban Renewal to find new locations. They fought unfair housing evictions, taught tenants how to get landlords to make repairs by putting rent into escrow and got streets paved by the City. They orchestrated a city wide selective buying campaign that resulted in jobs for black people in businesses that had not previously hired our people. A study done by Francis Redburn, a doctoral candidate at the University of North Carolina at Chapel Hill, concluded that the revenue lost to the affected stores during the selective buying campaign was nearly $1 million. But Ruffin was skillful in keeping protests out of politics. He also kept the goodwill of Operation Breakthrough, the local CAA, through which he had access to help from their staff and modest amounts of money for projects.

FCD-supported activities in Durham and across the state met with fervent criticism, not only from non-poor and non-black citizens but some middle and upper income blacks as well. The critics did not want disturbances. They feared that people would get hurt physically. They feared business slow-downs. They feared loss of jobs. They feared loss of whatever goodwill that had been established between the races. They feared, and they feared, and they feared. My own parents who ran drug stores and many of my friends who were professionals or who had good, secure jobs would often ask if I knew what I was doing or if I didn't think there was a better way to achieve our ends. They didn't object to the goals but they had serious doubts about the strategy.

Malcolm X Liberation University

In 1969 the black students at Duke University decided to boycott classes and to sit-in outside the Duke president's office to protest their treatment on that campus. Howard Fuller had been assisting them in strategies to bring their protests to the attention of the Duke administrators, though he assured me that the boycott was their idea, not his. They began to meet periodically at the FCD office with Howard. Sometimes they would be joined by one or two faculty members from either North Carolina College in Durham, Duke or the University of North Carolina at Chapel Hill.

I had some idea of what the parents of the kids might be going through. They were paying dearly for the tuition and fees and most did not approve of this form of protest. As far as I could tell, all education, other than what they were learning about the dynamics of social protest, had ceased. I hoped that Duke would make the concessions they were demanding quickly and felt that with the help of sympathetic faculty from both North Carolina College and Duke, perhaps they could continue their studies so as not to be too far behind when they resumed their classes.

Fuller thought well of the idea and quickly recruited a significant number of faculty to help. Classes were held in the FCD office. Fuller called the arrangement Malcolm X Liberation University. I was pleased with the activity, but not the name.

The boycott and sit-in ended fairly shortly after they began to study at Malcolm X Liberation University. A week or so after the students were back in class, Fuller asked to be assigned to formally organize and gather support for his new university.

The Tax Reform Act of 1969

The 1969 tax act forbade organizations like FCD from spending funds to influence legislation, either existing or proposed, by attempting to affect opinions of people through grass roots organization. Clearly, we were attempting to influence local ordinances (legislation concerning zoning, housing codes, etc.) and we encouraged the support of elected officials who would fight for the poor. The Act also forbade voter registration drives. Again, we were involved with voter registration as we preached about the importance of voting.

By the time of the 1969 Act, FCD's funding had shifted from the North Carolina Fund to the Ford Foundation. The Act placed "expenditure responsibility" on private foundations. This meant that if such a foundation gave money to another profit or nonprofit organization, the foundation would be responsible for the expenditures just as though it had spent the money itself. A private foundation is one whose funds in major part come from only a few sources as opposed to one that raises most of its money through gifts from many people or through grants from government entities. Ford is a private foundation and therefore had expenditure responsibility arising from transactions of FCD. If we continued to function as we had, the Ford Foundation could have lost its tax exemption.

In December 1969 Ford granted $90,000 to us for a three month period of study to see how best to redirect our focus. We agreed to shift our focus to economic development. We continued our support of UOCI, PPOP and Wilson Community Improvement, but the master organizers became FCD employees. We agreed with Ford to discontinue direct grants to the eight community organization we had been supporting. We also agreed to monitor the community organizations closely to prevent political activity. But we continued to provide seminars on black awareness, community organization, parliamentary procedure and communication skills for people with leadership potential.

A Shift in Emphasis to Economic Development

In 1968 and early 1969 I found that several of the community organizations we supported began to talk about the need for business development within their communities. Some had no food stores at all and those that did have them complained that they were not black owned, they did not hire black people and/or the prices were very high. Some felt an urgent need for the creation of high quality day care centers to allow parents to leave home for jobs with confidence that their children would be safe and well cared for. One community wanted a bookstore. Another wanted some kind of transportation system to enable people to get to work. Still another wanted to find a way to make single family housing available at a cost within the reach of low-income families.

We provided small grants and I provided training to help with some of these requests. These efforts effectively spread the word to other black communities and at least one white community that FCD was a possible source of help on venture development. For instance, Matthew Bacoate, a pioneering black entrepreneur in the mountain city of Asheville, called for help. His firm, AFRAM, had 25 employees and they were making non-woven paper nurse's hats and gowns and doctor's smocks. They needed $37,000 for working capital. FCD lent them $5,000 and helped broker a $32,000 loan from The Cooperative Assistance Fund, a national nonprofit venture capital firm, on whose board I sat. In another mountain area, the Blue Ridge Hearthside Crafts Association asked for help. They were a group of white craftspeople that had been organized in 1965 by the NC Fund-supported community action agency serving Watauga, Avery, Mitchell and Yancey counties. Aggie Lowrance, one of the crafts workers was on our board. We made them a grant of $1,000 and helped them get an SBA loan - the first SBA loan to a cooperative. Their membership grew from 68 to 700; they added a warehouse for their wholesale operations and expanded into three retail shops. They also started a program in which older people passed along their skills to the young.

It was clear that there would be strong demand for venture development so we formulated guidelines for FCD's involvement in venture development:

1. The venture had to be a corporation controlled by low-income people, but it had to include people with business and finance savvy as well.

2. The initial venture for the group had to be one that would provide a product or service that would be sold on a preferential basis to low-income people.

3. FCD would provide assistance to plan the venture free of charge, but the corporation had to raise equity capital so as to share the risk from the very beginning.

4. Those board members of the corporations who had not had training in management, marketing and finances were required to undergo the training provided by FCD.

5. Profits from early ventures were to be used to support expansion or to underwrite projects to help poor neighborhoods, not to pay cash dividends.

6. The debt should be no more that double the amount of equity.

7. The selection of ventures after the initial one should be ones that promised profits, stability and assurance of good jobs. The emphasis should be on providing jobs for skilled but underemployed people. Job training should be done by the technical institutes, not these ventures.

We called this "Community Capitalism" and the first major application of these guidelines was in support of UOCI

Experience would ultimately show that control by low income persons and selling to low income persons on a preferential basis were too socially oriented. United Durham, Incorporated found that these provisions were burdensome as that organization sought to operate profitably.

United Durham, Incorporated

With the help of William Marsh, our legal counsel, John Stewart and other members of the FCD board, I devised a plan for creating a local development company in Durham that would own and operate ventures. We reasoned that grants from the federal government and foundations might be possible if we could raise equity capital locally in support of these ventures. The State of North Carolina had a law that exempted local development companies from the securities laws that required expensive and burdensome filings for companies that attempted to sell stock to more than 35 people. That law had never been used by a black organization, however.

The local development company we created was United Durham, Incorporated. It was chartered in September1968. A majority of its board slots were filled by representatives from the neighborhood councils that had come together to create UOCI. The remaining slots were filled by business and professional people. The first venture was to be a supermarket to be located in the heart of a low income black community.

In consultation with the United Durham board, I devised a plan to sell two classes of stock. Class A stock could be bought only by low income people at a price of $10.00 per share. That $10.00 share entitled the owner to a five percent discount - given at the cash register - on purchases at the store for one full year beginning with the opening of the store. An additional $10.00 share had to be purchased each year in order to continue the discount. A means test was developed to determine that the person was, in deed, low income. Class B stock could be bought by anyone or any legal entity who resided in North Carolina. The charter for the corporation provided that regardless of the number of shares owned, whether Class A or Class B, the owner had one vote. Sixteen of the board members had to own Class A stock; eight had to own Class B stock.

We described the plan in grant applications to two federal agencies. The U. S. Department of Commerce promised $60,000 to plan ventures and the Office of Economic Opportunity (OEO), Lyndon Johnson's primary agency for his proclaimed "War on Poverty," promised $900,000 for capital to support the ventures. Both grants were made to FCD because United Durham was a for-profit corporation and therefore not eligible for grant money

Asa Spaulding, at that time the President and Chief Executive Officer of the North Carolina Mutual Life Insurance Company, chaired the campaign to sell stock. The campaign was a success. We raised $40,000. In April, 1969 OEO announced its grant and the Department of Commerce followed suit soon after.

However, Richard Nixon was sworn in as President in January 1969 and he ordered the Commerce Department and the Office of Economic Opportunity to stop the grants because of FCD's image as a troublemaker. James Holshouser the Republican Party Chairman who would later become Governor of North Carolina asked Nixon to hold up the grants because of Fuller. Also, a group of Southern congressmen who had supported Nixon sought to cancel the grants.

At this point I must tell of the courage of a black woman who worked for the Office of Economic Opportunity. Fully aware of Nixon's order to stop the grant, she managed to have a check issued to FCD for the full $900,000. When I opened the envelope I was amazed. However, within an hour of the time I had gotten the check, I had a call from a very high official in Washington asking me to return the check. He clearly implied that not to do so would mean the woman who arranged for it to be sent would be fired. Anyway, he said, the government had other means of recapturing the funds. I capitulated; I made a copy of the check and sent it back.

Soon after, a group of local Republicans that included one or two blacks whom I had considered my friends, asked Nixon to redirect the grants them. Their effort failed however because they could not show that they had the capacity to perform and could not make a case for voiding the grant actions.

But we were delayed for over a year by Nixon's order. Meanwhile, we used North Carolina Fund and Ford Foundation grant money to proceed with the plan for ventures that was to have been paid for with the Commerce grant. By the time the Commerce grant arrived, we had perfected the United Durham board, helped them recruit and hire Richmond Edward Stewart as the top executive and helped them plan for ventures beyond the super market. We were able to reimburse the Fund and Ford accounts when the Commerce money finally came in. A short time later, the $900,000 from the Office of Economic Development was received. We promptly invested that money in United Durham and that effort was launched at last.

A building was constructed using a black contractor to house the supermarket but the market failed for lack of a sufficient customer base that was non-black and non-poor. A later venture to manufacture homes at low cost failed because of poor construction management and insufficient markets, although several units were sold and are still occupied. Even though these initial ventures did not succeed, the Office of Economic Opportunity continued their support and urged United Durham to create a nonprofit successor - UDI CDC which, under the leadership of Richmond E. Stewart, has had a long history of success in a variety of projects including:

1. Creation of an industrial park that has brought jobs to people in southeastern Durham,

2. Housing renovations in low-wealth areas of the city,

3. Loans to support new businesses,

4. Building a shopping strip that houses a police substation and a very attractive hain (Food Lion) supermarket, and

5. A plant that makes steel framing for homes.

Fuller Leaves

Our funding, training and technical assistance for economic development in response to community requests increased, but, due to the 1969 Tax Reform Act and Ford Foundation policy, we had to discontinue direct grants to the eight community organizations we had been supporting.

Howard realized that FCD could not support him in his former role and he was not prepared to remain at FCD if he could not be a community organizer and public speaker. He wanted to work full time with Malcolm X Liberation University. I was genuinely sorry that he was leaving FCD.

Almost everybody predicted that he and I could never work together, especially with me as the boss. They correctly saw us as totally different personalities. I was the stiff-necked administrator who demanded that things be done right. I liked careful planning and insisted on accountability. Howard, on the other hand, was charismatic, given to spur of the moment judgments and unpredictable. Oil and water.

What people didn't know was that Howard was a good administrator. He believed that by following the rules I set to assure fiscal integrity, the organization would be safe and operations could continue. He turned in time sheets and documented expense reports as required. He followed FCD policy on purchasing. He never used FCD property in an unauthorized way. We agreed to always be totally honest with each other. If he was planning something that he knew would cause a public stir, he would come to talk it out with me and he would adjust his plans to make sure he broke no laws as an FCD employee.

Although Howard always cooperated, some on his staff grumbled about the fact that I was in charge. I learned from my secretary, who was intensely loyal to me, that I was often discussed in a negative way by Howard's staff. I told her they had a right to complain about me either in private or face-to-face and she must stop reporting what she heard to me. I told her that as long as they were getting the work done and staying within the boundaries the board, Howard and I had agreed upon, I didn't care what they thought.

I had frequent meetings with the staff at which we talked frankly about what was happening in the communities. In those meetings we critiqued what went well and where the problems were. We ironed out differences and laid plans. But my secretary continued to bring me stories and I sensed that morale was getting low because of her. Finally, I concluded that I had to let her go. I did not want a spy. Weak administrators need spies. I was not weak.

The FCD board approved a small grant to MXLU to get them started. Howard recruited faculty, found space in a former movie theater in black Durham, recruited students and faculty and started classes.

One of his gratis faculty members was Wanda who taught communications. Wanda had resigned her teaching job in the Durham Public Schools and was producing and hosting a television show that aired on Saturdays just before *Hee Haw*. The show was called *Black Unlimited* and on it she interviewed distinguished residents and visitors. Some of her visitors were Jesse Jackson, Julian Bond, Nicki Giovanni, Maya Angelou, Louis Farrakhan, George Shirley, Shirley Caeser, Pauli Murray, Mohammad Ali and Alex Haley. She also showcased an awful lot of little girls dancing in their *tutus*. She was the first black female ever to produce and host a television show in North Carolina. While doing the show, she completed her Master's Degree in communications at the University of North Carolina in Chapel Hill. For her Master's thesis she drove to Washington and taped an interview with one of her favorite black poets, Sterling Brown.

Howard Fuller changed his name to Owusu Sadauki. After a year, he moved Malcolm X University to Greensboro in hope of finding more community financial support. Two years later he was forced to close and left the state for his native Wisconsin where he has succeeded in several activities: life insurance salesman, superintendent of schools in Milwaukee and professor at the university of Wisconsin.

James Lee

James (Jim) Sumner Lee, the son of a college professor and a librarian who had nearly completed a master's degree in experimental psychology at North Carolina State University in Raleigh, joined FCD as a community organizer a year before Howard left. At Howard's departure, and on his recommendation, Lee became the Director of Training.

I had known the Lee family for many years. Mrs. Mollie Lee was one of the first, if not the first, black woman to become a public librarian in North Carolina. The family lived on Nelson Street, a block from where I lived. Mrs. Lee and my mother were good friends and shared membership in at least two social clubs. However, Jim was 10 to 12 years younger than I and, therefore,

I never knew him well as he grew up in Durham. When he joined FCD I observed his work at a distance. When I named him Director of Training I was satisfied that he had the education and experience needed to succeed Howard Fuller. But Jim was not as careful as Fuller about staying within the bounds of the law. Also, he did not confer with me on controversial issues to the extent that Howard had. This led to some problems for our organization.

I received a call one evening from Jim telling me that while driving to visit the community organization in Rocky Mount, he had been stopped and arrested for possessing an illegal automatic weapon. He explained that the weapon was his, that it was in the passenger side of the car, but completely under cover, and that it was a semi-automatic Carbine with a magazine that held 12 cartridges. Unlike automatic rifles for which pulling and holding the trigger allowed you to empty the magazine, the semi-automatic Carbine was designed to require a separate trigger pull for each round fired. Although a 12 cartridge Carbine was legal, North Carolina law provided that a weapon that allowed for more than 12 cartridges was illegal. The arresting officer alleged that, when found, Jim's Carbine had 12 cartridges in the magazine and a 13th cartridge in the chamber, thus making it illegal.

Jim spent the night in jail and was arraigned the next morning. Bail was set at $50,000. During that morning I conferred with several black lawyers and I was advised that the search of Jim's car was probably unconstitutional and that even if the Carbine was admitted in evidence, there was a chance that a jury could be convinced that there would be no reason for Jim to have loaded a 13th cartridge. I concluded that Jim was not guilty, and that I had to get him out of jail.

I did not, and Jim did not, have $50,000 in personal assets with which to post bond. I could have paid a bondsman 10% of the bail, and Jim would be released. But I did not have $5,000 in cash personally and, further, paying it would have meant that money was lost. Finally, I concluded that since Jim had been on FCD business when arrested, had a good chance of winning in court and was not the kind of person who would abscond, the best course of action was to post bond in cash, using funds we had on hand from the Ford Foundation grant. Therefore, that afternoon, I took a $50,000 certified check to the court and gained Jim Lee's release.

Battle with IRS

The papers had a field day with my decision, but all but one of the FCD board and the Ford Foundation supported me. When Jim returned for trial, the case was dismissed and the $50,000 was returned to FCD. However, our detractors, including some politicians, still howled about the incident. One result of their howling was a visit from Internal Revenue Service (IRS) to see if we should be allowed to keep our tax-exempt status.

IRS gave us a week's notice that we would be audited by a field agent. When the agent arrived, I instructed Sue Graham, our highly competent chief fiscal person, to find office space for him in the building and to give him everything he asked for. After three weeks of records examination, the agent stopped asking for data, but continued to come to the office. It was clear that his purpose was to observe our staff and our visitors. After the fifth week, I demanded that he share with me his preliminary conclusions and that he tell me when he planned to complete the audit. He had reached no negative conclusions based on the documents he had audited, but he could not tell me when his work would be completed. I then told him that, as far as I was concerned, the audit was over and he could not return to our office. He packed his brief case and left. He never returned and we never got a copy of his report.

Social programs that challenge the old ways of doing things will always generate powerful enemies. This episode with IRS reinforced the conclusion I had reached about how to prevent controversial, cutting-edge social programs from being shut down: stay true to your mission, stay within the law and keep your fiscal affairs in order.

A second consequence of Jim Lee's arrest and bailment was the resignation of John S. Stewart, our board chairman. As the CEO of the black owned Mutual Savings and Loan he was under pressure from depositors - both white and black - to curb our activity or to disassociate from us. His departure was a serious blow to our credibility at the time.

Reorganization

Not long after the trial on the illegal weapons charge, Jim Lee concluded that he should step down as Director of Training. He stayed for a while longer as a special assistant to me while I reorganized

The departure of both Fuller and Lee and the impact of the 1969 Tax Reform Act led the board to conclude that we needed a different structure. I continued as head of the Department of Policy and Administration. Working with me were Lottie Hayes, Shirley Mayfield, Jacquelyn Wilkins, Susan Graham, Norma Taylor, Jim Lee and William A. Marsh (consulting attorney).

The Department of Training was transformed into Leadership Development headed by Thelma Jean (TJ) Miller. Thelma had a degree in sociology from North Carolina College, had worked at the Bertie County Welfare Department and had been on the staff of the North Carolina Fund.

She had served as the master organizer for the Rocky Mount project. TJ's staff included Joyce Ruffin, Sandra Philpott, Cynthia Ruffin and Vaughn Glapion. The department's purpose was to train adults and youth who wanted to be active in economic development and other community projects. The curriculum included:

1. Analysis of social, economic and political systems

2. Problem solving and planning

3. Dynamics of group action

4. Sources of financial and technical assistance for problem resolution

5. Use of mass media

6. Writing, dictating and public speaking skills

7. Speed reading

8. Program planning and administration

9. Black history and culture

10. Principles of community organization

The Department of Research was formed to gather and disseminate information on law and social policy that affected the implementation of economic development projects or the problems that the poor would be attempting to solve through economic development. To that end, the department produced publications on such things as community organization, local government, board training for community-based organizations, economic boycotts, child care operations, the public welfare system, and how to use publicity to best advantage. One of its earlier thrusts was to help increase the supply of licensed black attorneys by giving law graduates internships with practicing attorneys across the state. Another effort was to establish an informal working consortium of the 11 black colleges in North Carolina to make more use of faculty talent in the social sciences to conduct research for black-supported programs and legislation. That department was headed by Etta Joyce Grant, a mathematics major in college. She was supported by Katherine Miller, Brenda Wilson, Vivian Gunn and O. A. Moses.

The Department of Community Venture Development was formed to give technical and financial assistance to UDI, the other community development corporations and a few black-owned business firms. The department had a small investment fund for equity injections, direct loans or loan guarantees. My memberships on the boards of directors of the Cooperative Assistance Fund of New York, Opportunity Funding Corporation of D. C. and the Inter-religious Foundation for Community Organization of New York resulted in the husbanding of investments from those sources with FCD investments. This department was headed by Allard Allston who was backed by Liz Cofer, Peggy Duncan, Pauline Bowman, Adolph Reed, David Lewis, Osman Admed, Linda Sauls, Joe Green, Lewis Brandon and Reginald Durante. Some of Allston's staff had previously been employed in the former Department of Training.

Allard Allston

I didn't find Allard, Allard found me. His father was an unusually successful black businessman in South Carolina and Allard had worked closely with him as a boy and a young man. Allard had graduated from Yale and had returned to South Carolina with the intent to carry on his father's business interests and perhaps to go to law school. He had also served for a while as the co-director of the South Carolina Council on Human Relations. He had heard about FCD and the black Yalie at its helm and decided he would put his plans on hold for a while if he could get an opportunity to work with me. He came to Durham to see if I could use his talent just as I was looking for someone to head the new Community Venture Development Department.

Much of the success that UDI has had and much of the expansion of CDCs across the state (there are now over 70) is due to Allard's imagination, analytical and planning skills, and his overall leadership.

My Departure from FCD

In the winter of 1972 the Ford Foundation retained Hugh Price [years later to become the CEO of the Urban League] to do an in-depth evaluation of FCD. His 84 page report was favorable to FCD and very kind to me. At page 60 he wrote:

"The survival of FCD after the tumultuous events of 1969 [tax Reform Act], its acquisition of widespread respect within the black and white communities, the establishment of its current successful programs a mere two years after 1969 – all are a tribute to FCD Executive Director Nathan Garrett and his surprisingly small but extremely capable staff.

"Nathan Garrett is hailed throughout North Carolina as an extraordinarily intelligent, sensitive, candid and pragmatic leader. Mayor James Hawkins of Durham, black bank president John Wheeler, National Sharecropper Fund Executive Director James Pierce and others respect Garrett as one of the most effective community leaders in the entire State. And . because of Nathan Garrett's personal and professional honesty, FCD has never been challenged in its accounting for the use of funds from private or government sources.

" Edward Stewart, executive director of UDI, indicates that the staff talent which FCD possesses is unusual in North Carolina. Other excellent judges of professional capability, such as Mutual Savings and Loan Vice-President [later President] F. V. Allison and North Carolina Mutual Vice-President [later President, CEO and Chairman] W. J. Kennedy, echo Stewart's praise of FCD's technical capability"

In his summary Price wrote:

"The Foundation for Community Development is a committed and capable organization which encountered and overcame a severe threat to its existence, which addresses itself to the basic needs of black people and which possesses vision and resourcefulness in developing solutions for meeting those needs. FCD's function as a black peoples' foundation for community development is a unique one in this country which has proven its validity in a very short period of time, although there are substantial adjustments in program focus and staffing patterns which appear to be warranted based upon the experience of poor peoples' CDCs in North Carolina and across the country. [emphasis added] In view of the impressive growth potential of the State of North carolina and the commitment of FCD to the needs of its constituents, the prospect that black people will enter the economic mainstream of the State is measurably enhanced by the presence of FCD."

The underlined portion of the previous paragraph was prophetic, though I did not know it at the time. The Ford Foundation staff had decided to continue the funding of FCD but with the important change that FCD would become the engine for black economic development and that its support for local leadership development and local partnerships would cease. FCD would become a statewide conglomerate as they saw it. And they anticipated that I would continue at the helm for this new approach.

I, however, did not see myself as the chief executive of this new approach.

The eight years since 1964 - the North Carolina Fund and then FCD - had taken a toll on me. Constantly breaking new ground and exploring new territories, not knowing if the steps you were taking were the right ones; broken friendships; negative publicity; the uncertainties of garnering the resources needed to continue; and perhaps most important, the time away from my wife and children all contributed to a near burn out. Wanda was fully aware of the stresses on me and was as supportive as any wife could be. However, she told me that she and the children were also stressed by my long hours and their genuine fear that I would meet a bullet or a club during one of my frequent absences from home. She wisely counseled that saving others at the expense of family seemed out of balance.

Also, during the previous six months I had noticed that when a bright staff member would bring in an idea to do something new or differently so as to reach a better result, I resisted. I was beginning to yearn for certainty in my life by following the practices that had produced good results in the past, though not always as good as we wanted. A yearning for stability and certainty has no place in the makeup of a person working to change society.

I also new that I could sometimes relieve the stress that came with my work in social engineering by throwing myself into building something simple like a garbage rack or doing some simple accounting procedures such as recording transactions, doing a bank reconciliation or preparing financial statements. I had never been any good at carpentry, but I was good at accounting. And fortunately, because Dewitt Sullivan (whom I had recruited from Detroit in 1966) and I had maintained something of an accounting practice by spending a few hours at it on weekends there was a little of such work to do. Unlike my work at FCD, accounting had clear objectives and if you followed prescribed procedures it produced the end product desired.

Dewitt and I often discussed our desire to start an accounting practice full time. He had left the North Carolina Fund in 1968 to become the controller at the Manpower Development Corporation (MDC), another Fund spin-off, but he was ready to join me in an accounting practice anytime I agreed to commit to it.

By May of 1972 I announced my decision to leave FCD and re-enter the accounting practice. My resignation was effective July 1; the board turned to Allard to succeed me.

The financial future was uncertain, but I had saved some money to help me over the rough spots. In late May, Wanda and I went to Detroit and bought her a new Cadillac. In June we were in New York for a meeting and I bought her a fur coat. In early July I went to New York for a board meeting, went to the Diamond District, and bought her a sizeable marquis shaped diamond ring. I told her I couldn't predict what our income would be as Dewitt and I tried to build a practice, but it was important to me that she have a fur coat, diamond ring and big Cadillac car.

On August 1,1972 I re-entered public accounting full time. That was eight days before my 41st birthday.

CHAPTER NINE

The Years as a Professional

Nathan T. Garrett, Certified Public Accountant

I decided that the best location for the office was Parrish Street in downtown Durham. It was a block east of the three black financial institutions - N. C. Mutual, Mechanics & Farmers Bank and Mutual Savings and Loan. It was a second floor office at 107 ½ East Parrish, the same space that had been occupied by the North Carolina Fund when I joined that organization in 1964. The sign on the door was Nathan T. Garrett, Certified Public Accountant. It had been ten years since I opened my practice in Attorney Floyd McKissick's office on Main Street and I was still the only black person in the state attempting to run a public practice as a CPA.

A month after I entered the office, Sue Graham resigned from FCD and joined me. Later, Dewitt Sullivan cut down on his hours at the Manpower Development Corporation and joined Sue and me part time to start building the practice.

All of the clients we had been serving on our nights and weekends during the social engineering years remained with us and we quickly added Ellis Jones Funeral Home, Pine Knoll Rest Home, and the Chicken Box. For all these clients we kept the records and prepared tax returns. But these clients did not pay enough in fees to support the practice. Therefore, Dewitt and I agreed on a two pronged strategy: we would form a corporation to buy and run several small businesses and we would build the CPA practice primarily on audits of nonprofit community-based organizations like the ones we had worked with at the North Carolina Fund and at FCD

Garrett & Sullivan, Inc.

Shortly after we formed Garrett & Sullivan, Inc., the owner of Pine Knoll Rest Home, for whom we were doing the accounting work, offered to sell to us. We bought it and Dewitt and his wife Kaye took over the management. That venture produced enough profits to provide both families with 20% of the income we needed.

Next we bought out a man who had been running a beer and wine store in an excellent location on a busy street very near Durham Business College and not far from North Carolina College. We named the business The Party Bag. We hired and trained sales clerks and made sure we checked the inventory and register after each shift to confirm that sales were what they should have been. This operation contributed another 10% of the income we needed.

A year or so later, a third business opportunity arose. The owner of the Chicken Box fell ill and was no longer able to run the business profitably. We had been doing his books, also. The business enjoyed a good customer base but was unable to generate enough gross profits to pay its overhead and a reasonable salary for the owner. Dewitt and I concluded that by instituting effective internal controls, the business could be turned around. So, we bought it. We found someone to manage it and Dewitt set up systems for inventory, labor and food preparation controls. However, the business continued to lose money and neither Dewitt, the manager nor I could figure out why. Our biggest sales were in carry-out chicken boxes and dinners, although we also had good sales volume in our cafeteria where we served a variety of other foods. We were careful to set the prices for both lines of business that should have produced decent profits. The cafeteria performed well but we lost money on the carry-out fried chicken. Our inventory control system required that we check all deliveries to make sure that the quantity and price agreed with our purchase order. We knew we were getting the right number of pounds of chicken because we weighed each box that came in. We instituted portion control to be sure that the people behind the counter were putting the right amount of food on the plates or in the chicken boxes. We made sure that spoilage was kept low by making careful forecasts of what the sales demand would be for each day of the week. Finally, we knew that our employees were not stealing fresh chickens.

It took several months to discover the problem. Though our pricing per chicken piece was based on which part of the chicken the customer ordered - breasts, wings, legs and thighs had different prices - the three of us failed to consider that if you buy chicken by the pound and sell it by the piece, you have to make sure you buy chickens of the right size. Our supplier always sent us the largest chickens it had. Two and one half pound chickens would have been perfect, but three and a half to four and a half pound chickens were what we were getting. It took common sense in addition to management know-how to make The Chicken Box a success.

By the time we solved the problem, the CPA practice had grown to the point that it needed full time from both Dewitt and me. There was no time to oversee the affairs of Pine Knoll, The Chicken Box and the Party Bag. The latter two especially demanded a large amount of time. The controls at both places still had to be maintained and at the Party Bag, it was not unusual for the clerk assigned on a Friday or Saturday night to call in sick or just not show up. This meant Dewitt, Kaye, Wanda or I had to sell beer and wine that evening. So, we got out of the chicken and beer business quickly. But Pine Knoll was much simpler to run and we had a strong person in charge. So we kept that business for several more years before finding a buyer.

Growth of the CPA Practice - Formation of Garrett, Sullivan & Company and the Garrett, Sullivan Group of CPA Firms

During the years from 1972 to 1975 we added considerably to the staff. Sue Graham attracted Lee Sanders, a young white man, whom she met while she pursued additional accounting courses at the University of North Carolina in Chapel Hill. Another addition was B. J. Abdullah, a young girl from Smithfield North Carolina whose family roots were Arabic from the middle east. Patricia Williams, Ron Douglas, Helmy Malek (an Egyptian) and Carolyn Kelley handled most of the bookkeeping clients. Juanita Bynum did the statistical typing and was the office manager.

Although Dewitt had a private room in which to oversee the Garrett & Sullivan businesses, six of the new staff members and I shared one large room where I could interact with them as they went about their work. Problems with accounting entries, balancing the books, financial statement preparation and tax return preparation were discussed among the six of us so that these junior staffers grew a great deal in a short period of time.

Walter Davenport, a young black Morehouse graduate from Raleigh, joined us in 1974. He had been invited to interview with Soul City as its chief fiscal officer. He had worked at the Arthur Andersen CPA firm for two years but was not yet a CPA. Soul City was our client. It was started by Floyd McKissick, the civil rights lawyer in whose offices I rented space when I started my practice in 1962. The mission of Soul City was to build a city in eastern North Carolina with help under the Model Cities Program within the U. S. Department of Housing and Urban Development. McKissick had been able to attract considerable debt capital from North Carolina National Bank (now BankAmerica) and other lenders both within and outside of North Carolina

Our firm was hired to oversee the bookkeeping for the purchase of what had been a ranch, and the administrative and pre-development costs such as surveying and city planning. The financial statements I prepared were to be the basis of the permanent financing closing that was to occur on Wall Street. I recognized that we would not get paid for our services until closing. I also knew that there was a chance that we would never get to closing because of strong opposition to the project from the North Carolina's Republican delegation in Congress, led by Senator Jesse Helms. Perhaps the remoteness of Soul City and or/the political heat it was facing caused Walter to decide he would not take the job. After his interview he came by to see me and asked if he could join my firm. I hired him.

> *The Soul City Project did get to closing. But before it closed, government auditors descended on the project to go through every transaction and to challenge every estimate that had been made. Over $3 million had been spent and the auditors found only a $293 error. I was both proud and embarrassed. It was a ridiculously small error, but the error was a payment I had classified incorrectly that had to be added to, not subtracted from the predevelopment costs. I went to New York for the closing on Wall Street to reaffirm the debts owed to each lender and wrote all the checks. I returned from New York with a check for $32,000 representing almost three years of work. The next day there were bonuses for all staff and a big party.*

In 1975, Dewitt, Sue, Walter and Lee passed the CPA exam, got their licenses, and we formed Garrett, Sullivan & Company, CPAs as a professional corporation with the five of us as shareholders. Later, B. J. (who by this time had married and become B. J. Keel) and Carolyn Kelley also passed the exam and got their certificates. We had the foundation for continued growth. Our decision to pursue an audit practice was the right one. As a result of the War on Poverty that had started in 1964-65, federal agencies began to provide grants to many community-based nonprofit corporations such as those Dewitt, Sue Graham and I had worked with at the North Carolina Fund and FCD. All these grantees had to be audited annually. The large CPA firms were generally not interested in these audits because the audit fees these clients could pay were much lower than the firms could get from profitable business clients. And the smaller CPA firms were not as familiar as we were with the accounting and auditing requirements of these new entities. Dewitt, Sue and I had a great reputations throughout the State among the CEOs and board members of organizations who were formed to fight poverty. This was the first of five niches that led to our firm's growth.

The second niche was the private black colleges in the State: Shaw and St Augustine's in Raleigh, Bennett in Greensboro, Livingstone in Salisbury, Barber Scotia in Concord and Johnson C. Smith in Charlotte. We did audit or management advisory work for five of the six.

The third niche was the black-controlled financial institutions of which there were seven: one insurance company, three banks, one savings and loan and two credit unions. At one time or another we did audit work for all except the insurance company.

The fourth niche was government contract work. Through the Minority Set-aside program administered by the U. S. Small Business Administration, we won government contracts to provide fiscal management technical assistance for grantees of the U. S. Department of Labor in 40 states of the nation. We also won contracts with the U. S. Department of Commerce to provide technical assistance to minority businesses in Durham, Fayetteville North Carolina and Atlanta. The 8A program was a serious attempt by the Carter Administration to give minority small businesses opportunities to sell products and services to federal government agencies and departments. Congress had sufficient evidence that, historically, these small businesses had been systematically excluded from government work and concluded that affirmative action was needed to help right the wrongs of the past. The program provided that a small portion of agency and department funds that were to be used to buy products and services from the private sector would be set aside in a pool. Minority small businesses would bid against one another for contract awards in the pool, but they did not have to bid against large majority-owned firms which, because of their size, could bid so low that no minority small business could hope to win. If the agency could not find minority small businesses with the capacity to perform on the contract, the set aside money was returned to the general pool.

To pursue the Labor Department work we formed a consortium of minority CPA firms consisting of Mitchell-Titus that had offices in New York and Philadelphia, Watson-Rice that had its office in Cleveland, and Ashby Armstrong and Johnson that had its office in Denver. Through the consortium and the Garrett, Sullivan & Company Group of CPA Firms we controlled the majority of black CPA talent in the U. S. The Garrett, Sullivan & Company Group of CPA

Firms resulted from our desire to help black sole practitioners expand. Our plan was to use our access to the Small Business Set-Aside program to get contracts that could be farmed out to members of the group. Each member of the group became a professional corporation in which Garrett, Sullivan

& Company was a minority shareholder. The corporations were: Martin-Garrett, Sullivan & Company in Charlotte, McNamee-Garrett, Sullivan & Company in Detroit and McQuay-Garrett, Sullivan & Company in Tampa. In addition to those locations, in order to provide services under the Labor and Commerce Department contracts, we opened offices in Fayetteville, North Carolina, Atlanta and the District Of Columbia.

The fifth and least profitable niche was bookkeeping and tax service for small businesses. However, Dewitt and I had decided that although it was always wise to offer these services, we would never allow this kind of work to represent more than 10 th 15% of our revenues. Our experience with bookkeeping and tax services at the Austin firm in Detroit (in which we had worked together for four years beginning in 1958) had soured us on that type of practice. But we always remembered that sometimes a bookkeeping client could become a big business as we had witnessed at the Austin firm where one struggling client became the hugely successful Motown run by Barry Gordy. Our decision to give every bookkeeping and tax client the very best of service despite their inability to pay was the cause of low, and often no, profits from that work. Although Dewitt and I kept our eyes open for our Motown, it never came.

We bought the building we were in, and with the help of Lee's brother who was a contractor, we turned it into a marvelous facility suitable for our size and for use limited public use. We had a huge conference room that was open to community groups. Four of the upstairs offices were leased to The North Carolina Voter Education Project headed by John Edwards, Randall Rogers Realty, Hayti Development Corporation headed by Nat White, Jr. and The North Carolina Institute of Minority Economic Development. The walls were covered with original paintings done by local artists. The furnishings were modern and color coordinated (thanks to Wanda). We invested in the very latest in computer networking technology.

The grand opening for our new and expanded home was on a Sunday, February 9, 1975. The night before the opening, the Klan and the Black Solidarity Movement in Greensboro had a shoot out at a public housing development. The Black Solidarity Movement was headed by Nelson Johnson with whom I had worked closely when I headed the Foundation for Community Development. We seemed to be succeeding as a professional firm, but the economic and racial problems continued.

Dewitt Sullivan and me, 1975. Photo by Billy Barnes.

Partners of Garrett, Sullivan & Company Group of CPA Firms. Left to right: Ronald J. Peterson, David McQuay, Jr., Richard J. McNamee, Walter C. Davenport, (center person not identified), Dewitt Sullivan, Susan B. Graham, me, Lee E. Sanders. Photo by Billy Barnes.

Garrett, Sullivan, Davenport, Bowie and Grant

These five niches allowed us to grow dramatically from 1972 until Ronald Reagan took office as President of the United States. When Jimmy Carter left office, our firm was finishing up $2 million in federal 8A contracts and had another $3 million in the pipeline that were nearly ready to be awarded to us. Three months after Reagan took office, we had zero federal contracts because he and his administration did not favor Affirmative Action and the SBA 8A Program. Since all of the Garrett, Sullivan partners and probably the vast majority of our staff, were Democrats, we decided to spend $25,000 with a Washington D. C. law firm in the hope that that firm's strong connections to the new administration would win us more federal business. Unfortunately, that didn't work. As a result, the partners made some major decisions. First, we would immediately lay off the 40% of staff who were working exclusively on federal contracts. Second, we would not pursue federal or state government work again until we had a mixture of Democrat and Republican Party members among the partners so that a change in political power in government would not be as devastating to us as had been Reagan's election.

The downturn in federal contracting caused a large reduction in profits and, therefore, in compensation for the five partners. Each partner was put under great pressure to attract new clients. We opened a branch of the firm in Raleigh with Walter Davenport as the partner in charge. We also opened an office in Greensboro under the direction of a young black CPA from Virginia. Walter did an outstanding job in attracting new clients. But, initially, we had poor results in Greensboro. The young man we hired resigned precipitously one day. We were able to find and hire Winston Chen, a black Jamaican who had graduated from East Carolina University and had earned his CPA. Unfortunately, Winston wrongly thought that golfing was the best way to attract clients and that did not work. We finally decided that I was the logical one to try to build the Greensboro client base. Therefore, Wanda and I took an apartment in Greensboro and Dewitt became the managing partner of our total operation. Dewitt found Oliver Bowie, a new black CPA, who after a period of seasoning was placed in charge of Greensboro, allowing Wanda and me to return to Durham after a year of work. Joyce Grant, who had worked with me at The Foundation for Community Development, earned her CPA certificate during this period and had successfully run our Atlanta office which was devoted to providing technical assistance to minority business enterprises. We closed that office and brought her back to Durham when our federal contracts ran out. The same was true for Charles Hobgood, another black CPA, whom we had placed in charge of our Fayetteville, NC office to provide minority business enterprise assistance under a federal contract.

Ultimately, the two white partners - Sue Graham and Lee Sanders - concluded that despite all their efforts, they were unable to attract white clients. They explained that those whom they approached would not give them their tax, audit or bookkeeping work because they could not see themselves entrusting their work to a black CPA firm. They retired as partners. Lee moved to eastern North Carolina and opened his own office and Sue joined the staff of a competing CPA firm in Durham.

Law School

Following Sue and Lee's departures, we formed Garrett, Sullivan, Davenport Bowie and Grant consisting of four black men and a black woman. I resumed leadership of the firm, but the partners agreed to allow me to reduce my required time by 80% so that I could attend law school at North Carolina Central University. This was something I had long wanted to do. I had actually been accepted twice before. The first time was in 1964. That time I enrolled and took classes for a semester. Maynard Jackson, who later became mayor of Atlanta, was a classmate. But the prospect of taking on a substantial new client (the North Carolina Fund) dictated that I withdraw. The second time I was accepted I declined to enroll because the businesses needed my full time attention. This third time I almost made the same decision as before and for the same reason, but Wanda, who also applied, challenged me. She said that we would be able to make it on the money we had accumulated and that it was something we needed to do together. She was right. We enrolled. Our nest was empty because our older son, Marc, had left Durham and Nathan Jr. had entered Dartmouth. I ran the CPA practice on a part-time basis and Wanda and I studied together every night and every weekend. We ate fast food or took our meals in the cafeteria on campus. Wanda, at age 52, was elected president of our senior class. At the beginning of our senior year (1985-86) Marc returned to Durham and was inspired to return to A&T State University to finish out his undergraduate degree because he knew that his younger brother and his parents were all going to get degrees in Spring 1986. Marc commuted to A&T, some 55 miles away, and finished 45 hours of course work in two semesters. We all got our degrees in May and/or June 1986.

I returned to the CPA practice full time after passing the bar examination in August 1986. But then Dewitt decided that he needed to relocate to Hattiesburg Mississippi, his boyhood home, to open his own practice. Two things drove Dewitt's decision. The first, and most important, was that Mechanics & Farmers Bank, which had been our auditing client for years and for which audit Dewitt was the partner in charge, decided to drop our firm in favor of Deloitte-Touche, one of what was then the Big Six CPA Firms. He took the bank's decision as a personal insult. He told me that his second reason was that the accolades I had received as a local boy who had met with success.made him want to return to his native Mississippi to do the same thing. I said and did everything I could to change his mind, but he was resolute. At the farewell party for the Sullivans, I said that Dewitt and I had been partners for over 20 years and that during that time we showed complete trust and confidence in each other. I said that our families were so close that their departure would be almost like losing the very air we breathe. It was a heart-wrenching event.

With Dewitt's departure, the remaining partners agreed to break up the firm. Bowie and Grant decided to go it alone in separate firms; Bowie in Greensboro and Grant in Durham. Davenport also wanted to continue his practice in Raleigh, but implored me to join him. I had decided not to practice any more and had taken a tenure track full-time position on the faculty of the School of Business at North Carolina Central University to teach law and accounting. I had also decided to start a limited law practice to serve corporate clients in the financial services industry and nonprofit clients involved in community economic development. Wanda had been appointed to the North Carolina Parole Commission by then Governor Martin. There are five commissioners for the whole state and it is their job to determine eligibility and to grant paroles to prisoners. Two of the five commissioners must concur in granting a parole; in life cases, three signatures are required. The combination of incomes from all the sources was quite enough to buy and do almost anything we wanted. However, Walter kept after me and offered me a package consisting of equality in decision-making, 25% of the profits and a requirement to spend not more than five hours a week on firm business. Walter and I had grown very close during the years since he joined us in 1975 and I felt my name and advice could help him add clients from Durham to help assure his continued success. We formed Garrett and Davenport, CPAs with offices in both Raleigh and Durham in 1987.

Garrett and Davenport

Under Walter's excellent leadership, Garrett and Davenport enjoyed good growth and profits. But by the 10th year it became clear that continued growth was unlikely, primarily because the large international CPA firms had decided that they were interested in pursuing all of our larger clients such as black colleges and universities, local school boards and local governments. Many of the board members or elected officials who provided leadership for these clients and many of the banks and other lending institutions who financed some of these clients felt that audits done by the big firms carried greater assurance of reliability. Despite a well integrated staff and extensive marketing, we had not been able to lure white owned small businesses as clients. We had succeeded in getting work with a few North Carolina corporations such as Duke Power and Burlington Industries, but these were relatively small engagements and could not make up for the loss of our biggest clients to Price Waterhouse, Deloitte, Ernst and Young and Peat Marwick. Also, some of the smaller clients were being lost to smaller black-owned CPA firms who cut costs drastically to win those engagements.

Walter and I went through a lengthy analysis before reaching the painful conclusion to merge our practice into Cherry, Bekaert and Holland (CBH), the largest non-national firm in the southeast. CBH did not have a presence in Raleigh or Durham and had only one or two black staffers in any of their offices in the seven states in which they operated. They approached us and a smaller white-owned Raleigh firm, and we consummated the merger January 1, 1999. Walter stayed on as a full time equity partner in the merged entity. He was not put in charge of the Raleigh office, but he was made the partner in charge of attracting and servicing nonprofit clients throughout the southeast. I, however, remained as an income partner for only one year after which CBH paid me for my equity in Garrett and Davenport. When Walter retired from

CBH in 2008, it left them with no black partners and only a few more black staffers than they had in 1999.

The nearly 40 years I had spent as practicing CPA enabled me to provide well for my family. Wanda and I supported our children and some of our grandchildren, nieces and nephews as they studied to earn their baccalaureate degrees. Although the economic result of the practicing years was satisfying, I draw greater satisfaction from the fact that there are hundreds of black and white men and women who were inspired to become CPAs because of the reputation of the firms that carried my name. My only regret is that we were not able to become a regional or national firm. One of my dreams was to be a part of the leadership of a CPA firm that was better than any competitor in providing service to clients and in providing opportunities for employment for segments of society who, though talented, were not welcomed by other firms. I never wanted to be known as a black-owned firm and I never wanted the ownership and staff to be all black. I simply wanted to be the best. That dream died with the merger with CBH, but I had other dreams - for status and service to community and my profession- that are being fulfilled even today in what is probably the last decade of my life. The next chapter describes some of the service I have been privileged to provide.

CHAPTER TEN

Take a Penny, Give (at Least) a Penny

I honestly do not know what motivated me to volunteer my services in so many ways. The practice started early in life when I volunteered to be an acolyte in the Episcopal Church, despite the fact that my family was Baptist. I think that episode was inspired by my involvement in a Cub Scout group that met at the neighborhood center located behind St. Titus Episcopal Church on Fayetteville Street, two blocks from 1502.In high school I volunteered to run, and won the elections, for class president for both my junior and senior years. I also volunteered to serve as editor of the high school newspaper for my last two years.

At Yale I volunteered to serve as a member of the Dwight Hall Board. Dwight Hall is an independent, student run, educational and religious organization that started in 1886 at Yale. In my sophomore year at Yale I volunteered to serve as editor of my college's (dormitory) newspaper.

In Detroit, I agreed to serve on the board of St. Peter Claver Nursery where our son, Marc, attended school.

In 1964, after returning to Durham from Detroit, I agreed to be the treasurer for a $500,000 fund-raising campaign for Lincoln Hospital. In the '70s, after the hospital had closed, I became a member of the initial board of the Lincoln Community Health Center. I chaired the South Side Division for one of the United Way campaign. My mother and I served together on the board of my old kindergarten, Scarborough Nursery. I served as Treasurer for the Durham Committee on the Affairs of Black People. In that position, I led the effort to increase the Committee's revenue from the sale of advertisements in the program booklet for its annual fund-raising dinner.

During my days at the helm of the Foundation for Community Development, I was on the board of the Inter-religious Foundation for Community Organization based in New York (IFCO). IFCO was a co-sponsor of the National Black Economic Development Conference held in Detroit at which James Forman, an activist, seized the microphone and made his very moving Black Manifesto speech that included demands for reparations and a call to overturn the table if we, as a race, were not invited to sit at the table. Forman's speech, the crowd's reaction to it and my association with IFCO earned me a spot on the Federal Bureau of Investigation's watch list. I discovered this some 13 years after the conference when the FBI sent me the secret file they compiled on me for several years

During President Carter's term in office, I agreed to serve as the chairman of the Minority Economic Development Advisory Committee to Philip Klutznick, the U. S. Secretary of Commerce.

For the State of North Carolina, I served as the chairman of the People Panel for the Commission on the Future of North Carolina formed by Governor Hunt and later served as a member of the Advisory Committee to the North Carolina Revenue Secretary on State Tax Policy. The line on our Individual Tax Form on which taxpayers can volunteer to pay Use Tax on out of state purchases was one of my recommendations.

For Fayetteville State University, one of the campuses of North Carolina's university system, I served as chairman of the search committee for a recent chancellor and then served for two years as chairman of the University's Board of Trustees.

At the request of Brenda Brodie, wife of former Duke University President, Keith Brodie, I served for several years on the board of Seeds, an organization Brenda started to promote urban gardens to encourage consumption of healthy and home grown food, to train urban youth and to help neighborhood beautification. I also represented Duke University for two years as its representative on the Research Triangle Institute Corporate Board.

For the City of Durham, I was the initial chairman for the Parrish Street Advocacy Group, a group of volunteers formed to assist the City in developing and implementing plans for the revitalization of that historic section of downtown Durham. Also for the City, Wanda, Cynthia Brodhead (the Duke University first lady) and I co-chaired the "8 Bonds for a Better Durham" committee that successfully promoted the voters' approval of bond issues to pave streets, renovate public structures including parks and garages, improve the water/sewer utility and to improve neighborhoods in several ways. The voter turnout was unusually large and the eight bonds were approved by an average of 72%

But I think it was the name recognition that resulted from my work with the North Carolina Fund, The Foundation for Community Development and the CPA practices that helped bring me to the attention of a lot of influential people: John Wheeler, president of Mechanics and Farmers Bank; Terry Sanford who was named president of Duke University shortly after his terms as North Carolina Governor; Asa Spaulding and William Kennedy, III, both of whom served as chairman, president and chief executive officer at North Carolina Mutual Life Insurance Company; and North Carolina Governors, Jim Hunt and Jim Martin. What follows is a description of my experiences and my observations on some of the issues faced on two corporate boards and several nonprofit boards.

Mechanics & Farmers Bank

John Wheeler, who had been one of my mentors from the day I returned to Durham, recommended me as a board member of the bank in 1974. By the time I joined the board, the bank, under Wheeler's leadership, had five offices: two in Durham, one in Raleigh, one in Winston Salem and one in Charlotte. Two additional offices, one in Raleigh and another in Charlotte, were added while I served on the board.

The bank's customers were, perhaps, 90% black and their accounts, both the commercial and individual ones, held small balances, reflecting their relatively small wealth. The cost of maintaining records for small balances and small deposits, withdrawals, loans and loan payments is as high as it is for larger ones. Therefore, relative to deposits and loan balances, operating costs were higher at M&F than for banks with wealthier customers.

M&F's growth has been steady, but slow. A bank in western North Carolina, where very few blacks live, was started in the mid to late '70s. Its capital was less than that of M&F. That bank is now many times larger than M&F in deposits, profits and capital. I don't think that that bank's management was superior to that of M&F. I think their growth was caused by their ability to penetrate entirely an under-served commercial and consumer market in our state's mountainous region. M&F, on the other hand, served only the black market - partially because most whites would not even consider banking with M&F, and partially because the management of M&F did not make serious efforts to penetrate the white market.

On the several occasions when I suggested that we find additional capital from within the white community and that we market heavily in that community as other start-up banks have done in the past 30 years, I was told that the board and management wanted to keep the ownership in black hands. Although stock ownership was dispersed throughout the black community, stock ownership was concentrated within a very small group of families and the North Carolina Mutual. That group, also, wanted to make sure that the percentage of black ownership would not be diluted. When a stockholder died, M&F bank executives would find a suitable black buyer for the stock if the heirs wanted to sell.

Perhaps they were right to stay away from white investors and white customers. The experience (recounted in the previous chapter) I had when we merged our CPA firm into a large white one, suggests there is wisdom in that policy. There is a place in our economy for businesses that are black-owned and that cater almost exclusively to black customers. But I think such businesses are destined to be small and marginal in terms of jobs created and wealth produced. However, in today's world, there are many blacks who are getting graduate educations in business, are gaining experience in corporate America and are finding investments from wherever the money is in order to follow their entrepreneurial dreams. Once in business they sell their products and services to the entire market, domestic and international. They hire the best people they can find, regardless of race or ethnicity. I think many of them know that any time a person is hired, the company takes a risk that the employee will not perform as desired. I fervently hope that these new entrepreneurs will have the heightened desire and insights needed to identify talent and potential among black applicants.

I resigned from the M&F board in the late '70s when our firm was selected to perform the bank's annual audits.

MECHANICS & FARMERS BANK BOARD, CIRCA 1972. STANDING: J. C. SCARBOROUGH, III, ALBERT WHITING, ME, ARTHUR E. SPEARS, JOHN WHEELER, JOHN GREENE, JJ SANSOM, JOE GOODLOE, JOHN WINTERS, W. J. KENNEDY, III. SEATED: CHARLES CLINTON SPAULDING, JR., JAY WALKER, VIOLA TURNER, W. J. KENNEDY, JR., J. C. SCARBOROUGH, JOHN STEWART, D. HAYWOOD

Foray into Politics

In 1970 there was one black person serving on the Durham Board of County Commissioners. It was Asa Spaulding, an actuary who had headed the North Carolina Mutual Life Insurance Company. The Commission runs county government. The Sheriff's office, Elections, Social Services, Zoning, Mental Health, the county hospital, and the libraries are among departments for which the commissioners are responsible. They hire and oversee the County Manager, determine the annual budget for both the county departments and the county schools and set property tax rates. In the 1970s, the Commission members devoted 40 or more hours a month preparing for and attending public and private meetings. Additionally, every two years for at least a month before the primary and the general elections, they spent additional hours campaigning.

William Bell, a black man who was an engineer and an executive at IBM, won one of the five Democrat slots for Commissioners in the 1972 primary. Spaulding also won a slot for re-election, so there were to be two black candidates among the five Democrats running against Republican opposition in November. However, for reasons of health or family, Spaulding decided that he could not continue to serve as a Commissioner. He recommended to the Democratic Party and to the Durham Committee on Negro Affairs that I be put on the ballot to replace him for the November election. Spaulding knew my family and also had gotten to know me through my work in getting UDI started. The political organizations followed his advice; I was put on the ballot and Bell and I won.

I worked hard as a Commissioner and my expertise in general management and fiscal affairs earned me the respect of my fellow Commissioners. Most of my recommendations on budgets and management changes were adopted. However, none of my initiatives on matters related to appointments or policy changes that were designed to bring about parity of treatment between blacks and whites ever got past a second at our meetings. Bill Bell would usually support me, but the three white members never did. The three were not bad people, but we simply could not see eye to eye on social issues.

After two years of frustration I reluctantly decided to run for re-election. I was very pleased when I heard that Elna Spaulding, the wife of Asa Spaulding, was considering a run for one of the five seats. She and I talked and I encouraged her to run. I reasoned that if we could manage to get blacks in three of the five seats, we could change Durham for the better. During the campaign, I expressed my feeling publicly that I was wasting my time as a Commissioner unless we could get Mrs. Spaulding elected along with Bell and me. Dumb!

Mrs. Spaulding, Bell and I won the primary, but I came in 6th in the general election. Although many in the black community criticized Mrs. Spaulding for running (thinking that was the cause of my defeat), I always praised her for doing so. She and Bill Bell served successfully as members of the Commission for many years. Bell also served as chairman for twelve years. The county was better off with the two of them than it would have been with Bell and me. Both of them had the patience and fortitude to take defeat after defeat on social issues and keep coming back. At that stage in my life, patience was not one of my strengths. (When Wanda read this last sentence, her comment was "*ha*.")

Duke University Board of Trustees

I was delighted to say yes to Terry Sanford's request for permission to submit my name for election to the Duke Board of Trustees. Terry, Margaret Rose Sanford, Wanda and I had gotten to know one another during my work at the North Carolina Fund when he was North Carolina's Governor. Following a good deal of student unrest during the late '60s, Terry was tapped to lead the University. The Board of Trustees had concluded that, instead of an academician, they needed Terry's reputation and his political, management and legal skills to steer a new course for Duke.

My name was put forward to replace Dr. C. E. Bouleware, a math professor at North Carolina College and a local black political activist. Bouleware had completed his six-year term and because of age was not eligible for re-election. At that time the formula called for one of the 36 trustees to be black. Two or three years later there were two additional blacks on the board. Dr. Samuel Dubois Cook, who had earned a Duke law degree in 1979, had been a faculty member at Duke and who was then President of Dillard University (an HBCU) in New Orleans was elected in 1981. Still later, Kevin Moore, a black student who had been elected President of the Student Government Association, was named to the "young trustee" slot for a two-year term..

When I was ready for Duke when I graduated high school in 1948, Duke was not ready for me. It was not until the early 1960s that the first black undergraduates were accepted. As a sub-teenager I had gone to a football game or two and sat in the section reserved for "the colored." - the very last section of that beautiful horseshoe stadium that looked down on the goal post. Before I arrived, Terry had already made significant progress on increasing the black student enrollment, although the black students tended to socialize mostly with other blacks. But he was having great difficulty in getting black faculty. Shortly after I joined the board, he invited Wanda and me to the presidential home for a private dinner to get my opinion on how best to get the black students to interact more with the whites and how to recruit black faculty, given the fact that it is the deans and department heads who decide on faculty appointments, not the president. My answers disappointed him. As to the students' social habits, I relayed to him my experiences at Yale: the blacks needed one another for some purposes, but the opinions offered in classrooms, the exposure resulting from working on assignments as a team, the occasional sharing of a meal or of music and the participation in intramural sports were sufficient for white and black students to learn more about their respective cultures. I told him that although a goodly number of black students was essential, black faculty were not. Even the limited mixing of racial and ethnic cultures inside and outside the classroom resulted in a graduate who was better prepared to contribute to making ours a better society. A multi-cultural faculty could help, but, in my opinion, not as much as student diversity. I told Terry that I was ambivalent about recruiting black faculty to Duke because they would have to come from the black schools. If those schools lost their strongest professors, the impact on the HBCU students would be a huge negative. I suggested that Duke and other top schools needed a long term plan of recruiting black students into PhD programs who, perhaps, could be convinced to remain as professors.

Many of the administrators and my fellow board members assumed that I was their expert on black affairs. On more occasions than I can remember, I had to tell them that the views and actions of the black race are as varied as one can find in the white or any other race. I could no more speak for the black population than they could speak for the white. I did, however, freely give my advice on how Duke might deal with several racial issues. One issue that arose concerned the state's plan to build an expressway that would come within a quarter of a mile of the campus and directly through a nearby stable, but low wealth, black community populated mostly by maids and janitors who worked at the University. Duke's concern was that the road would cause a heavy increase in traffic, especially trucks, resulting in noise, congestion and greater air pollution near the campus. The residents of the low wealth community were opposed to the road because it meant the destruction of their homes and churches and the pains of relocations. The State assured Duke that the traffic problem would not be as great as was feared because the expressway was not to be connected to the Interstate Highway that passed through Durham on an east-west path that was well north of campus. Had the roads been connected, traffic coming from Raleigh going west and traffic from the west going toward Raleigh would have found that the expressway was the shortest and fastest route. With that assurance, Duke was ready to drop its objection to the road. I talked to Terry about the plight of the low-wealth community and told him that Duke was in a position to help save those homes and churches. I also told him that, in my opinion, the assurances of the state about not connecting that road to the Interstate could not be relied on for long. Terry got Duke involved in a dialogue with the residents of the community and the state to work out a route that would be further removed from campus and would disturb only a small portion of the targeted housing. Furthermore, Duke helped with a program of housing rehabilitation and, even today, the targeted community is an attractive, stable area. I must add, that the expressway is now connected to Interstate 85 northwest of Durham and to Interstate 40 southeast of the city as I predicted.

A second issue involving race was the national initiative to have universities and pension funds divest themselves of stock in companies that did business in South Africa. Several universities had decided to do so. The theory was that divestment would cause a decline in the market value of the companies' securities and thus bring pressure on them to discontinue their operations in South Africa and/or to push harder with the South African government to end apartheid. Those who opposed argued that if divestment led those companies to discontinue their operations in South Africa, the result would be that corporate voices to end apartheid from within the country would be silenced. The opposition among the Duke Trustees also feared that the University could suffer losses in its investment portfolio if the securities were sold.

Because many students and faculty members for months had been petitioning Duke's administration and demonstrating in favor of divestment, Terry decided to place the question on the agenda for a Trustee meeting on May 3, 1986. The night before the Trustees met, the issue was taken up by the Executive Committee to decide on its recommendation to the Trustees the next morning. Knowing that I favored divestment, Terry asked me to attend the Executive Committee meeting to present my views. There was good discussion and although several Committee members agreed with my position, the majority did not. I do not recall how many Committee members were top-tier corporate executives, but I know that easily half of the full Board of Trustees were captains of industry. When I arrived at the Trustee meeting the next morning, students were on the quadrangle outside the meeting place (the Allen Building) holding placards and making speeches in favor of divestment. When we reached the divestment question on the agenda, the Chairman of the Board reported that the Executive Committee recommended against divestment, but opened the meeting for discussion before voting. Trustees spoke on both sides of the issue, but it was the remarks of one of the emeritus trustees that seemed to have the greatest impact. That trustee was George C. McGhee, a Texas oil millionaire who had served as the United States Ambassador to both Turkey and West Germany. He sat in one of the leather armchairs that ringed the huge mahogany table at which the active trustees sat. He was elderly, splendidly dressed, had a full head of totally white hair and used a cane to steady himself as he rose to make his comments. He stated that his granddaughter was among the students demonstrating outside, that he had talked with her extensively and he had concluded that divestment was the right thing to do. He then asked Eugene McDonald, the officer in charge of Duke's investments, if divestment would result in serious harm to the value of the University's investments or its investment income. McDonald answered, "No, it would not." At this point Phillip Jackson Baugh, Jr, class of 1954 from Kentucky and the Vice Chairman of the Board, nudged me. He had been at the Executive Committee meeting the evening before. He leaned to my ear and whispered that he thought we had the votes to win and said he would make the motion if I would second it. He did. I did. And the Trustees voted to sell the securities it held in companies that were doing business in South Africa.

Four years later, as a result of external pressure on its economy, international criticism and protests from within the country, South African President F. W. De Klerk announced that apartheid would end.

As I had learned in the segregated theater incident back in 1963, attacking the weakest link was the right strategy. Maggie Dent, the white theater operator in Durham who wanted to integrate the theater but who could not because of a clause in her equipment lease, when faced with a boycott of her business by the NAACP youth, went out and found the financial backing she needed to give an ultimatum to the lessor: "I am going to integrate this theater. You may remove your equipment in accordance with the terms of your lease. However, I have the money to buy my own equipment." Maggie was a weak link among Durham's white businesses that supported racial segregation in theaters, restaurants and other commercial enterprises. Many of the corporations that were doing business in South Africa abhorred apartheid, but did relatively little to bring pressure on the South African political leaders. Those corporations were the weak links in the political, social and economic chain that made it possible for apartheid to continue. The decline in the market value of corporations' securities that resulted from the divestment decisions of Duke and many other universities provided incentives for the corporations to do more than they had been doing to get the law abolished.

At the beginning of my second six-year term I was named to the Presidential Search Committee. Terry had decided to step down to pursue his interest in more electoral politics. During this process I learned that it is important not to divulge the names of candidates for university president. If the candidate is in a top position at another institution, sometimes the news that he or she has agreed to be considered for a new position can cause the candidate's colleagues to question the candidate's loyalty. If not chosen for the new position, the candidate not only would be embarrassed about not being good enough but also might not be treated as well as he or she might have been treated if the person's loyalty had not been questioned. Often, once it becomes public that a person is being considered, the person will withdraw his or her name, thus devaluing the pool of candidates.

Several years later, I was one of three finalists for the position of Chancellor of NCCU. At the time, I had committed myself to Walter Davenport to help with the Garrett and Davenport firm, I had started my law practice and I was a tenured faculty member at the NCCU School of Business. Had the search committee not agreed to keep silent on my candidacy I would have declined the nominations made by Richmond Stewart, Bert Collins, Elliot B. Palmer and several other close friends. Knowledge of my candidacy for a position that would require me to discontinue my professional and teaching work would have reduced my capacity to attract and serve accounting and legal clients and would have resulted in changes in my relationships among the faculty at the School of Business. The President of the University system, Dick Spangler, chose one of the other two finalists: famed civil rights attorney Julius Chambers as Chancellor. Spangler called me when Wanda and I were vacationing in Anchorage, Alaska to tell me his selection. Julius had been a client of our CPA firm, we shared memberships in Alpha Phi Alpha, Sigma Pi Phi and the Guardsmen, and he was a good friend. I was pleased for him and me. He served the University well for six years. I, on the other hand, was able to continue my work as a CPA, broaden my legal work and continue my work as a professor, all of which I was enjoying tremendously.

The Duke Search Committee was given the charge to do a nation-wide search and to recommend three names ranked in order of our preference to the Trustee's Executive Committee. One of the three names we agreed upon was Dr. H. Keith H. Brodie, a psychiatrist who had a long history at Duke and who was, in effect, the number two man to Terry. However, the Committee had selected two other names, one of whom was a non-Christian who had made a great impression during the interview. The information on the names and backgrounds of the three people was leaked to the Executive Committee and just before the Search Committee was to meet to rank the three for its report, Terry informed us that the charge had been changed and that we were to give the names without ranking. The Executive Committee chose not to interview any of the three candidates and chose Brodie, the candidate with whom they were all familiar. I have often speculated on the reasons for the change in the charge but I never asked why of Terry, John

Forlines, who chaired the Search Committee, or any member of the Executive Committee.

At the end of my second term in June, 1989, I was made an emeritus trustee, but because my firm won a contract to audit one of Duke's pension plans, I had to make the choice of resigning my emeritus status or losing the audit contract. The professional literature and federal guidelines clearly indicated that there was no conflict of interest in this situation. The emeriti have no voting or debating rights in University affairs and I was not going to be involved in the audit in any manner whatsoever. Therefore, our firm's independence was not in question. However, one highly placed person within the school's administration with whom I had had a somewhat tempestuous relationship, pushed the independence question very hard. I concluded that even an unreasonable question of independence had to be respected and so I resigned my emeritus status. This was the first, and I believe only, time that a person had resigned emeritus trustee status. To have done otherwise would have cost us an important and prestigious engagement. Several years later in 2000 after the CPA firm had been disbanded, Nan Keohane who then was the Duke President, took action to have me reinstated as an emeritus trustee.

I have enjoyed my association with Duke tremendously. I have made many good friends among the trustees, faculty and administrators in the process. Wanda and I have served the University in many capacities over the years and we remain strong supporters. Most recently, we served for three years as members of Patient Advocacy Council for the Duke University Health System. I was the first of the council members who were not employees of the Health System to serve as chairman along with Dr. Karen Frush, one of the top executives of the System and a pediatrician. Wanda and I feel our pioneering efforts are, in some small way, partially responsible for the fact that our good friend, Attorney Daniel Blue, a black attorney who graduated from Duke Law School in 1973, was elected Chairman of the Board of Trustees. His term began July 2009.

North Carolina Mutual Board of Directors

Company President William Kennedy, III called in late 1978 to say he wanted to recommend Bert Collins and me as new members of the Mutual Board of Directors and the board's Executive Committee. Bert and his wife Carolyn and two of their children had come to Durham in 1968 as a result of my contacts with James Cheek, president of Shaw University, and Joe Goodloe, who at that time was president of the Mutual. Bert and I had worked together at the Austin CPA firm in Detroit. He had earned his CPA certificate and his MBA a year or two after I left the firm, but we stayed in touch. Cheek asked me to recommend someone to serve as the vice president for finance at Shaw and I called Bert. After the interview, Cheek told Bert he also wanted him to be interviewed by the Shaw board chairman, Joe Goodloe. Goodloe was so impressed with Bert that he told him that if he did not take the Shaw job, he wanted him to join the Mutual. And so, Bert joined the Mutual. Bert worked closely with Goodloe, Kennedy and other Mutual executives and moved quickly up the ladder. He also earned a law degree at the N. C. Central School of Law during this period. When Kennedy succeeded Goodloe as Chairman and CEO, Bert was elevated to Senior Vice President.

By the time I was approached to serve on its board, the company had moved from its six-story office building and several annex buildings on and around Parrish Street to its twelve story office tower that sat on the land that had been the home of Doris Duke. That parcel of land - a full block- is the highest point in the downtown area and, as a result, the Mutual building was higher than any other structure in Durham, even though at least one of them had more floors. When the structure was built, company president Asa Spaulding and his planner Murray Marvin had decided that to the maximum extent possible, African American contractors would be used. To that end, joint venture companies were formed from among black-owned electrical and plumbing companies based in Durham, Raleigh, Greensboro, Winston-Salem and Charlotte. The joint venturers were advised to use me for accounting and internal control services. The white companies that were hired to do the plumbing and electrical work were required to subcontract with these two joint venture companies for as much work as possible. The building was completed in 1965 and U. S. Vice President Hubert Humphrey was the featured speaker for the grand opening celebration.

North Carolina Mutual Executive Committee and Corporate Counsel 1988. From left to right: me, Bert Collins, Attorney W. Wayne Perry, William J. Kennedy, III, Cicero Green, Dr. Charles Watts. Photo courtesy of North Carolina Mutual Life Insurance Company.

My service on the Mutual board has been eventful, to say the least. The company's business model has changed several times and I have been an important part of these changes. The company was started in 1890 when blacks could not buy insurance polices from white insurance companies. The business grew under Charles Clinton Spaulding, William J. Kennedy, Jr., Asa T. Spaulding and Joe Goodloe by selling small face value insurance policies in Southeastern, Mid-Atlantic and Mid-Western states. At that time, the vast majority of policyholders - domestic workers, laborers, small business owners, professionals - all lived in tightly knit, racially segregated sections of cities and of rural areas. The agents who went door to door, usually on foot, collected the premiums. The areas served by these agents were called debits. The agents were respected and trusted members of the communities they served. They dressed better than most of their clients. They also were generally better educated with high school diplomas and perhaps even a college degree. When a baby was born, they knew about it and could counsel the family on the need for more insurance. When a child graduated from school at any level, the agent was often there to offer congratulations. When an insured died, the agent delivered the death benefit check, brought condolences and provided more counseling on how the surviving spouse should handle the family's financial affairs. It was a good business model that was protected by segregation, intolerance and discrimination. But the model eventually failed for two primary reasons: (1) when it became unlawful to discriminate racially in the housing market, the middle and upper income blacks began to move into other parts of the city making it more expensive for the agent to collect premiums and making it more difficult to have the kind of relationship with his clients that led to repeat sales; and (2) the white controlled insurance companies began selling insurance to the middle and upper income black families, thus competing with the Mutual and other black-controlled insurance companies.

These developments caused our agents to sell almost exclusively to the lower income blacks who, because of life styles forced on them by low income, often had higher mortality rates. Also, these policyholders, because of automation, employment discrimination and/or health problems, were faced with frequent lay-offs and, thus, the inability to continue to pay the policy premiums. Claims became a larger and larger percentage of premium income and policies began to lapse at an alarming rate. Faced with these conditions, Kennedy concluded that it was no longer possible for a black-controlled life insurance company to earn profits from its operations. He, therefore, with the backing of the Board of Directors, launched the company into new business areas. At one time, we owned a radio station in Tidewater Virginia, a cable station in South Carolina, an asset management firm and a housing development company based in Durham. We also owned a significant percentage of a start-up commercial airline company that was black-controlled. Kennedy's strategy was to earn profits from these subsidiaries and affiliated firms so as to offset the continued erosion of profits from insurance operations. It was a model Kennedy knew was employed by companies such as Mobil Oil, Pfizer and Quaker Oats on whose boards he sat. However, none of our subsidiaries and affiliated firms made money for us. It did not take me long to realize that one of the reasons the enterprises were failing was that Kennedy did not recruit executives and board members with experience in the lines of business being pursued by the subsidiaries. Instead, he was using top-level people at the Mutual to serve as the executives and board members of these new enterprises. These people were good at their jobs for insurance operations but had no backgrounds suited for their new assignments. And to make matters worse, they were being distracted from their full time responsibilities for insurance operations. After several years of operating losses and shrinking surplus, board member Dr. Charles Watts (the former medical officer and husband of Constance Merrick who is the granddaughter of two of the Mutual founders) and I led the board in securing Kennedy's resignation as president and CEO. He retained his title as board chairman, but Bert Collins was named as the new president and chief executive.

Bert was convinced that it was possible to make money from insurance operations and set about to do so. First, he sold or closed down all of the subsidiaries. Fortunately, he was able to sell the asset management firm to a new investor so that we recovered all of the funds we had invested in that enterprise. He, along with Willie Closs, his Senior Vice President, then set about the development of a new business plan. Top-staff, the board of directors and outside consultants worked together on a new four-pronged model for the company. The first prong was to sell group life insurance directly to major corporations and large governmental units. The second was to sell group health policies to small businesses and local governments, and student health policies to colleges and universities. The third was to sell whole life insurance policies to middle income blacks through a unique program for developing sales leads for our agents. The fourth was to get the clients whose premiums were being collected by agents to mail the payments to the office or to pay by having their bank account drafted so that the agents could focus on selling policies to the middle-income blacks instead of going door to door to collect premiums. The four-pronged approach under leadership of Closs and Collins produced profits for several years until we discovered that we had made a bad mistake in going into the student health business. That mistake resulted in huge losses for us. Bert was able to disengage the company from that line of business and shortly thereafter decided to step down as CEO.

James Speed, a CPA with a BA from North Carolina Central University and an MBA from Clark-Atlanta University was named as Bert's successor. Speed had managed the Mutual audit when he worked at Deloitte-Touche and had served as the top fiscal person for Hardees Restaurants. Bert recruited Speed to come to the Mutual after Willie Closs moved from financial affairs to head up marketing.

Before stepping down, however, Bert got board approval for the Mutual to invest in Piedmont Investment Advisers, another start-up asset management firm, headed by Isaac Green. Green is a graduate of Duke University, has an MBA from Columbia and has had many years of experience in asset management. Green is also the grandson of James E. Shepard, founder of NCCU and one of the early promoters of North Carolina Mutual. Bert and I served on the initial managing board for Piedmont. Unlike the Kennedy approach of using Mutual staffers to manage subsidiaries, Piedmont was staffed by experienced professionals who had an ownership stake in the firm and had a managing board loaded with investment know-how. Today,

Piedmont is doing very well. It is profitable and has over $2.5 billion under management.

During most of Bert's tenure as president and CEO, I served as chairman of the Mutual's Board of Directors and worked very closely with him. When I became chairman, Bert and I agreed that if he ever wanted to be chairman, I would step aside. I did so when he retired as CEO. I became Chairman Emeritus.

The business model under James Speed calls for greater focus on selling policies to middle income blacks, acquisition of blocks of premium paying business from other insurance companies, reduced emphasis on selling direct group policies and eliminating excess capacity, much of which was built up to enable us to sell and service direct group policies. The problem with direct group sales is that the larger companies now price their direct group premiums at such low levels that losses are almost certain to occur. They do so in order to have access to the employees to sell them more profitable individual policies. The profits from the individual policies more than offset the losses from the group contract. We concluded that we could not afford to compete for group sales when major losses could be expected. During Speed's term in office I aged off the board under our by-law provision requiring retirement at the first annual meeting of the company following the attainment of age 72. I had been off the board for almost a year when I was asked to return for a year. The request was made because they thought I could help in implementing the new business model. The board and policyholders have voted to suspend that by-law provision each year to allow me to serve six consecutive one-year terms.

Speed has assembled an extremely competent group of executives and has a very talented Board of Directors that includes Ambassador Carol Moseley Braun (former U. S. Senator from Illinois), Willie Closs (CPA, MBA and former Executive VP of NCM), Joe Dudley (cosmetics manufacturer and national distributor), Elliott Hall (attorney and former Ford Motor Company executive), Theodore Long (CPA and retired partner of Ernst and Young) and Richard Moore (former Treasurer of the State of NC). I am convinced that the company will return to profitability in the very near future and will continue to thrive thereafter.

Minority Business Organizations

Shortly after I re-entered practice in 1972, I joined the North Carolina Association of Minority Business, a statewide organization of businessmen and women. Two years later, I became president and served for three years. During my presidency, with the help of Larnie Horton, a businessman and minister, the Association initiated an annual event called "The Golf and

Tennis Weekend." The purpose was to help minority firms get more business from major corporations. We did so by getting the executives from the minority firms and the big corporations to eat, play golf and tennis, and get to know one another to the end that business relationships could be formed. Also, during my term as Association president I worked with Lew Myers and Julian Brown to create the North Carolina Institute of Minority Economic Development. The Institute still operates and, under the leadership of Andrea Harris, is the leading source of training and marketing aid for minority and women-owned businesses in North Carolina. Studies have concluded that, largely because of the Institute, North Carolina minorities and women lead the nation on a per capita basis as to the number and sizes of business firms. Although the Institute has continued "The Golf and Tennis Weekend," it has appropriately re-named the event as the "Executive Networking Conference." It is still held at Pinehurst in late March or April of each year.

National Association of Minority CPA Firms

The minority-owned CPA firms that developed in the mid to late '70s pulled together to form the National Association of Minority CPA Firms. Most of the owners had gotten to know one another through their memberships in the National Association of Black Accountants (NABA). NABA was largely concerned with encouraging blacks to major in accounting and providing advice and networking opportunities for black accountants in industry and government. Those of us who were running CPA firms saw the need to form the new Association as a means of bringing our firms to the attention of government and big corporations. I served as president of that Association in 1978.

Minority Enterprise Investment Firms

I became deeply involved in three organizations whose missions were to provide investments and technical assistance to minority-owned firms throughout the nation. The first one was The Opportunity Funding Corporation (OFC), headquartered in Washington, D.C. OFC received grant support from the U. S. Department of Commerce in response to President Nixon's "Black Capitalism" thrust. I served OFC as a member of its Executive Committee and as Chairman of its Investment Committee. Jack Gloster, a Morehouse graduate, was the CEO and Paul Pride, an energetic and innovative young man, was Jack's top assistant. The second organization was the Cooperative Assistance Fund (CAF), an organization formed under the leadership of Yale law professor, John Simon. John solicited funds from several New York-based private foundations to provide equity and loan capital to firms all over the country that agreed to establish themselves in low-wealth communities. I served CAF as a board member, as its CEO for a brief period to span the gap between the resignation of Ed Sylvester and the hiring of Tex Wilson as CEO, as Chairman of its Investment Committee, and as Chairman of its Board of Directors. The third one was Structured Employment and Economic Development Corporation (SEEDCO) based in New York and headed by Tom Seessel with Ernest Osborne as Tom's top assistant. SEEDCO was funded principally by the Ford and Mott foundations and it focused on assisting colleges all over the country to create community development corporations (CDCs) to address residential blight, and the lack of attractive and efficient retail establishments in the areas surrounding the campuses. Most of SEEDCO's work was with historically black colleges and universities (HBCUs). I knew of their work and they knew of me because of my involvements with The Foundation for Community Development, OFC and CAF. Tom and Ernie retained me to do a mid-course review of the HBCU CDCs to serve as a report to the Mott Foundation from which much of the SEEDCO's funds had come. Later, I was asked to join the SEEDCO board. I served the organization for several years, but resigned my board position when, under the CEO who succeeded Tom Seessel, the focus of organization shifted from support for CDCs to the operation of a variety of projects in New York and other major cities. Since my resignation, SEEDCO has become one of the largest and most influential economic development organizations in the country.

Durham Colored Library

Dr. A. M. Moore, one of the founders of North Carolina Mutual and Durham's first black physician, started a reading room in a section of White Rock Baptist Church on Fayetteville Street in Durham. That was 1910. The reading room was later moved to a nearby location so that the whole black community would have access to it. It was called the Durham Colored Library (DCL). Ultimately, when a black physician donated the land for the construction of a new facility, a new building was constructed and was named for him: The Stanford L. Warren Public Library. However, DCL continued to run the library and provided the financial support. Much later, the library became a branch of the Durham County Library system. As a child and young adult, I spent many hours reading and attending special programs at "our" library; the only one in the all-black southeastern quadrant of the city and the only one at which blacks could feel truly welcome. DCL continued to provide support for special projects after the County took it over.

In 1922, John Washington, an abandoned blind baby, lived for a time in the home of Lyda Moore (Dr. Moore's daughter) and her husband, John Merrick, son of another North Carolina Mutual founder. Mrs. Lyda Moore Merrick became chairman of the DCL board in the early '50s and, because of the continuing relationship she had with Washington, she was aware of the lack of Braille reading material that featured news and feature articles about black people. Therefore, she set about the task of raising money through the DCL to create what now is called the Merrick-Washington Magazine for the Blind. Braille and a large-print magazine are published twice a year and copies are distributed to libraries here and abroad. Mrs. Merrick's daughter, Constance Merrick Watts became chairman of the DCL board when advancing age made it impossible for her mother to continue. I was asked to join the board in the early '70s and have served ever since. The current president is Mrs. Watts' daughter, Eileen Watts Welch.

Regulation of Accountants

North Carolina State Board of CPA Examiners

In 1986, I was appointed to the State Board by Governor James Martin, one of a handful of Republicans who succeeded in becoming the Governor of North Carolina. I had supported him in his race against a Democrat for whom I had no respect. Larnie Horton, a friend who had worked with me when I was president of the North Carolina Association of Minority Businesses, and who was a Republican, knew of my dislike for the Democrat nominee. He encouraged me to look closely at Martin and I liked what I saw. Horton also encouraged me to switch to the Republican Party, which I did against my better judgment.

The State Board licenses and disciplines CPAs in our state. The purpose of the Board of Examiners is to protect the public from being harmed by substandard work. Of course, it is impossible to provide complete protection, but the board does the following things in furthering that purpose:

1. Prescribes how much education, what examinations and how much and what kind of experience a man or woman must have to become a CPA in North Carolina.

2. Prescribes the type and amount of continuing professional education a CPA has to have each year in order to keep the license.

3. Prescribes that each North Carolina office of a CPA firm that does audits or reviews or compiles financial statements must undergo a review of its professional work periodically and provide evidence to

the Board that major deficiencies uncovered during the review have been corrected.

4. Defines what conduct by a CPA is improper.

5. Investigates complaints about the work of CPAs and decides what, if any, disciplinary action is warranted, ranging from a private censure to revocation of license.

6. Determines if a CPA from another state has credentials comparable to those of North Carolina CPAs when that CPA wants to serve a client based in North Carolina.

I became secretary-treasurer of the state board during my two three-year terms that ended in 1992. Any North Carolina CPA who was licensed during most of that period has a certificate that was signed by me.

State Boards of Accountancy

There are over 400,000 CPAs in the United States; each one is licensed under the laws of one or more of the 55 jurisdictions and each one is subject to disciplinary actions of the jurisdiction that granted the license. The federal government has no say at all as to who may be granted a license. In response to the audit failures for Enron, WorldCom and other giant corporations, Congress passed the Sarbanes-Oxley Act (SOX). To help assure independence and objectivity on the part of CPA firms, SOX prohibits audit firms from performing major consulting services for the firms they audit and calls for the rotation of auditors after several years. While the federal government may provide evidence of substandard audits, substandard tax work or improper conduct, and may bar firms from performing audits on corporations whose stock is publicly traded, only the jurisdiction that granted a license to a CPA can take the license away.

Each of the 55 jurisdictions has a board that oversees professional accountancy. The board members are appointed by the top executive – usually the governor – of each jurisdiction. In North Carolina, there are five board members who are, themselves, CPAs and two who are "public" members; i.e., people in business or government who understand the importance of the work of CPAs in our state. Other jurisdictions have similar arrangements.

American Institute of Certified Public Accountants (AICPA)

The AICPA is an organization controlled by its members, all of whom are CPAs. The AICPA serves the needs of its membership in many ways, most importantly by promoting high professional standards and by constructing and grading the Uniform CPA Examination that is used by all jurisdictions for the licensing of CPAs.

The AICPA has always constructed and graded the examination. It owns it. The boards of each of the 54 jurisdictions annually make the decision to purchase the exam from the AICPA and to have it graded by the AICPA. After grading, the AICPA gives notices to the various boards as to the scores of their candidates and recommends what score ought to be considered a passing score. Although each board is free to decide what score is passing, historically, all adopt the recommendation of the AICPA. The problem with this relationship among the AICPA, the licensing jurisdictions and the candidates was that some considered the AICPA to have a conflict of interest. As a membership organization it responds to the needs of its members. It is conceivable, therefore, that if the members felt the need for more CPAs to be licensed, the AICPA could make the exam easier. If the membership felt that fewer CPAs should be licensed, the AICPA could do the opposite. There is absolutely no evidence that the AICPA has ever constructed or graded the examination in response to demands from its members, however, the arrangement looked bad on its face.

This arrangement with the AICPA is somewhat unique among the major professions. The licensing examinations are usually under the control of the licensing bodies, not the membership associations. In some cases the examination is a joint enterprise between the licensing bodies and the professional associations, but in no instance is the professional association in complete control as it is with the AICPA.

The licensing boards needed assurance that the examination questions, grading and administration were appropriate for determining who could enter the profession. But what was the best way of securing that assurance? Each board could have hired its own experts to determine the validity and reliability of the AICPA's exam with the result that the AICPA would have been subjected to up to 54 different teams looking at its work. The boards could have agreed on a single firm of experts to do the work for all of them, but the processes of selection and oversight of the firm would have been very difficult for 54 independent boards, each subject to the unique purchasing and contract laws of their respective states and territories. Each board could have decided to develop its own exam but that would have made it very difficult, for example, for North Carolina to allow a person from New York to do work in North Carolina if that person had only passed an examination designed by the New York board. The solution to the problem was to have the National Association of State Boards of Accountancy (NASBA) provide the assurance needed.

NASBA

During my first two years on the North Carolina CPA Board, I learned of NASBA. NASBA's history is traced to 1908 when 17 men from ten states assembled in Atlantic City to discuss the need for uniformity of procedures by the boards that were responsible for licensing certified public accountants. The initial organization was the National Association of CPA Examiners. The name was changed to the current one in 1956.

NASBA is controlled by its members, the boards of accountancy of the 54 jurisdictions that license Certified Public Accountants and regulate professional accountancy in the United States. The four jurisdictions beyond the 50 states are the District of Columbia, Guam, Puerto Rico and the U.S. Virgin Islands.

NASBA serves the needs of its members in many ways, but there are two that are primary. First, it encourages uniformity among the jurisdictions as to the licensing of accountants as it has done from its beginning in 1908. Second, beginning around 1975, it audits all aspects of the Uniform CPA Examination to assure the member boards that the test can be relied upon to determine that those who pass it have enough knowledge and skills so that people and organizations who rely on the accountant's work are less likely to be harmed.

The AICPA nurtured and provided financial support for NASBA's predecessor and NASBA itself for many years. In fact, NASBA was housed within the AICPA offices until 1975. In that year, however, NASBA established its own offices on Fifth Avenue near the AICPA offices at 1211 Avenue of the Americas (Sixth Avenue). The chief executive officer for NASBA at the time of the move was William Van Rensselaer. If NASBA was to be the auditor of the Uniform CPA Examination, there needed to be a separation between the two entities: NASBA needed to have an independent board, its own staff and it had to come out from under the AICPA wing. NASBA now performs audits of the construction, administration, and grading of the Uniform CPA Examination for the benefit of its membership, the 54 licensing boards. If the questions are not appropriate, the grading not correct or the security surrounding the examination inadequate, the auditors can reveal it and require corrective action by the AICPA. If the AICPA does not make the necessary corrections, the auditors could recommend that the boards make other arrangements for an examination and not use the AICPA's Uniform CPA Examination. Thus, NASBA serves as a shield for the AICPA and the Boards against critics who may assert that the AICPA has complete control over the licensing examination

As to the first of the two primary services that NASBA provides for its membership, the reader must know that the laws and regulations that govern the practice of accountancy are determined by each of the 54 states and territories. The lack of uniformity is an impediment to the interstate mobility of CPAs and it can make it difficult for businesses with operations in more than one state to select auditing firms. For example, at one time North Carolina required a college degree whereas Minnesota required only a high school diploma in order to become a CPA. Therefore, North Carolina would not permit a person from Minnesota to get a license or to serve a client in North Carolina. Also, California's licensees were required to have a specified number of hours of experience in auditing, but North Carolina did not specify the kind of experience the person had to get; it could have been all audit, all tax or other kinds of work. North Carolina only said the work had to be done under the supervision of a CPA Therefore, if a North Carolina CPA had only done tax work he or she could not get licensed in California until getting experience in auditing.

Because of the work of NASBA, the legislators and boards of the various states, the AICPA and state CPA societies, there is much greater similarity among the jurisdictions today than ever before, but the quest for uniformity continues. It must continue. Differences in laws or regulations that prevent competent practitioners from crossing state lines to serve clients are a burden to interstate commerce. The United States Congress has not yet decided that the burden is great enough to cause it to mandate national standards under its Constitutional power to regulate interstate commerce.

NASBA has divided its membership into eight regions that meet in June of each year. In June 1987 the Mid-Atlantic regional meeting was hosted by the North Carolina Board and was held in Asheville, a city in the mountains in the western part of the state. As it turned out, I asked one or two questions and offered my opinion on several issues during the sessions. Though I did not know it, members of the NASBA Nominating Committee were on hand. I guess they noticed me because I was the only African-American in attendance and/or because they concluded that I had good communication skills. In July 1988 the chairman of the nominating committee asked if I would consent to be nominated for a one-year term as the regional director for the Mid-Atlantic Region: South Carolina, North Carolina, Virginia, Maryland, the District of Columbia, West Virginia and Delaware. I readily said yes. I was elected.

A year later at the 1989 Annual Meeting I was elected to a four-year term as one of eight at-large directors and was also made a vice president. In May 1990 I was among three or four candidates that were under consideration to become NASBA president-elect. The normal process was for the Nominating Committee to meet in late June to decide on the slate consisting of the president-elect and board members to be presented at the Annual Meeting.

The president-elect is an officer, a member of the Executive Committee and automatically succeeds to the presidency after one year. Once the slate is decided, the chairman of the Nominating Committee calls the prospective nominees to confirm their willingness to serve. The slate is then presented to the membership for a vote at the Annual Meeting in October.

It had been a month since the Nominating Committee had met and I had not received a call.

Why hadn't I been called?

Why Hadn't the Call Come?

I was in the second year of a four-year term as an at-large member of the NASBA Board of Directors. I had served for a year as a Regional Director. I had headed several committees and was representing NASBA on the Education Change Commission, a body comprised of leading educators and authors in the field of accounting. I had also been voted a vice president for each of the past two years. My credentials were good: Yale undergraduate, managing partner of a CPA firm for many years and a license to practice law. Clearly I was in the running to become president.

But it was mid-July and I had not been called.

Was there someone else whom the Committee felt was a better candidate? There were two others on the 19-member board who had, during the last year, shown something extra in leadership. One was a partner in a local firm who was elected to the board as a regional director the same year I was elected as the Mid-Atlantic Regional Director. He was bright, articulate and energetic. He was also perceived as a maverick and an impatient person. I liked him a lot, but I did not feel he had the temperament to lead a board consisting of volunteers. The other was Noel Kirch, a partner in one of the big international firms who had been elected as an at-large director. Noel exuded competence, wisdom, and even-handedness in everything he did. In comparison to the other man, he was reserved. I respected him greatly, as did the rest of the board. I felt Noel would be a good President *to follow me*. After all, I had served a year longer than he had. I felt that seniority ought to count if your credentials are good, and I knew mine were good. Certainly the Nominating Committee must have known that if they passed over a good man and nominated as President a person with less seniority, they would likely alienate the man who had served longer. The contributions he might have made could be forever lost to the organization.

Or was the Committee not willing to recommend me because I was the only African-American ever to have served on the board? Jim Armstrong, an African-American CPA who was on the Colorado CPA Board, was named as a member of the NASBA nominating committee that met in June 1989, eight months after I had been elected as the Mid-Atlantic Regional Director (October 1988). I had gotten to know Jim through The National Association of Minority CPA Firms that I had served as President in 1978 and through a joint venture engagement between our two firms. Jim shared with me that the Nominating Committee and the NASBA board members with whom he had talked just "didn't know what to do with me." Few African-Americans had been involved in state regulation of accountancy before 1988. They had served on a few committees but rarely attended either the regional or annual meetings. It was the Nominating Committee on which Jim sat that had decided to nominate me to a four-year term as Director-At-Large.

After my first year as an at-large director I asked then-President Jerry Solomon if he thought I had a chance at becoming President. Jerry is from Massachusetts, is Jewish, was managing partner of one of the large national firms and was one of the most capable, honest and genuinely nice people I met during my service to NASBA. This says a lot because every board member was possessed of great ability and character. The person scheduled to follow Jerry was Dick Goode of Nevada. He was named President-Elect in October 1990. In answering my question, Jerry looked me straight in the eye and said, "Yes, if I have anything to do with it." He didn't elaborate and we never discussed it again.

The job of Nominating Committee chair always fell to the Immediate Past President and that meant Jerry Schine of Florida; Jewish and a partner in one of the international firms. He had followed Sam Yellen as president. Sam, of California and also a partner in an international firm, was the third member of what they, themselves, called the "NASBA Jewish Mafia" – Yellen, Schine and Solomon

I also knew, however, that Jerry Solomon, as President, would name the rest of the Nominating Committee. Although he had been able to assess my performance for the three years during which he served as President-Elect, President and as Immediate Past President, I wasn't sure about what Schine thought of me. We had butted heads a few times on issues that were before the NASBA board. Also, I recall one instance when he and I were the last to board a bus at a meeting in Rhode Island. Schine made a joke of the fact that he and I would have to sit in the back of the bus, but that at least I was used to it. This caused me to question this Floridian's sensitivity to racial issues. Blacks joke about this all the time, but we don't really appreciate it from whites, especially southern whites. Schine and I always treated each other with cool cordiality. I did not feel he would try to pressure the committee against me for overtly racial reasons, but I did feel he thought I would not make a good president. Before the committee met, Schine asked me if, in the event I was nominated, would I be willing to serve as president-elect? I am sure he asked the other two likely candidates the same question. Schine was questionable, but Solomon was not against me and Solomon would be appointing the other members of the nominating committee. I was satisfied that I was in the running. I had a chance.

And the Call Came

I have never asked anyone within NASBA why the Committee took so long to decide, but I strongly suspect that they initially decided to nominate one of the two competitors I described. I also suspect that Noel Kirch, one of the two, would have declined the nomination for a combination of reasons. His wife was not well and he knew that the position of President would require a huge amount of time and energy – a time and energy consumption that would make it difficult for him to tend to his wife's needs. Second, I think he genuinely felt that I would make a good President and that I deserved the chance. If he did, in fact, decline and indicate his support for my candidacy, that action might explain two of the things he did a year later.

The call finally came in late August. I said *yes*.

Then, three weeks later, a tragedy.

Dick Goode, the NASBA President-Elect, was killed when he stepped off a curb on The Strip in Las Vegas and was hit by a motorist. Dick was such a good human being. We were all devastated.

A week later, after the funeral, NASBA had to address a leadership problem. Presidential terms had always been limited to one year. The President-Elect had the opportunity to observe and plan for a full year before taking on the job of President. The question was, was I ready to become President without the advantage of that year of preparation? I thought I was, but others saw it differently.

The decision was to have Jerry Solomon serve as President for two years instead of one. This would give me the year of preparation called for by the scheme. Therefore, at the Annual Meeting, Solomon was re-elected as President and I was elected as President-Elect. I wondered if one of the other two men had been nominated as President-Elect, would the decision still have been to keep Solomon on for a second year. Was it racial? I will never know, but it wasn't long before I agreed that the decision was the right one. First of all, Jerry Solomon had been an excellent President and his firm and family were willing to support him for a second term. Second, there was a lot I needed to learn about the program and administrative issues confronting NASBA, including questions about the quality of the then Executive Director, before I assumed the burdens of leadership

I was installed as NASBA's 36th President at the end of the organization's annual meeting in Washington, D. C. in October 1992. Noel Kirch was elected President-Elect.

I am President, Now What?

In my inaugural address I warned the member boards that the lack of uniformity in licensing among the states meant that we were impeding interstate commerce and therefore were in danger of losing the power to license. Under the Commerce Clause of the United States Constitution, Congress has the authority to pass laws that override state laws if it concludes that the state laws are a serious impediment to interstate commerce. Thus, Congress could create a federal agency to establish and administer licensure rules for CPAs. I urged increased attention to achieving uniformity in licensing standards.

My plan was to achieve greater uniformity during my year as President through encouraging all boards to adopt a rule called the "Five in Ten Rule." Under that rule a CPA from state "A" would be deemed acceptable to state "B" if he or she was in good standing with the board of state "A" and if he or she had been in public practice in state "A" for five of the last ten years.

The "Five in Ten" rule was not a perfect answer to the uniformity problem, because it did nothing for the newly minted CPAs or those who had not had at least five years of public practice. But I reasoned that the rule would solve the problem for the "seasoned" practitioners who constituted the vast majority of the licensed accountants in the country. If they could move freely from state to state despite minor differences in education, conditions under which the examination was passed, or differences in experience, etc. there would be no appreciable negative impact on interstate commerce.

My major message for the state boards from 1992 to 1994 was "Five in Ten; all 54 by '94."

Unfortunately, the staff was distracted by other developments and did not work with me as I had hoped during my presidential year.

The first distraction was that Noel Kirch, the newly elected President-Elect, told the Executive Director that he was going to be replaced. He did not confer with me before doing so. In conversations at meals, or during leisure times when the staff was not present, many of the board members, myself included, had decided that the organization needed someone at its helm who was a member of the profession. Our Executive Director had served under William Van Rennsalear for several years, was a good writer and had taken course work in association management. However, he had no training or experience in accounting. He even had difficulty interpreting NASBA's own financial statements. That was bad enough, but it also placed him at a severe disadvantage when he tried to represent NASBA with organizations such as the AICPA, The Society of Public Accountants, state CPA societies and associations created by chartered/certified accountants in other countries.

The premature disclosure had a terrible impact on the entire staff. The Executive Director asked me if it was true and I had to be truthful. I told him that although no official vote had taken place, it was likely that such action would be taken at some time during my term in office. The process was to have taken around nine months and it would have been orderly. Confusion and anxiety within the staff would have been minimized because there would have been a well thought out plan, and staff questions could have been answered. Instead, there was near chaos followed by rock bottom morale. Productive work came to a virtual standstill. Without a focused, enthusiastic Executive Director to lead the staff effort, my "Five in Ten; all 54 by '94" initiative made very little progress.

The second distraction was an accelerated push to develop new paradigms for the relationship between NASBA and the AICPA as to the CPA examination and the relationship between NASBA and the boards of the 54 jurisdictions. The accelerated "push" was initiated by Noel, but it was supported by a highly vocal group of board members. One of them was the other director who was in contention for the President-Elect position when I got the nod.

The group wanted the AICPA to convert the CPA examination from paper and pencil to computer. They also wanted the boards of the 55 jurisdictions to have a much stronger voice on all examination matters to the ends that the passing standard would be established in a more scientific way and the reliability and validity of the questions would be improved.

As to the relationship with the boards of the 55 jurisdictions, the group wanted to help assure that persons elected to the NASBA Board would understand how jurisdictions operated and that terms of NASBA board members would be limited in order to achieve turnover in not more than six years.

These were all good ideas and I supported them. I knew, however, that the examination issues ideas would require time to do the politics and technical homework. I estimated at least a three-year time line for them. As it turns out, it took even longer. The stronger voice on examination matters was achieved in 2003 when the AICPA increased the number of state board representatives on the committee that is responsible for the CPA examination. The first computerized examination was offered in 2004. However, the by-law changes regarding board elections were doable within six months and I authored almost all of the changes that were adopted at the 1993 annual meeting.

I knew the push on examination issues would make it difficult to focus on my "Five in Ten" rule priority, but I felt it unwise to stand in the way of the momentum that was developing. Therefore, I embraced the new thrusts and appointed Noel to chair a special *ad hoc* committee to pursue them.

By the end of my year as President I had worked out a deal whereby the top executives agreed to remain until a new chief executive officer could be recruited. I announced the forthcoming changes in my report to the membership. Also, the delegates passed the changes to the by-laws I had recommended concerning board seats

The continuing Quest for Uniformity; Local Preferences

Long-term, the work of the *ad hoc* committee resulted in important changes. The threat of the 54 jurisdictions losing the licensing authority did not materialize. The push for uniformity continues in the form of a NASBA – created National Qualifications Appraisal Board (NQAB).

The NQAB reviews the certification requirements established by various jurisdictions and determines if they are substantially equivalent to the requirements outlined in the Uniform Accountancy Act. The Uniform Accountancy Act is a model act developed by NASBA with the assistance of the AICPA. Legislators in the 54 jurisdictions are encouraged to adopt the Act as written or to amend existing laws to make them similar to the Act's provisions. All jurisdictions that are substantially equivalent are encouraged to accept one another's licensees.

The differences among the jurisdictions are relatively minor. One area of difference is the education requirement. Most jurisdictions now require a candidate to have a baccalaureate degree plus thirty additional hours of college level work before sitting for the examination. A few states require the baccalaureate in order to sit for the examination but mandate that the additional hours must be taken before licensure. So, in those states, the candidate who passes the examination can get a job with a CPA to satisfy the experience requirement and take the added course work evenings or weekends to meet the licensing requirement. North Carolina is one of the states with this type of arrangement and I am proud to say that I played a significant role in influencing how our law reads. The added course work requirement is not intended to impart more knowledge of accountancy. The eight or nine accounting courses that constitute a major in the subject are really all that are needed to pass the examination and the purpose of the examination and of the 54 jurisdictions is to determine which candidates have just enough knowledge and skills to avoid serious mistakes in serving the accounting, auditing and tax preparation needs of clients. Though we want as many truly bright people as possible to join our profession, the licensing procedure is designed only to determine who is minimally qualified. Other licensing bodies operate the same way. However, the AICPA and other practitioner groups felt that it was time to make accountancy more like other professions, many of which, such as attorneys and physicians, require masters or doctoral degrees. Historically, accountants were considered to be just above the blue-collar worker; the green eye shade and pen were the symbols most associated with us; we were considered smart people but narrow minded and unable to see and understand anything beyond the numbers with which we work. The members of management to whom we present our audit findings often have more education than the typical CPA does. The purpose of the 150 hours campaign (baccalaureate plus 30 hours) was in large part intended to improve our image. Ultimately, I think we will require a master's degree, a small step from the 150 hours requirement.

I supported the need for additional course work as a means of adding to the student's knowledge of such subjects as economics, political science, history, computerized information systems and foreign cultures and languages. These make the CPA a more rounded individual; more at home in a global, multi-cultural world. The additional education will help the CPA understand the societal implications of business practices and to provide better advice to clients. But as a regulator concerned with determining what candidate is just good enough to be admitted to the profession, the additional hours of education are nearly irrelevant. Therefore, as a compromise, I lobbied to have the North Carolina Legislature to pass a law requiring the 150 hours as a condition for licensure rather than as a condition for sitting for the CPA examination.

Because North Carolina permits candidates to sit for the examination with the baccalaureate, some states resisted allowing our licensees to practice. However, the National Qualifications Appraisal Board has determined that North Carolina is substantially equivalent to the 150 hours requirement contained in the Uniform Accountancy Act. In recent years several states that had decreed 150 hours in order to sit for the exam have decided that 150 hours for licensure is a better requirement.

Other minor differences among jurisdictions involve what we call "conditioning" on the examination. The national examination prepared by the AICPA has four parts. Before the computerized examination, the exam was given twice a year and most jurisdictions required a new candidate to take all four parts. If the candidate passed at least two parts and made at least a score of 50 on the other two parts he or she received credit for those two parts. On the next sitting the candidate would only have to take the remaining two parts. If he or she passed one of them and got at least a 50 on the other, credit was given for the one passed and at a subsequent sitting the candidate would take only the single remaining part. If, however, the new candidate passed two parts but scored a 49 on one of the other two parts, no credit was given and at the next sitting the candidate would have to take all four parts again. Several jurisdictions had different "conditioning" schemes. Some allowed credit for parts passed regardless of the scores on the failed parts. Others established a threshold lower than 50 on the parts failed. The licensees from such states found it difficult to have their credentials accepted in those states that had the more stringent requirement.

With the advent of the computerized examination, "conditioning" is much less of a problem. All jurisdictions have agreed to allow the computerized examination candidates to take one part at a time. If they pass it, they get credit. However, in most jurisdictions, they must pass the remaining four parts within 18 months or they will lose credit. Unfortunately, some jurisdictions grant longer than 18 months, thus barriers to uniformity persist.

Experience requirements still differ among the jurisdictions. One year under the supervision of a CPA is the standard used in the Uniform Accountancy Act. However, some jurisdictions require more than one year of experience, while some don't require any. Some require that the experience must be under a CPA in public practice while others say that teaching accounting can satisfy the experience requirement. A master's degree reduces the amount of experience required in some states. These differences may never be resolved other than through application of the "Five in Ten" rule.

A Labor of Love (mostly on the CPA examination) After the Presidency

I served NASBA in many capacities following my year as president. I was "Immediate Past President" for the ensuing year and spearheaded additional changes to the by-laws, one of which was to change the title of the Executive Director to President and to change the top volunteer leader from President to Chairman of the Board. I was very active in finding the right person for our top staff position. Happily, the new person was hired six months after the search began.

The second year following my year as President, I chaired a committee to work with the AICPA to develop a new procedure for setting the passing score on the CPA examination. For many years, grade adjustment points were added to the raw scores of the candidates sufficient to result in approximately 30% of the candidates passing each of the four parts. This meant that a candidate's chances of passing the examination depended on how smart the other candidates were. If you were with a really smart group, there would be fewer grade adjustment points needed to reach the 30% target. If the group was not very smart, more grade adjustment points were needed. These adjustments had been necessary because, historically, the questions were released to the public following each examination. The candidates took the question booklets home with them. This meant that new questions had to be developed for each new examination. However, it is not possible to know if a previously unused question is a good one. Some candidates come up with reasonable answers that had not been anticipated by the question writers. The wording of some questions may be such that very good candidates cannot come up with the right answers. Other questions may be so easy that virtually all candidates get them right so that you can't determine which are the weak ones. Since the AICPA could not be certain that questions used were really good ones they could not be certain that the most recent examination was at the same level of difficulty as prior ones. Without grade adjustment points, a group of strong candidates could fail on a really difficult examination and large numbers of weak candidates might wind up passing an examination that turned out to be an easy one. Neither result was acceptable to the regulators who needed to identify the minimally competent candidate.

Partially as a result of pressure from NASBA, the AICPA changed its policy and stopped sharing the questions with the public. The candidates were required to turn in the question booklets along with the answer sheets. After two years, the AICPA had excellent statistics on how their bank of questions performed and therefore could be reasonably satisfied that the examination given in the fall, though not identical, was of comparable difficulty to the one given in the spring. Furthermore, they were able to insert new questions in an examination to observe how they performed. These new questions were not used in determining the candidate's raw scores. Once they were satisfied with the quality of the new questions they were placed in subsequent examinations and used to determine who failed and who passed.

The non-disclosed examination made it possible do away with the 30% rule and to establish a passing score based on one of several methodologies employed by professionals in the world of testing. The job of the committee I headed was to be a participant-observer in the process of selecting and testing a new methodology and to recommend adoption of the new procedure by the 54 jurisdictions.

It took two years, but at the end, my committee and the AICPA testing experts were agreed on a procedure that was fair and legally defensible. Panels of experienced CPAs who regularly supervised the work of newer CPAs were assembled and asked to give their judgments as to whether a new CPA would know the answer to the questions contained in a recent examination. Following discussions of why they reached the judgments they did on each question, the panelists were given the opportunity to revise their judgments. The average of the revised judgments was used to determine what should have been the passing score on that examination.

In order to be reasonably certain that examinations had comparable difficulty, a process of "equating" was instituted. Equating requires a series of steps and the application of sophisticated mathematical calculations. First, the testing experts select a small group of questions from the prior examination on which the panelists had made judgments as to whether a new CPA would know the answers. Next, they review the statistics on how well the strong, average and weak candidates actually did on those questions when they encountered them on the prior examination. That small group is then embedded in a new exam and the testing experts analyze how well the candidates taking the new exam did on the embedded questions. By comparing the performance of the new candidates with that of prior candidates on the same questions, the experts have a basis for determining if the two groups of candidates have nearly the same in ability. Finally, the distribution of scores on the rest of the new examination is compared with the distribution of scores on the prior examination. If the ability of the two groups of test takers had been deemed nearly the same, the distribution of scores on the new and prior examinations should be about the same. If not, they can determine the extent to which one examination was harder or easier than the other. The cut score for the prior examination that had been established by the panelists is adjusted to account for any difference in difficulty and then used to determine who passed and who failed the new examination.

The testing experts are called psychometricians. They are mathematicians who specialize in testing and measurement.

The procedures for determining the passing score were not perfect for several reasons. The major reason relates to the use of the panels. I think the AICPA did the best it could in selecting the panels. They also assembled two panels to render judgments on the same questions and they compared the resulting passing scores. However, one could never conclude that a passing score established in this manner is absolutely accurate. But I believe it was the best any organization could do.

I wrote a 10-page document describing the procedure and NASBA disseminated it to the boards of the 54 jurisdictions. I explained and answered questions on the document at the regional meetings. Before the year was out, each of the jurisdictions had approved the new procedures for determining the passing score on the Uniform CPA Examination

The computerized examination on which I worked for over two years presents a new set of problems for determining the cut score primarily because a new type of question, called a "Simulation", is now being used. For some of the Simulation questions, the candidate must search a database for answers to questions on auditing, accounting or taxation. For others, he or she must construct a worksheet by cutting and pasting data and perhaps write an explanation of what the data on the worksheet means. The procedures for determining the cut score for such questions require the use of panels also, but how the scores are used and how equating is done are different from the way it was done for the paper and pencil examination. The procedures for determining the passing score on the computerized examination are evolving. There are certain to be changes in the way it is done as we gain more experience with this type of testing. I believe this new examination was superior to the paper and pencil one on the day it was launched. I am confident it will get even better as we gain more experience with this type of testing.

International Reciprocity

Reciprocity for foreign accounting professionals was another of my involvements during my more active years with NASBA. NASBA and the AICPA were approached by the Canadian Institute of Chartered Accountants about the desire of a few Chartered Accountants to get licensed as CPAs. Also, a few CPAs who wanted to serve clients in Canada, expressed their desires to get the Chartered Accountant designation.

After an exhaustive study, NASBA and the Canadian Institute concluded that the educational, experience and examination requirements for the two professional designations were substantially equivalent. However, there were slight differences in auditing standards and accounting theory and substantial differences in law and taxation. The two bodies agreed to allow CPAs to become Chartered Accountants by passing a special examination prepared by the Canadian Institute that tested on the differences. The AICPA did the same for Chartered Accountants and if the candidate passed, one or more of the 54 jurisdictions could grant the CPA license.

NASBA has been trying to work out a similar arrangement with the Chartered Accountants in the United Kingdom. As with Canadian Chartered Accountants, the education, experience and examination requirements are substantially equivalent. The barrier to reaching agreement has been an agency of the British government that licenses accountants to perform audits within the United Kingdom. That agency licenses United Kingdom accountants with less stringent examination, education and experience requirements than the Chartered Accountants. Although they are satisfied with the credentials of CPAs, they will not allow reciprocity unless all their licensees are included in the deal. NASBA has determined that the non Chartered Accountants are not substantially equivalent to CPAs, so we have an impasse at this time. As I write this, however, there are changes being implemented by the UK that give us hope of reaching an agreement.

Arrangements similar to the one worked out with Canada have been consummated for professional accountants in Australia, Mexico and Ireland. The qualifying examinations for all of these foreign designations are prepared by the AICPA and administered by NASBA.

As a result of my service over a thirteen year period I was given NASBA's highest honor in 2001: the William H. Van Rensselaer Public Service Award. Also, I was given the "Being a Difference Award" by NASBA's Center for the Public Trust in 2008.

I am proud of my work with and recognition from NASBA. There were, and still are, many extremely talented and dedicated staff at NASBA. They and the volunteers on the NASBA Board and the staff and volunteers from the State Boards made possible whatever successes I have enjoyed from my efforts. The current President and CEO is David Costello. The staff members with whom I worked most closely were Lorraine Sachs (Executive Vice President) Louise Dratler- Haberman, Tom Kenny and Lisa Axisa. NASBA Board members, state board members and state board staff whose counsel I sought regularly, in addition to those already mentioned, were Noel Allen (North Carolina), Barton Baldwin (North Carolina), Bernard Blum (Connecticut), Robert Brooks (North Carolina), O Whitfield Broom, Jr. (Virginia), Milton Brown (New Jersey), Gerald Burns (Oregon), O. Charlie Chewning (North Carolina), Walter Davenport (North Carolina), Robert Ellyson (Florida), Gary Fish (Illinois), Welling Fruehauf (Pennsylvania), Robert Gray (New York), John Greene (South Carolina), Princey Harrison (Mississippi), Gary Heesacker (Washington), Asa Hord (Kentucky), Donald Howard (Maryland), Richard Isserman (New York), Joe Lawrence (Alabama), Theodore Long (Ohio), John Peace (Arkansas), Will Pugh (Tennessee), Anthony Pustorino (New York), Donald Roland (Georgia), Ronnie Rudd (Texas), Wilbert Schwotzer (Georgia), Carol Sigmann (California), Dennis Spackman (Utah), Susan Stopher (Kentucky), Charles Taylor (Mississippi), Jerry Tobin (New Jersey), William Tonkin (Idaho), William Treacy (Texas), David Vaught (Iowa), George Veily (Connecticut), Michael Weatherwax (Colorado), Harris Widmer (North Dakota), JaniceWilson-Marcum (California) and Martha Willis (Florida).

I am also proud that black CPAs are now more involved than ever in NASBA as committee and board members. No black person had ever served on the NASBA board before my election. But, as of this writing, there are two. One of them is Walter Davenport from North Carolina, my partner for 25 years and the other is Theodore Long of Ohio with whom I sit on the Board of Directors of North Carolina Mutual Life Insurance Company.

Historically Black Colleges and Universities (HBCUs)

One hundred and six colleges and universities in the United States have the distinction of having been started to educate African Americans. Not all of them are active today due primarily to bankruptcies or mergers. The first HBCU was Lincoln University of Pennsylvania, founded in 1854. The first in the South was Shaw University in Raleigh, North Carolina, founded in 1865. Some were started by regional or national church organizations. Some resulted from the philanthropy of wealthy individuals. Others were created and supported by state government, or in the case of Howard University, by the federal government (supported initially through the Freedman's Bureau and later by special appropriations of the U.S. Congress). Because of the Morrill Act of 1890, which amended the Morrill Act of 1862, some HBCUs are land-grant institutions that received either cash or land from the federal government to be used by the former Confederate states to create schools for the teaching of agricultural and mechanical skills to African Americans. (The Morrill Act, however, did permit the teaching of science, the classics and military tactics in all of the land-grant institutions.) Thirteen HBCUs were created in Alabama; eleven in North Carolina; ten in Georgia; nine each in Texas and Louisiana; eight each in Mississippi and South Carolina; six in Tennessee; four each in Arkansas and Florida; three each in Missouri and Maryland; two each in Pennsylvania, Virginia. Ohio and the District of Columbia, and one each in West Virginia, California, Michigan, Illinois, Delaware, West Virginia, Kentucky, Oklahoma and the Virgin Islands.

Before the *Brown* decision in 1954, African Americans who had the intellect, means and desire to go to college in the South were restricted to the HBCUs. It is not surprising, therefore, that the Southern HBCUs can boast of a huge number of African American business, professional, religious and political leaders who were educated on their campuses. But since 1954 there has been a slow and steady change on almost all southern college campuses. Many of the best-prepared African American students and faculty now find their way onto the campuses that formerly excluded them, and almost all of the HBCU campuses now have white and other races as students, faculty and administrators. West Virginia State University has become so integrated that it no longer considers as its mission the education of African Americans. The law school at North Carolina Central University (NCCU), an HBCU, now has a majority white student enrollment. (Mike Easley who completed two four-year terms as Governor of North Carolina in 2008 is an NCCU Law School graduate.)

Recent national studies show that all but a few of the private HBCUs are in serious financial difficulty due to low enrollments, high uncollectible student fee balances and negligible alumni giving. North Carolina studies show that the high school grade point averages and the college entrance examination scores of the African American freshmen at HBCUs are low compared to the rest of the college-going students. And finally, the studies here in North Carolina show that the four, five and six year graduation rates at the five state-supported HBCUs are much lower than they are on the other eleven campuses that comprise our university system. These data cause many to ask: is there still a need for the HBCUs? My answer is *YES, THERE IS!*

My answer and comments in this section are based on my observations of students, faculty and administrators at HBCUs and discussions with over twenty members of my family and a host of friends who studied at one or more HBCUs. I was on the Board of Trustees at Fayetteville State University, an HBCU, for six years, including two as its chairman. Wanda taught English at NCCU for over 10 years. Wanda and I earned our law degrees at NCCU. Wanda is a graduate of the University of Arkansas at Pine Bluff, an HBCU founded in 1873 that became a land-grant college in 1890. I am currently teaching business law at in the School of Business at NCCU.

Most, but not all, of the students who come to my classes, whether African American, white, Hispanic or Asian, do not have college entrance examination scores or high school grade point averages that are good enough for admission to the formerly all-white campuses that constitute North Carolina's university system. I estimate that 30% of my students have communication skills that are well below what one would expect from a high school graduate. (According to Professor Leonard Greenbaugh of Dartmouth, pre-school students from low-income families have a 1,500 word vocabulary compared to 3,500 for those from other families, and the low-income students never catch up.). Half of my students have never developed skills needed to solve law or accounting problems. Perhaps as few as 10% of them have had any exposure to accounting, business management, the legal environment of businesses, or finance prior to enrolling in college.

Despite these negatives, it is clear to me that these students have promise. They are not among the high number who drop out before completing high school, or the number who get their high school diplomas, but do not seek, or are unable to obtain, admission to any post baccalaureate institution. (Greenbaugh states that 50% of 9th graders do not graduate from high school and 50% of those who do graduate cannot read, write or decipher.) The fact that they enrolled in NCCU says that they have achieved at least minimal levels of competence and that they have a desire for a college degree. My job is to help them turn those desires or dreams into reality. But the reality must be a degree that says to the outside world that these students have succeeded in getting through a rigorous program of learning. I am thankful that NCCU attracts at least a few students who could have succeeded on non-HBCU campuses. These "Chancellor's Scholars" help to establish competition on exams, homework completion and class discussions. However, I have to guard against lowering my expectations for any of the students, scholars and non-scholars alike. It is not unusual for the scholars to decide that they need not extend themselves to learn as much as they can because they have no competitors.

I am also thankful for the agreements that have been made to allow students to transfer credits for college-level courses taken at one of North Carolina's 58 community colleges to the four-year institutions. Entrance requirements at the community colleges are lower than they are at the four -ear campuses. The year or two period students spend at the community colleges often help them overcome some of the deficits described above. When they enroll at the four-year institutions, they tend to be more capable and more serious about pursuing their educations.

I know what knowledge and skills these students will need to succeed as employees or entrepreneurs. My goals are for each student to master the basic concepts in my course, improve his or her communication skills, develop the ability to think critically and learn how to search professional literature to aid in problem-solving. Achieving these goals requires more than lectures, class discussions and being available a few hours each week for advising. I estimate that at least 80% of my students are working from 15 to 40 hours a week. This means that I often need to make appointments to meet them when their schedules permit, not just during my posted hours. I also have to be available to them via my home phone and e-mail address. In class, I try to give them examples of how concepts might be applied to situations with which they might be familiar. I require them to read articles about business and to relate the subject matter of the articles to the topics covered in the course. I try to help them see the relationships among business law, accounting, marketing, finance and management. Ethical issues are discussed with great frequency in class. I encourage them to think of themselves as employers or executives, rather than low-level employees. I am aided in all this by university policy that limits class sizes to a relatively small number of students.

I am not unique in using these measures. My colleagues at NCCU and faculties on other HBCU campuses are all doing pretty much the same with their students. We all recognize that the students who come to us with deficits in their education and narrow exposure to cultures other than their own need nurturing and extra efforts to help them see the relevance of the subjects we teach. I am not saying that faculties at the former all white colleges and universities are not interested or capable of doing what we do at HBCUs.

However, the need for it is less because they teach students that are better prepared for the rigors of higher education.

But despite all my efforts, it is not unusual for a third of my students not to pass my course. Some try again at a later time and some withdraw from the university. However, I feel that even those who withdraw gain measurably from the college experience. Several members of my family dropped out of college. But, each one of them was perceived with slightly more respect by their peers and performed slightly better than their peers in their careers as a result of their experience at HBCUs.

We are approaching an era in which African Americans and Hispanics will be major parts of a new majority in this country. The nation cannot afford to ignore the special needs of students from low-income families, most of them from African American and Hispanic families, who seek a college education. We must grow and harvest intellectual potential wherever it is found. HBCUs are doing that now and are uniquely qualified to do so.

ESSAY ON RELIGION

Thank God!

Mother grew up in St. Paul's African Methodist Episcopal Zion Church in the little eastern, Coastal Plains North Carolina town of Tarboro. However, I never remember a time when she was not a member of White Rock Baptist Church in Durham. Dad had been a member of Union Baptist in Tarboro, and although he did not transfer his membership from Union Baptist until he was 90, mother and the children joined White Rock and we all attended there.

We never talked much about church or religion at home. On occasion during Sunday dinner, mother and dad would discuss the sermon delivered by White Rock's pastor, the Reverend Miles Mark Fisher, a truly outstanding preacher, composer and writer. We didn't study the bible but we did say a brief grace before dinner. Before bed I was taught to say:

Now I lay me down to sleep

I pray the Lord my soul to keepError! No bookmark name given.

If I should die before I wake

I pray the Lord my soul to take

God bless momma and daddy and all my family,

Amen

Going to church was just expected, and we attended more Sundays than we missed. I honestly don't know whether the motivation for attendance was religious belief or business development. Dad was the only pharmacist who attended White Rock.

From early childhood through early teens I liked Sunday school but rarely attended. I liked sleeping late on Sunday much better. I went to the eleven o'clock service much more than Sunday school and Reverend Fisher gave me a lot to think about. The sermons I enjoyed most were those that told us how we ought to treat one another based on the teachings of Jesus.

As a young child I found the church experience helpful in explaining the world around me. The "how, when, why and where" questions about creation, nature, heaven and hell were all answered satisfactorily in the Sunday school lessons or the sermons. Many times I would lie in bed, close my eyes, and focus on God hoping I would see a vision or feel His presence. On one occasion I thought I saw a strong blue light with a halo around it, but on reflection, I concluded I must have been dreaming and never mentioned it to anyone.

The Commandments about having no other gods, honoring parents, adultery, stealing, lying and coveting made sense to me (though the male chauvinism inherent in the one on coveting escaped me at the time). But even at age ten it seemed that the remaining four about not having graven images, killing, taking God's name in vain and keeping the Sabbath holy needed a lot of exceptions to be workable. Every church had images of Jesus and God and we bowed before them and the cross. A lot of very good people cursed and swore. Killing was justified in self-defense or in war. I was ten when the Japanese attacked Peal Harbor and we entered the Second World War. Garrett's Drugstore was open every Sunday before and after church and what was wrong with that? The pastor and his family often came to the store for ice cream on Sunday.

By age thirteen, having learned a little science and history, I could not accept the biblical stories about creation, the Garden of Eden, Noah and the ark and Jonah and the whale.

I accepted the statement that Jews are the chosen people of God until college where I met and talked with people of Jewish faith for the first time. Those talks caused me to read and think about the Jew's journey from Egypt, Moses on Mt. Sinai speaking with God and the killing that took place to enable the Jews to overcome the inhabitants of the "promised land." Why would the God of all creation not love all people the same?

At about the same time, I began to question the notion of a personal God with whom you could converse and who would intervene in your life. Also, I decided I could no longer accept that Jesus actually performed miracles or that he was resurrected.

By the time I finished college I had decided that religion was not important but church was. Religion caused misunderstanding, and encouraged hatred and war. However, church, as an institution, was almost totally positive. It helped you to meet new people. The pastor and the members did good things like visiting the sick and comforting the bereaved. White Rock had after school programs to provide food, clothing and tutoring for young students who needed them. Reverend Fisher spearheaded the creation of a recreation center for the boys of White Rock and the community that surrounded it. The center was a four or five room frame house on an unpaved street near the church. There was room for a ping-pong table, checkers, card games, a reading room and, in the rear, a very short dirt basketball court. Some of the mature adults sponsored scouting and arranged field trips. White Rock was extremely important to the Garrett family. Many churches are now partnering with government and private enterprises to create much needed housing for the low income and elderly, day care for children and adults, and health centers to serve the total community. We are a better society because of what our churches are doing.

After college and serving my two years in the army and marriage to Joyce, my first wife, I went to Detroit, her hometown. Joyce had the same reservations about religion that I had, but she was a member of an Episcopal church on 14th Street. The priest, Father Henri Stines, was a young man from Haiti who had been a pastor at a non-Episcopal church before he converted. Whatever the church was, he learned well how to preach and for my purposes was a good substitute for Miles Mark Fisher. I had no strong preference for any denomination, but because Father Stines was good in the pulpit and because I believed that a family should attend the same church, as I had been brought up, I joined Grace Episcopal.

Episcopalians must go through instruction to learn the rituals of the denomination, so I went to weekly classes for about a month. What I learned I have long since forgotten, but I have not forgotten how strongly I felt that the rituals were pointless. Baptists have their rituals but they are few compared to the Episcopalians and Catholics. I attended a Catholic church in New Haven a few times while I was a student at Yale because I was courting a New Haven girl who belonged.

Even after my divorce I continued my membership in Grace because of the quality of Father Stine's sermons and because I had come to know him and many members of the church. Joyce had stopped attending. So, when I met Wanda, my wife of nearly 52 years as I write this, I was still an Episcopalian. She had always been a Baptist.

Wanda's mother, Georgia Hockenhull Jones, was as strongly Baptist as she was religious. Her comment to Wanda on learning that we would be attending Grace Episcopal after marriage was that she guessed we could serve God anywhere, even in an Episcopal church.

Georgia was a beautiful woman with a brown face tinged with a little red and long hair (Wanda looks a great deal like her.). Georgia's mother, whose picture hangs in our living room, was named Katie Rainwater Hockenhull, and she was a full-blooded Cherokee Indian. Georgia was a serious student of

213

the Christian bible and believed it to be the holy word of God, inconsistencies in its text notwithstanding. She prayed on her knees morning, noon and night. She fasted each Wednesday. Her devotion to Christianity had helped make her a very kind, generous and loving person. I never saw her interacting with non-Christians, though there is a large population of Jews and worshipers of Islam in Detroit. Her beliefs in Christianity and her allegiance to the Baptist Church were so strong that I am sure she tried to convert anyone she spoke to to the Baptist church. But she would have been motherly and patient with them. Wanda has told me that when Georgia operated a shop on Oakland Avenue in Detroit, she interacted with respect, friendliness and disbelief with The Honorable Elijah Muhammad, leader of the black Muslims, whose temple was one block away. At a later time when Georgia operated another neighborhood store, a young man shoved a gun in her face and demanded her money. She stared at the criminal during the entire episode and he threatened to shoot her if she didn't stop staring. She told him that she was staring so that she could give God – not the police – a good description of him when she asked God in her evening prayer - or in Heaven - to forgive and heal him. The young man didn't shoot, but he did take the cash register receipts.

After a few spirited debates with Georgia about our respective beliefs I concluded that it was nonsense for me to challenge her beliefs. The important thing was that I loved and respected her and that she returned those feelings to me.

When Wanda and I relocated to Durham from Detroit in 1962 we attended St Titus, a black Episcopal church, until our youngest child, influenced by my mother, joined White Rock. White Rock's preacher at that time was Lorenzo Lynch. Lynch was a good man in my estimation and there was good content in his sermons even though he was not a good speaker.

Wanda and I have discussed religion many, many times and we are pretty much at peace with our respective positions. She is a believer in Christ and prays at meals and at other times when she feels the need. She is also very careful to respect the religious preferences of others. She believes that most religions offer a civilizing impact on most behavior. Our daughter, Andrea, married a Muslim, converted to that faith, changed her name to Shahida and reared her four sons as Muslims. We discuss religious matters with Shahida and the boys, but no one attempts to proselytize. For the last 20 years when Wanda says prayer in their presence she omits her customary ending. "for Christ's sake." She also omits those words when she is before groups that include non-Christians.

If I am pulled into a discussion on religion with people with strong faith in any religion, I usually tell them how much I envy their faith without exposing my lack of it. This is not insincere. I have seen many people who, like Georgia, accept calmly the calamities and uncertainties they encounter by simply believing that it is in God's hands and that God knows best.

When others want to pray at meetings or meals, I participate by closing my eyes and listening to the words. Prayer often helps set the proper tone for what it precedes in that it encourages people to be truthful, civil, helpful, forgiving, and most importantly, loving.

Until recently when I was called on to pray I would do so and would end the prayer with "for Christ's sake." But I have now decided that such an ending, and the prayer itself, is dishonest because of what I do not believe about Jesus and God. This new attitude has left me struggling to create statements that are helpful to others but do not run counter to my current beliefs.

So what do I believe right now?

There is one God.

God is the creator of all physical things, known and unknown.

God created all the laws of science, known or unknown.

God is a force or a power, is the source of all life and resides within each of us.

God cannot die unless all matter ceases to exist.

God does not communicate with us but is the source of our urges to preserve self, find happiness and love.

God does not intervene in what happens to the things created; He has built into our genes the ability, over time, to change (evolve) so that we are able to thrive in our environment.

There is no heaven or hell.

There have never been prophets that were truly divinely inspired or instructed.

Jesus was not God.

Love is not possible without life.

Life without love is meaningless.

When I am called upon to speak at a religion-oriented group, I find a passage from the Christian bible to illustrate a point I want to make. For example, several times I have used the 5th chapter of John, verses one through four, to make a point about people who change things for the better. I got this from Reverend Reginald Van Stephens at White Rock. The story is about the angel coming down to stir the waters of the pool at Bethesda in Jerusalem so that the first sick or infirmed person entering the water would be healed. I infer from this that still waters don't make things better and that he who stirs up the waters can make things better. Therefore, the person who pushes for change or will not accept the status quo is, like the angel of the Lord, "troubling the waters" and can cause life to be better. The Christian bible has passages that can be suited to almost any occasion.

For prayers at meetings I usually decline, but when pressed I say something like:

We are gathered to deliberate and communicate to the end that this organization can prosper and do good things for those whose lives we touch. I ask you to listen with an open mind, speak with respect and love for all and think always of what is good for all rather than for self. I believe the spark of God that is within each of us will help us during this time together. Amen.

When Dr. Charles Watts died, his family asked me to give the prayer at the funeral service at St. Joseph's African Methodist Episcopal Church. Charles was a pioneering surgeon and the leader of dozens of important causes in Durham and elsewhere. When I relocated to Durham and established my CPA practice he became one of my early clients. He served the medical needs of most of my family. His family and ours were extremely close. I was surprised at the request to pray at his funeral, but I could not say no. I knew that people of several races and religions revered him and would be present at the funeral services. Here is what I said:

In this assembly, in addition to the many, many Christians, there probably are Jews and Muslims. There may also be Hindus for whom the Supreme Being or Eternal Spirit is Brahman or others who revere Buddha whom they call the "Enlightened One." There are agnostics who believe it is impossible to know God and possibly atheists who believe there is no God. But whatever your belief, I ask you to join in this brief prayer because of your love for Charles Dewitt Watts. Regardless of who we are and what we believe, we are here because he touched our lives in a good way.

Dear God, it is fitting that this gathering include men and women of differing beliefs, especially in this time when people all over this world are struggling and looking to their beliefs to find what is the right thing to do about our fellow man - in Iraq, Israel, the Palestinian Territory, the Sudan, the Philippines, the Pakistan-Indian border, Korea and, yes, right here in Durham.

The fact that we are here, oh Lord, says that there is something about the way Charles Dewitt Watts lived his life that helps us see what to do about helping our fellow man. His ministries of medical care, community service, corporate leadership and as a family patriarch teach us much. All that he did was done with skill, with dignity, with a desire to help and, I sincerely believe, with great love. Charles was a Christian and the great message of Christ is love. Help us to honor his legacy by perpetuating his ministries with love.

And now I ask all who are thankful for the life of this great man who showed us great love to please join me in saying, AMEN.

Dozens of people, about half of them non-Christians, praised me for the prayer. Some said they usually feel left out or forgotten at public gatherings when prayers are said. One old friend who is an elected official in a nearby town asked for a copy of what I said for use at open meetings of his governing body. Dr. Watts' son recently asked for a copy of the prayer to help him in developing a version of it for use at meetings of NC Department of Transportation board on which he sits.

The first draft of the above did not include the words "prayer," "Dear God," and "oh Lord," but Wanda didn't approve. She pointed out that I agreed to pray and, therefore, I was going to pray no matter how I felt about it. After years of relying on her to edit my stuff I could not ignore her protest. My need to be forthright in expressing my religious beliefs when called upon to do so is not stronger than my need to perpetuate my bond with my wife.

When called on to pray at meals, currently I am satisfied with:

God, the creator of life and all things, commands us to eat this food to sustain his creation in accordance with His laws of nature. Jesus, whom Christians believe is God's greatest creation, commanded us to pray, and above all, to love. Please join me in saying "Amen."

Or.

Please bow your heads for a moment of meditation or prayer, whichever you choose. (Pause for five seconds)

May the worship of your God lead you to seek to understand and tolerate the religion of others.

May the worship of your God impel you to serve others as you would have them serve you.

(And, If appropriate for the occasion.)

[May the reunions of family and friends represented in this gathering strengthen the bonds of love.]

[May this food nurture or bodies, minds and spirits so that we may better serve our fellow man.]

Amen

I am comfortable with using the word "amen" because according to Webster, the word is used at the end of a prayer or statement to express approval.

Now my major problem is to come up with an expression to use when we have had good fortune or good luck with a serious matter: a narrowly avoided car collision; a recovery from an illness; your son finds a job; or a business decision turns out well after early indications that things would go badly. So far, nothing I have thought of is as satisfying as "Thank God!" So, I'll continue to use it.

Dialogue On Love And Marriage

I was member of Sigma Pi Phi, the oldest fraternity of black college graduates. It was started in Philadelphia in 1904 by a few black professionals who wanted social interaction with men who had achieved success in their lives. Today there are approximately 6,000 members throughout the United States. The membership is divided into chapters, called Subordinate Boules. The national organization is called the Grand Boule. There are Subordinate Boules in practically all of the major cities. I was inducted into the Durham Subordinate Boule in 1977

The Durham Subordinate Boule has a dinner dance at Christmas to honor our wives and sweethearts. Our slogan for the event is "Christmas is for the Archousai." Usually one of the Archons gives a tribute to the Archousai through a special toast or poetry. However, in 2003 our Sire Archon, Frank Anderson, asked me to do something special. I enlisted the invaluable help of my Archousa and this is what we presented.

NATHAN & WANDA IN UNISON: Good evening Archons and Archousai.

NATHAN: In the words of Charles Becton, our, Master of Ceremonies:

> Our yesterdays sculpt all of the tomorrows
>
> Our past is the mosaic of our future
>
> And the grandeur of your artisan hand
>
> Makes our love an ever-unfolding work
>
> Wanda, those lines make me think of love and marriage as being like a garment that starts out with two panels of material

that are sewn together. In other words, through marriage the two separate people, or panels, are united into one.

WANDA: Not a bad analogy, Nathan, but I think of love and marriage more as a beautiful tapestry. But, you know, either way, it is the stitching that is important. For the garment, the more stitches you use, the stronger it is. For the tapestry, the more the stitching, the more beautiful it becomes.

NATHAN: I agree. And each stitch represents an important episode or pleasant moment in the couple's joint lives. The more such episodes and pleasant moments, the more stitches and therefore, the stronger the garment – or should I say the more beautiful the tapestry?

Archons and Archousai, do you remember the very first stitch, when first you met?

WANDA: I remember that very well. I was a young widow, you were a divorcee and you had a girlfriend. You came to pick her up from a bridge party, saw me, and secretly picked up my earrings as well.

NATHAN: Kept them for a month before I could afford a date with you to return them.

WANDA: I thought you were so clever.

NATHAN: Archons, how about meeting her parents? For me, it was Easter Sunday in 1958. We had been to a sunrise service and had breakfast with Wanda's family.

WANDA: My mom thought we were buddies and asked if I were helping you to reconcile with your former wife.

NATHAN: Didn't happen!

WANDA: I asked my sainted Mother if she was deranged.

NATHAN: Moving on, we all got married. Archons, I know you remember your wedding day.

WANDA: A great big stitch in the fabric. Then, for some, the uncertainties associated with parenthood created some knotty stitches in the fabric.

NATHAN: Some were knotty stitches of joy.

WANDA: Yes, like traveling 12 hours with children in the back seat of car… "He touched me!" "Are we there yet?"

But there were stitches of sadness, too, with the deaths of loved ones.

NATHAN: That's for sure. Together we've lost both sets of parents, five brothers and two sisters. Each death seemed unbearable at the time, but you were certainly there for me to see me through and I hope you feel I was there for you because I was, with every ounce of love and compassion within me. (Pause) Archons, other stitches have come from school and careers.

Nathan and Wanda

WANDA: I remember 1986 when our last-born got his degree from Dartmouth, our first-born received his baccalaureate from A&T and you and I got our law degrees from N. C. Central. That was a great time for celebration.

NATHAN: Not just for the joy of the accomplishments, but for the liberation from all those bills for tuition, books and whatever. ...

I also remember the long nights of study in preparation for the CPA exam and the agonizing three-month wait to get the results. I probably wasn't very easy to live with during that time, was I?

WANDA: Right. Joining the Boule was another memorable stitch in the fabric. I remember asking, "I'm going to be called a what?"

NATHAN: At my induction, Wanda was asked to respond for the new Archousai.

WANDA: In Greensboro, over 30 years ago.

NATHAN: And 30 years later, our current Sire Archon has involved you again in an important part of Christmas for the Archousai.

WANDA: On behalf of the Archousai, allow me to say:

> Love is never easy, but
> It turns life into song.
> There is no bit of circumstance
> That love cannot transform
> There is no weary moment
> Of anger or despair
> That love cannot convert
> And render whole and fair.
> When time and situations put our closeness to the test,
> Recalling favorite memories is what our hearts do best
> When the cares and worries of the day consume the lives we lead
> Overwhelm us with want and need...
> It's time to take a moment to smile
> And dwell on the cheerful thoughts –the stitches that make life's fabric worthwhile.

NATHAN: Archons and Archousai, I will close with a few lines by the comedian, George Carlin, written sometime after September 11, 2001 – 911:

> Remember to hold hands and cherish the moment, for someday that person will not be there again.
>
> Give time to love, give time to speak, and give time to share the precious thoughts in your mind.
>
> And always remember, life is not measured by the number

of breaths we take, but by the moments that take our breath away.

And now, I ask each Archon to stand, take the hand of your lovely Archousa and say "Merry Christmas and I love you" with all the passion your stitches have created.

Wanda, I love you with all my heart.

WANDA: And I, you.

WANDA & NATHAN: (Each took up a glass touched it to the other's glass and then faced the audience holding the glass high until the audience raised their glasses. Then all took a sip together.) "To love."

*　*　*　*　*　*　*　*　*　*　*

Family gathering at 3923 Northampton, 1994. Bottom row: Devron Marc Garrett (son), Sophia Easley (grand niece), Nathan Taylor Garrett, III, Christina Easley (grand niece) Lalia Corinne Garrett (granddaughter). Second row: Wanda. Third row: Yvonne Easley Moore (niece), Gail Garrett (daughter-in-law). Fifth row : (standing) Malik Mausi (grandson), (sitting) Shahida Mausi-Johnson (daughter), Sixth row: Audriana Grant (grand niece), Nathan Garrett, Jr. Top row: Sulaiman Mausi (grandson), York D. Garrett, Jr. (father), Dorian Mausi (grandson). Photo by Devron Marc Garrett.

Family gathering for my father's 100 birthday at 3923
Northampton, 1994. Photo by C. R. Stanback.

Garrett-Hockenhull-Jones-Williams Family Renunion,
Durham, 2008. Photo by David Harrison, Jr.

225

Nathan T. Garrett. Photo courtesy of North Carolina
Institute of Minority Economic Development.

CPSIA information can be obtained at www.ICGtesting.com
Printed in the USA
LVOW08*0250260914

405995LV00002B/56/P

9 781450 248761